PARADIGM AND PARODY

Images of Creativity in French Romanticism—Vigny, Hugo, Balzac, Gautier, Musset

PARADIGM & PARODY

Images of Creativity in
French Romanticism—
Vigny, Hugo, Balzac,
Gautier, Musset

Henry F. Majewski

UNIVERSITY PRESS OF VIRGINIA
Charlottesville

THE UNIVERSITY PRESS OF VIRGINIA
Copyright © 1989 by the Rector and Visitors
of the University of Virginia
First published 1989
Design by Pat Crowder

LIBRARY OF CONGRESS
Library of Congress Cataloging-in-Publication Data

Majewski, Henry F.
Paradigm and parody : images of creativity in French romanticism—
Vigny, Hugo, Balzac, Gautier, Musset / Henry F. Majewski.
p.   cm.
Bibliography: p.
ISBN 0-8139-1177-X
1. French literature—19th century—History and criticism.
2. Romanticism—France.   3. Creativity in literature.   4. Artists in
literature   I. Title.
PQ288.M35   1989
840'.9'007—dc19   88-15419
                                    CIP

Printed in the United States of America

Contents

Acknowledgments

I am indebted to many of my students, both graduate and undergraduate, who patiently listened to my ideas about French romantic literature and whose enthusiasm stimulated my interest and thought. My colleague and friend Professor Albert J. Salvan of Brown University read my manuscript in a spirit of generous and helpful criticism, for which I am deeply appreciative. I owe special thanks to Yvonne Morin, who typed several more or less legible versions of my text without complaint, and to Betty Lou Reid, who offered valuable assistance to me on many occasions. Brown University provided me with travel funds for summer research in the Paris libraries, which I gratefully acknowledge.

Some sections of the book appeared earlier in a different form in the following journals: *Romanic Review* 67 (November 1978), *Hebrew University Studies in Literature* 7 (Summer 1979), *Nineteenth Century French Studies* 9 (1980–81), *Studies in Romanticism* 20 (October 1981). For permission to reprint in a revised form I wish to thank the respective editors.

PARADIGM AND PARODY

Images of Creativity in French Romanticism—Vigny, Hugo, Balzac, Gautier, Musset

Introduction

In his study of Balzac's philosophy Henri Evans concluded that even Balzac, the self-appointed social analyst, had adopted the belief in art as "la véritable religion du monde moderne, et que le voyant futur c'est l'artiste." Postulating that this intuition was essential to Balzac's own experience as a creative person, "une idée vécue," he adds, "cette certitude est d'ailleurs universelle chez les romantiques, elle est le fond même du romantisme."[1]

The visionary side of European romanticism has often been examined, especially in the works of William Blake and the "fantastic" or dream literature of Germans such as Hoffmann, Novalis, and Jean-Paul. Those who inherit the idea of poetry as *voyance* and the concept of the artist as prophet (i.e., Rimbaud's seer or Nietzsche's mystique of the superman) have been given much critical attention.

The low status of the visionary figure in French romantic literature, however, is endemic to the treatment of this period in general. French critics traditionally refused to see French romanticism as other than an aberration in the general development of rationalist thought and discourse from Cartesianism to structuralism. To cite just two examples, the music of Berlioz is still misunderstood and neglected in France, and the "classical" side of Delacroix is stressed in order better to appreciate his masterworks. It was Albert Béguin's influential study *L'Ame romantique et le rêve* (1939) that first emphasized the importance of the "irrational" modes of thought—dreamwork, myth, and the concept of poetry as a means to knowledge—in French literature from Rousseau to Nerval.[2] Thanks to the surrealists and critics like Béguin, Nerval (the "French Blake" as he is characteristically termed) has finally been recognized as the great visionary creator of mythological worlds in his masterpiece *Aurélia*.

My study thus attempts to foreground the importance of the visionary strain in the major French romantics, not from the perspective of biography, but from the perspective of the fictional and poetic representation of creative persons and the creative process itself. Other writers than those I treat here might have been included; Nerval's entire production could be the object of such an enquiry. Lamartine and George Sand certainly contribute to the myth of the romantic artist as a privileged interpreter of experience—but perhaps more significantly in their own lives than in specific texts about the artist figure.[3]

Many important studies of romantic writers have, of course, analyzed their central concept of imagination as a truly creative faculty.[4] Scholarly works have been concerned with the romantic idea of poetry as a privileged means to knowledge resulting from the imaginative discoveries of resemblance: the belief in the analogy between metaphoric structures in poetic discourse and the very order of nature. Critics have also examined the exalted romantic view of the artist as a prophet or seer (Icarus, Orpheus, and Prometheus[5]). The specific ideas and theories of individual romantic writers and artists have also been commented upon in detail. I propose rather to emphasize the fictional representations of the creative process by a major group of French romantics through close reading of the texts, with particular emphasis on the archetypal and structural patterns that shape them. Major French romantic works will be analyzed in which characters and situations give form to the three basic aspects of creativity—the origins of a work of art (personal, collective, intertextual), its elaboration into a complete form, and finally the interplay of work and audience.

While it has become a commonplace that modernist texts are self-reflective, representing, as it were *en abîme,* their own patterns and problems of creativity, this phenomenon has been much less frequently considered as a characteristic of the texts of romanticism.

My study proposes, therefore, to focus upon the romantics as a group from the standpoint of their self-consciousness, and to explore systematically the self-knowledge displayed by their texts. I would like to place the question of the creativity of romanticism in a new context, by examining how the texts reflect or reflect upon their own conflicts of artistic production and audience reception.

This study is not organized chronologically, although all of the texts chosen were written between 1820 and 1870. They were selected because they offer the richest and most characteristic examples of the major romantic writers' representation of creativity. The order in which they are studied is designed to reveal a dialectical pattern that I believe accurately reflects the French romantics' great confidence in the signifying power of the language of art, and yet, concurrently, their own serious doubts concerning the value of the individual, creative act as a revelation of truth or a force for action in society.

It is not my intention to repeat the extensive debates about the meaning of romanticism[6]; only too often we are left with the uncomfortable impression of at least two romanticisms competing for our attention—a negative one imbued with the pessimism of individual and social failure (Byron, Musset, Balzac), and a positive or "dynamic organicist" version, stressing a philosophy of unlimited progress, personal and social evolution (Michelet, Hugo).[7] I personally discover the link between these apparently contradictory modes in the importance accorded to creativity itself by the romantic writers and thinkers. Romantic irony or pessimism stresses the illusionary aspect of reality, including the products of art, since all of life is essentially defined by the tragic limitations imposed by time, reason, and matter. This ironic stance, characteristic of much romantic writing, is in fact opposed by a new idealism. A positive, even progressist ideology develops in the first half of the nineteenth century, an ideology based on a growing confidence in the power of the creative person's vision in society to aid in the amelioration of a flawed reality.

It would be false to claim a shift from the negative or ironic position (of Musset and Petrus Borel) to the positive worldview (of Michelet and Hugo) in clearly chronological and historical terms; to state, for example, that the visionary capacity of the artist is only recognized after the July Revolution of 1830, as a kind of spiritualist reaction to the bourgeois, materialist ideology newly victorious in

France. It is much more accurate, as my study will illustrate, to see the problem of creativity through the perspective of a continuing dialogue.

Pessimistic, or negative, romanticism and visionary romanticism are not successive phases marking a historical change in worldviews, but rather two essentially connected aspects of a dialectic process. My study is structured to represent these two interacting aspects, first in microcosm in the works of Vigny and then by the interplay of succeeding chapters on Balzac, Gautier, and Musset. Victor Hugo serves as a master voice to which the others respond either in agreement or in denial.

The model or paradigm of the artist as a visionary endowed with a special energy, who can use the power of language to uncover the profound spiritual order beyond the apparent disorder of phenomena, is best studied in the works of Hugo, whose presence spans the century. Throughout his long and prolific career, Hugo constructed what we may call the myth of the artist as seer and prophet. In the earliest odes he presents a poetic persona who enjoys the special gift of intuition; in the later works published posthumously, *La Fin de Satan* (1886) and *Dieu* (1896), he practices the gift of poetic prophecy. Through apocalyptic visions of the end of time and the world of the supernatural, he develops the visionary impulse already present in the final sections of *Les Contemplations* (1856) ("En Marche," "Au Bord de l'infini"). Many of his poems treat the well-known "fonction du poète," and his early prose work *Littérature et philosophie mêlées* (1834) offers important discussions on art and aesthetics. *William Shakespeare* (1864) is unique, however, since it provides a splendid synthesis of Hugo's conception of Western art in the form of an archetypal figure and exemplary model of the artist, a "fictional" creation he names—Shakespeare. The creative life of Shakespeare is compared with that of Aeschylus. Both are understood and illuminated by the mythical figure of Prometheus, the Titan who was sacrificed for the gift he gave to humanity, but who survived spiritual death to be reborn in the minds and works of posterity. Through the structure of an archetypal rebirth pattern Hugo imagines the development of Western art. He traces the origins of the creative impulse, the elaboration of the artwork, and ultimately the complex relationships between artist, work, and the public that, in Hugo's view, the artist must serve through his special vision of spiritual and moral truth.

The Hugoesque model can therefore be seen as the thesis or text with which the other romantic texts interact and that they echo or contradict. The works of Alfred de Vigny I have chosen encompass the fundamental dialectic, and manifest an evolutionary process whose stages appear through various representations of creativity. The *Journal d'un poète* (1823–63) provides an excellent beginning, since it gives us insight into the mind of a romantic poet attempting to define and represent his own efforts to create; it reveals the anguish of alienation from society and a belief in the supreme value of art as he comes to terms with the ambivalent gift of poetic imagination.

Stello (1832) and *Daphné* (1837), the two Consultations of the Docteur Noir, offer fictionalized versions of the same precarious situation of the artist that preoccupied Vigny throughout his life: the potentially active role of the poet-philosopher in a society that rejects him. In both of these works the artist figure becomes the prophet/scapegoat, victim of a society incapable of comprehending his value. The central importance of *Stello* in Vigny's canon, for knowledge of his aesthetics, was stressed by François Germain in his important study *L'Imagination d'Alfred de Vigny.*[8] The complex function of poetic imagination and its inevitable conflicts with material and social realities are richly personified in the dialogue (an early suggestion of a psychiatric session) between the idealistic, anguished poet Stello and his realistic, storytelling Docteur Noir. An important example of romantic doubling, Stello and his doctor also represent the divided self of the artist who experiences the fragmentation of his personality in a hostile environment.

Little attention, however, has been given to the unfinished "sequel," *Daphné,* in which Vigny transforms his preoccupation with the psychology of the artist's personality into a meditation on language and symbolism. In the case of Julian the Apostate, the hero of *Daphné,* the artist's failure can be seen in terms of romantic language or discourse itself; the poet-emperor, a historical actualization of a romantic dream, fails to recognize the importance of symbolic discourse, or the proper choice of signifiers, in his efforts to determine and impose the religious faith of his followers.

The mythological poems of *Les Destinées,* however, do contain a genuine dialectical movement. Thematically and structurally they place in binary opposition the negative view of the artist as scapegoat and the optimistic faith in the power of the creative mind, which is finally resolved in favor of the second. In the last analysis, although Vigny in his Hellenistic phase can doubt all but the beauty of art as pure illusion for its own sake, he finally opts for the Hugoesque model: the exalted view of the artist that he and Hugo had begun to elaborate in the twenties in the early "Odes" and *Poèmes antiques et modernes*. "La Maison du berger," centerpiece of his poetic master-work, presents the image of a poet-Prometheus, freed from his spiritual death, transformed by his love for Eva, and newly confident in his own creative force.

Balzac's interest in the artist as a visionary was, of course, already signaled by Baudelaire as a caution to those who would overemphasize the mimetic concerns of his fiction.[9] In the "Avant-Propos" to the *Comédie humaine* and many other texts, Balzac insists that a novelist's ability to describe the real world must be accompanied by an intuitive capacity to discern the essential laws and spiritual principles that underlie the appearances and surfaces of phenomena. His fascination with the role of the artist in general, and especially the patterns of failure and destruction that define his efforts to create, is projected in the lives of the protagonists of the *Etudes philosophiques* (such as Frenhofer and Gambara) and fully developed through the Parisian rise and fall of Lucien de Rubempré (*Illusions perdues*).

Louis Lambert (1832–33) and *La Recherche de l'absolu* (1834), undoubtedly offer the most complex representations and analyses of the intricate mechanisms of creative energy to be found in the entire world of the *Comédie humaine*. Rather than emphasize the actual productions of the visionary mind, as they are exposed in the revelations of Balzac's *Séraphita* (or Hugo's "mage" in "Ce que dit la bouche d'ombre"), Balzac concentrates in these novels on the inner workings of the creative process.

Louis Lambert poses the fundamental problem of the creative person's conflict between instinctual needs and the impetus of intellectual activity. His basic inability to transform his quota of sexual energy into a force for creative work results in Louis's isolation in a world of inspired madness. Balthazar Claës, protagonist of *La Recherche de l'absolu,* is a modern incarnation of the Faust myth. Driven by his desire for absolute knowledge through science, he expends his energy in a desperate struggle with time itself to realize his dream of dominance over nature. The success or failure of his enterprise is indeed secondary in this novel to the narrator's exploration of the dynamics of the creative process. The static resistance of material reality (environment and family needs, love, sexuality, and matter itself) to the dynamic spiritual aspirations of the genius figure, produces a heroic struggle that for Balzac exemplifies the very laws of creativity: "Le mouvement, en raison de la résistance, produit une combinaison qui est la vie; dès que l'un ou l'autre est plus fort, la vie cesse." [10]

Théophile Gautier's relationship to romantic literature has often been misunderstood. After his initial association with "romantic ideology," as Victor Hugo's lieutenant in the battle of *Hernani,* and his close friendship with Nerval, he was linked primarily to Parnassian and presymbolist aesthetics. His numerous articles and reviews of painting, literature, and music written between the thirties and the seventies constitute a unique record of decades of cultural life in France; they reveal an enrichment of his critical judgment, not necessarily a rejection of the tenets of romantic writing. Instead of the celebrated and even infamous preface to *Mademoiselle de Maupin* (1835) (always credited with the justification of the principle Art for art's sake), I have therefore chosen to analyze a later essay, "Du Beau dans l'art" (1865). In this study, which affords an interesting parallel to Baudelaire's "Le Peintre de la vie moderne" (1863), Gautier similarly discusses the elements and stages constitutive of the creative process.

In spite of its date, this essay maintains a Neoplatonic version of romantic idealism, and even a fairly strict adherence to the Hugoesque model of the artist as visionary. Although Gautier totally rejects the concept of the socially committed function of the artist, he insists in this text, as he had throughout his long career, on the importance of a rich interior life as the true source of the creative impulse. He reverses Hugo's version of the relationship between the Ideal and real phenomena, however, for nature is not, for Gautier, the possible source of truth about the spiritual world, a readily accessible network of signs and symbols to be interpreted by the poet-prophet. Nature in the form of the artist's raw material or media must be infused with the individual creator's own personal apprehension of the ideal dimension of being. Still a Promethean figure, the artist now acquires the task of assigning a spiritual value to the phenomenological world. In the terms of current critical terminology, the artist no longer sees reality as "lisible" (to be interpreted) but as "scriptible" (to be created).

It is precisely the lack of individual inner resources that Gautier and Musset both mock in their satiric and parodic portraits of romantic painters and writers in *Les Jeunes-France* (1833) and the *Lettres de Dupuis et Cotonet* (1836–37). Both early works attest, however, to the self-reflective, ironic, and critical dimension of romantic writing in the 1830s that produced important parodies of its own paradigm of the creative experience. Gautier satirizes the romantic and perhaps universal tendency of artists to imitate previous forms; texts always mediate life for Gautier's hapless nonheroes, who attempt to force human reality to conform with artistic models in order to produce works of art. Total lack of originality, dependence on exaggerated cultural models, and a refusal to confront the "real" world before them—these are the errors of the young romantic generation. Through the use of parody, irony, and intertextuality (Alexandre Dumas's *Antony* as a romantic intertext), he attacks the pretentions of the young artists who destroy the talent they possess through a slavish imitation of texts.

Musset develops his ironic judgment of romantic aesthetics even beyond that of Gautier. Although he does present the portrait of an artist figure who recognizes the limits of his talent and energy, and achieves a masterpiece in *Le Fils du Titien* (1838), most of his many representations of creative persons reveal tragically fragmented personalities. Titian's son, whose story can serve as Musset's ideal model, is, after all, a late-Renaissance figure. The cultural codes of contemporary France after the July Revolution of 1830 are seen by Musset to be void of significance; their signs correspond to no recognizable human reality. The *Lettres de Dupuis et Cotonet* anticipates Flaubert's *Bouvard et Pécuchet* as the protagonists examine the essential words and concepts of romanticism ("romantisme," "humanitaire," "progrès") only to discover that these signifiers have no perceptible signifieds—words in the postrevolutionary July Monarchy definitely do not correspond to things.

Musset's almost modernist critique of romantic discourse pre-

scribes the need to approach social and personal reality with
plicity" or directness unmediated by the accumulated layers
mantic texts. Writing is obliged to return to a kind of zero degree,
since the failures of social and political systems (revolution, empire,
and restoration) necessitate new cultural codes.

In a sense we have completed the circle: Musset's statement of the
failure of romantic discourse due to its exaggerated forms ironically
complements Stello's experience of the conflict between his need to
produce poetry, and the destructive impact of political languages and
ideologies that prohibit him from functioning as a poet in society.
Musset develops the self-reflective, ironic mode to its final conclusion; romanticism, in this curious text that seems to herald Flaubert's
iconoclastic and modernist attitude, is identified with an abuse of
adjectives.

Hugo's romantic, idealistic, and essentially optimistic version of
the creative life (maintained even by Musset in his Renaissance portraits) is therefore seriously questioned by Vigny and is modified,
even parodied and satirized, by his contemporaries Gautier and Musset. The fiction of the *Etudes philosophiques* of Balzac remains perhaps
the central and most profound representation during the romantic
period of the necessary and heroic ("sublime" in his terminology)
conflict in the creative personality. The opposing forces of materialism and spirituality seem to define Balzac's artists; the worlds of
things, matter, and language itself resist their desire to transform and
thus to idealize and recreate them. Stello and Louis Lambert choose
to renounce the struggle and Balthazar engages himself in it totally
although it destroys him. Only Hugo's *mages* transcend the process;
these mythical men of genius, reborn and renewed after their descent
into hell, offer us above all a positive and exemplary model of the
romantic experience of creativity.

I

Alfred de Vigny and the Creative Experience:
Le Journal d'un poète

Le Journal d'un poète remains the best source for precise knowledge concerning Vigny's understanding of the creative personality. From 1823 until the last months of his life Vigny carefully noted the progress of his own oeuvre, recording numerous projects for poems, reactions to criticism, and concise interpretations of some of his works. He repeatedly analyzed his own personality as well as that of the artist and creative person in general. In a kind of dialogue between his public and private selves, between the active, philosophical Docteur Noir and the sensitive, secretive poet Stello, Vigny often probed the very nature of creativity.

François Germain in his excellent study *L'Imagination d'Alfred de Vigny*[1] relies most heavily on *Stello* and the poetry for his analysis; I propose to concentrate on the *Journal* because it is an extraordinarily rich and beautiful text that has been neglected, and also because it provides an opening into the mind and conscience of a major romantic artist grappling with the essential problem of his existence—the meaning and function of art. My discussion will be limited to two elements of Vigny's preoccupations with creativity: first, his view of himself as a creative personality and his efforts to define his own methods and techniques; second, his ideas on aesthetics (e.g., definition of the role of imagination, the concept of the correspondence between the arts) as they pertain to his portrait of the ideal creative person and the laws of the creative process itself.

Throughout the *Journal* Vigny stresses the dual nature of his own personality, the existence in himself of two distinct natures: the "dramatic" rational self who attempts with limited success to lead an active life in society (who is named Docteur Noir) and the meditative dreamer, the solitary Stello. He defines his life as a perpetual drama, a struggle between the two natures, and deplores the fact that he has always found it necessary, in order to function in society, to repress the "poetic" side of his nature (the "côté divin")[2] in favor of the human side. Since childhood, "le Docteur Noir seul parut en moi, Stello se cacha" (*Journal,* p. 960). His capacity for tenderness and extreme sensitivity and his tendency toward reverie were not only repressed but hidden under a cold, social mask; the vulnerable or "feminine" anima aspect of his personality was therefore carefully protected and controlled by the strong and impassive will of the soldier stoic. The sadness of a lonely childhood and the disappointments of his adult life, complemented by his scorn of all forms of contemporary power, concretized his feeling of alienation and served to strengthen the importance and value of the inner dreamworld. In fact, "ce qui se rêve est tout pour moi" (*Journal,* p. 1221); Vigny repeatedly emphasizes the importance of reverie, and the world of dreams as the center of his real life, his unique happiness, and the point of departure for his art: "Une rêverie perpétuelle, que l'action et la parole dérangent, voilà quelle a été ma vie et quelle elle doit être jusqu'à mon dernier jour. C'est le rêve qui est ma vie réelle, et la vie en est la distraction" (*Journal,* p. 1285).

The dreamworld is the source of his ideas, of the ideas and ideals that become the matrix of all his poems and fiction: "J'ai toujours été trop rêveur, cela dès l'enfance m'isolait: invincible distraction, une région heureuse où je vivais des idées qui me ravissaient" (*Journal,* p. 1227).

In a very profound sense "un artiste ne doit et ne peut aimer que lui-même" (*Journal,* p. 904); the self and its riches must be cultivated and protected. Solitude is necessary to permit the constant inner study or "secret travail" (*Journal,* 1320) of the mind that transforms dreams into ideas. The self and self-analysis are thus the major source of inspiration according to Vigny, but this perpetual study cannot take place without passionate effort and suffering, "le feu est notre seul élément" (*Journal,* p. 936).

Vigny understands this constant work of the mind or *esprit,* not only as the very essence of his own character but as the impetus to creativity for all men. Man is creative precisely when he struggles with the forces of nature on all levels; whether he be the artist with his unconscious impulses, the ship captain–hero of "La Bouteille à la mer" pitted against the fatality of the sea, or humanity itself torn between the forces of liberty and order.[3] The principle of struggle dominates the writer's situation, and it is precisely this special combat between the poet and his own idea that he had tried to dramatize in *Stello:* "La perpétuelle lutte du Poète est celle qu'il livre à son idée. Si l'idée triomphe du Poète et le passionne trop, il est sa dupe et tombe dans la mise en action de cette idée et s'y perd. Si le Poète est plus fort que l'idée, il la pétrit, la forme et la met en oeuvre. Elle devient ce qu'il a voulu, un monument" (*Journal,* p. 1071). For man in general, however, "tout se réduit donc à cette lutte du caractère contre la destinée" (*Journal,* p. 957). This latter phrase could serve as an epigraph for Vigny's entire production.

A refusal to accept the tragic imperfections of man's fate, defined by time and death and cruelly limited by reason and his material condition, becomes the impetus to create works of art that can withstand the destruction of time. A complex and interesting variation of this "romantic" concept of the meaning of art[4] as a revolt against the fatalities of human existence is developed by Vigny in the following notation in his *Journal:*

De la Vie.—Mon sentiment intime, profond, inné, c'est le déplaisir et le dégoût de la vie. Non le désespoir ou la douleur en aucune sorte, mais l'horreur de la *laideur.* Dès l'enfance j'eus l'idée et le désir d'une beauté physique et morale de la Création qui me la fit souhaiter et rêver meilleure. Nourri, enveloppé dans les langes de la *beauté,* vue à travers les chefs-d'oeuvre, et de la *convenance* vue à travers les récits et les moeurs des plus nobles familles, je n'ai jamais pu voir les réalités grossières sans un mépris profond, sans une horreur secrète de la laideur.

La beauté de la Création et de la Nature, je la rêvais à travers les chefs-d'oeuvre de la peinture: après avoir passé des heures de rêverie pendant des années devant Raphaël et la famille de Niobé, je trouvai peu de femmes dignes d'amour. Mais celles que j'aimai, je les adorai parce qu'elles avaient quelque chose de cet *idéal.*

Après avoir contemplé les mers dans le *Déluge* de Poussin, je trouvai la première tempête que je vis sur mer d'une petitesse ridicule.

On ne voyait pas autour de moi assez d'étendue d'eau, assez de soulèvement des vagues, contre les rochers. (*Journal,* p. 1297)

The beauty and harmony of master paintings and great literature alone give form to the ideals through which man can dream of a world different from the ugly realities of this one. To create a poem or a painting is, thus, for Vigny, to find the appropriate form for the idea or ideal, the spiritual value that should be preserved because it corresponds to the highest goals or aspirations of mankind.

The superiority of art over the flawed world of nature and man is a concept that becomes even more pronounced in the *Journal* toward the end of Vigny's life. *L'atticisme* (atticism, or unusual refinement in taste and language) is the term he selects to designate the love of all beautiful forms, artistic illusion, and pure ideas that he proposes as a necessary choice for modern man: "Il faudra bien que la société moderne choisisse entre deux destinées: Ou l'abrutissement matériel et industriel, ou bien le choix, *purifié* de plus en plus, des Idées, l'Atticisme partout" (*Journal,* p. 1385). Not only does art influence life: the ideal beauty of a Raphael figure, for example, is seen reflected in the imperfect beauty of a real woman, who thus becomes more admirable; but art is perhaps, in the last analysis, the illusion that alone makes the nothingness of existence tolerable: "Les insensés positivistes qui ne voient pas que l'idéal est le charme, l'illusion la seule consolation de la vie" (*Journal,* p. 1280).

Vigny's concept of art manifests a kind of negative or pessimistic Platonism, an adoration of ideas, the ideal, and artistic beauty for themselves, with full awareness of their illusory quality and perhaps their nonexistence. This attitude parallels his continued support of the supernatural and Christianity even though he no longer believes in God or the Church. In fact Vigny has made a religion out of art, and ideas must be seen in his language as mystical entities that, in a perfected state in which they are developed to their purest, clearest possibilities, represent a truly spiritual reality. The "esprit pur" of the artist, philosopher, or poet seeking to incarnate these ideas by discovering the most beautiful forms for them is actively repeating the gesture attributed to divine creativity. For Vigny man as creator has become his own god,[5] whose ambition is to "soumettre le monde à la

domination des esprits supérieurs en qui réside l'intelligence divine"
(*Journal,* p. 897).

The metaphysical value of the ideal world, or Vigny's mysticism
of ideas, is clearly expressed in early sections of the *Journal,* when he
is experiencing a loss of orthodox faith and is disillusioned by the
collapse of traditional social and political values. In 1832 he compares
himself to Dante's heroine: "Mon âme tourmentée se repose sur des
Idées revêtues de formes mystiques. . . . Ame jetée aux vents comme
Françoise de Rimini! Ton âme ô Francesca, montait tenant entre tes
bras l'âme bien-aimée de Paolo: mon âme est pareille à toi!" (*Journal,*
p. 941). When his intellectual idealism is developed to its final conclusions, however, Vigny realizes that his "atticism" means that the
artist creates illusion primarily because man needs illusions of meaning and beauty in order to survive the emptiness and ugliness of
reality:

Du Néant des Lettres. — La seule fin vraie à laquelle l'esprit arrive, en péné-
trant tout au fond de chaque perspective, c'est le néant de tout. Gloire,
amour, bonheur, rien de tout cela n'est complètement. Donc, pour écrire
des pensées sur un sujet quelconque et dans quelque forme que ce soit, nous
sommes forcés de commencer par nous mentir à nous-mêmes, en nous fi-
gurant que quelque chose existe et en créant un fantôme pour ensuite l'adorer
ou le profaner, le grandir ou le détruire. Ainsi nous sommes des don Qui-
chottes perpétuels et moins excusable que le héros de Cervantes, car nous
savons que nos géants sont des moulins et nous nous enivrons pour les voir
géants. (*Journal,* p. 1126)

Vigny's atticism and love of ideas explain the pleasure the artist
himself enjoys as the creator of beautiful forms and spiritual "pensées," but they also illuminate certain aspects of the creative process
itself. The artist's real happiness comes literally from the play of creating, from the interplay of ideas: "De La Pensée Pure. — La Pensée
seule, la Pensée pure, l'exercice intérieur des idées et leur jeu entre
elles, est pour moi un véritable bonheur" (*Journal,* p. 1337). The value
of solving aesthetic problems that he sets for himself (numerous
projected works attest to this in the *Journal*) and the mastering the
composition of difficult forms are important aspects of the creative
life. Vigny's thought resembles Gautier's particular brand of classicism—the challenge of transforming hard materials into beauty—
but prefigures as well Mallarmé's notion of the virtue found in in-

comprehensibility or obscureness: "Atticisme. — Il faut choisir dans les lettres entre deux mépris: celui que l'auteur a pour lui-même s'il écrit des vulgarités populaires et celui que le vulgaire a pour lui s'il enveloppe sa pensée d'une forme d'art qui la rend plus belle, plus abstraite et plus difficile à comprendre" (*Journal*, p. 1288).

The choice of atticism and the aesthetics of the mastery of difficult formal problems are attributes of Vigny's version of the ideal man, "l'âme contemplative." In a long entry of December 1835 he analyzes the essential qualities of the thinker or creator, far superior to the man who lives only for the present moment. Memory, judgment, and imagination are the three faculties of his triple "vision," and they correspond to a profound knowledge of the past, a solid appraisal of the present, and an almost prophetic intuition of the future. Reinforced by reason and a strong will, the contemplative man "rapporte au coeur les émotions que lui donne sa triple vue et à ce centre d'amour et de bonté se perfectionne et s'agrandit sans cesse la grandeur et la puissance de son être" (*Journal*, p. 1036). Vigny judges such a person capable of growing in moral stature and eventually producing immortal works and actions beneficial to humanity.

This humanistic conception of the ideal man can serve as a point of departure for an examination of Vigny's analysis of his own method of creating and can lead to his conclusions about the creative process, for it contains in generalized form the main thrust of his argument.

The impulse to create, in Vigny's case to write a poem or a work in prose, does not come from what he calls his active personality, his conscious or present experience. He severely criticizes the biographical approach to criticism, in particular that of Sainte-Beuve, and insists, perhaps excessively, that his life has never been the source of his oeuvre.[6] The mysterious impulse that becomes an obsession, and a source of delight (*jouissance* and *délire* are the terms he uses to designate the joy of creating), is born from memory, reverie, a sentiment, or on rare occasions is triggered by direct observation of reality. This initial stage of the creative process, akin to what Jung calls an autonomous complex, related to a neurosis but distinguished from it precisely because its impulse is toward joy and work, remains for Vigny an involuntary inspiration that causes him to feel ecstatic and to know a happiness he experiences at no other moment. It takes him out of the course of present time, bringing him into contact with the needs and aspirations of his deepest self: "Aujourd'hui, malgré moi, l'idée d'une pièce de théâtre sur la primitive Eglise chrétienne m'a préoccupé fortement. Cette idée m'a tenu en extase tout le jour à travers les conversations" (*Journal*, p. 962).

It is certainly no exaggeration that the romantics began to uncover and express the force of the unconscious self. One of the most important and least recognized contributions of the *Journal* is precisely Vigny's description of the role the unconscious plays in the creative life: "Ce qui se rêve est tout pour moi. Le rêve est aussi cher au penseur que tout ce qu'on aime dans le monde réel et plus redoutable que tout ce qu'on y craint" (*Journal*, p. 1008). Here he makes the connection between the impulse from the unconscious to the second level of the creative experience, the obsessive idea. Perpetually writing a "livre intérieur" (*Journal*, p. 1326), dominated by the ideas that force themselves toward a form, Vigny speaks of the "laboratoire intime" (*Journal*, p. 1359) where the movement toward conception and composition takes place, suggesting both the science and the magic of creating. "Ma tête pour retenir les idées positives, est forcée de les jeter dans le domaine de l'imagination. Où me conduiras-tu, passion des Idées, où me conduiras-tu? J'ai possédé telle Idée; avec telle autre j'ai passé bien des nuits. Vous m'avez donné mon imagination pour maîtresse. La volupté de l'âme est plus longue, l'extase morale est supérieure à l'extase physique!" (*Journal*, p. 1008).

For Vigny the idea is the matrix, or rather the organic source of every work that grows in him like a seed: "L'Idée. — Lorsqu'une idée neuve, juste, poétique, est tombée, de je ne sais d'où dans mon âme, rien ne peut l'en arracher, elle y germe comme le grain dans une terre labourée sans cesse par l'imagination. En vain, je parle, j'agis, j'écris, je pense même sur d'autres choses, je la sens pousser en moi, l'épi mûrit et s'élève, et bientôt il faut que je moissonne ce froment et que j'en forme un pain salutaire et quotidien pour la multitude" (*Journal*, p. 1180).

This romantic comparison of creativity to a dynamic, organic, and yet mysterious natural process, contains the fundamental elements of Vigny's aesthetic: the mysterious origins and growth of the idea, the necessary labor of the imagination, and the final harvesting of the wheat, i.e., the formation of the work that in time becomes the bread or spiritual nourishment for humanity.

If the origins of the idea remain the secret of "inspiration," born in the individual consciousness and yet related to unconscious collective experience, the work of the imagination, the major creative faculty for Vigny, is a conscious and well-defined effort. In many texts of the *Journal* as well as in *Stello* and certain poems,[7] Vigny analyzes the function of imagination as a synthesizing, fusing power that discovers the structures—that is, develops the fables or myths into the narratives and verse forms that permanently incorporate ideas: "l'imagination donne du corps aux idées et leur crée des types et des symboles vivants qui sont comme la forme palpable et la preuve d'une théorie abstraite" (*Journal*, p. 880). The central work of the imagination then, is that of discovering, creating, organizing, and composing the living symbols and palpable forms that will permit the passage from the mind of the artist to the world of his audience. It translates the matter or sensory experiences of beauty and pleasure into a language that makes the reception and communication of ideas possible.

In a text entitled "De ma manière de composer" Vigny delineates this organizing faculty of the imagination both in terms of its revelation of sensuous forms, in this case the spatial and temporal setting, and of its truly creative aspect, "une fable qu'il faut inventer."

L'idée une fois reçue m'émeut jusqu'au coeur, et je la prends en adoration. Cent fois par jour elle revient à ma pensée dans le cercle toujours mouvant des pensées. Je la salue et la perfectionne à chacune de ses évolutions. Puis je travaille pour elle, je lui choisis une époque pour sa demeure, pour son vêtement une nation. Là je fouille les temps et les débris de la société de ces âges qui conviennent le mieux à sa manifestation. Ces précieux restes une fois assemblés, je trouve le point par lequel l'idée s'unit à eux dans la vérité de l'art et par lequel la réalité des moeurs s'élève jusqu'à l'idéal de la pensée-mère; sur ce point flotte une fable, qu'il faut inventer assez passionnée, assez émouvante pour servir de démonstration à l'idée et la démonstration incontestable s'il se peut. Travail difficile s'il en est et qui ne peut produire que des oeuvres rares. (*Journal*, pp. 1355–57)

The *Journal* contains numerous references to the role of the creative imagination both in the composition of prose works (historical novels or short stories such as the previous quotation would suggest) and of poetry. In this respect Vigny's most interesting observations about his own imagination lead to a better knowledge of the romantic appreciation of a meaningful correspondence between the arts. Vigny's contribution to this phenomenon has passed virtually unnoticed, although his formulations recall certain ideas of both Diderot and Baudelaire, who in their theoretical writings frequently suggested elements of comparison and unity in the arts. In an early poem (1824) written as a eulogy to the dead painter Girodet and as a prelude to his own "Le Déluge" (itself inspired by Girodet's painting), Vigny invokes the romantic dream of a total art that Wagner would later attempt to realize. He already suggests, moreover, the use Baudelaire would make of the possible relationships or correspondences between the sensory experiences in music, painting, and poetry. The poem indeed evokes the possibility of a harmonious unity, complementarity, and interpenetration of sound, color, and language:

La Beauté idéale

Où donc est la beauté que rêve le poète?
Aucun d'entre les arts n'est son digne interprète,
Et souvent il voudrait, par son rêve égaré,
Confondre ce que Dieu pour l'homme a séparé.
Il voudrait ajouter les sons à la peinture.
A son gré si la Muse imitait la nature,
Les formes, la pensée et tous les bruits épars
Viendraient se rencontrer dans le prisme des arts,
Centre où de l'univers les beautés réunies
Apporteraient au coeur toutes les harmonies,
Les bruits et les couleurs de la terre et des cieux,
Le charme de l'oreille et le charme des yeux.
Descends donc, triple lyre, instrument inconnu,
O toi! qui parmi nous n'est pas encore venu
Et qu'en se consumant invoque le génie.
Sans toi point de beauté, sans toi point d'harmonie:
Musique, poésie, art pur de Raphaël,
Vous deviendrez un Dieu . . . mais sur un seul autel.[8]

In his own inner world, memory presents ideas to the imagination in the form of colors to be painted: "L'obstination de la mémoire m'est à charge et souvent je suis obsédé de ses retours, qui me ramènent sous les yeux des verres de couleurs vives et des tableaux et des rayons de pensées qu'il me faut peindre. Après les avoir conçus la crainte de les oublier me les fait écrire, et jusqu'à ce que le papier m'en ait délivré, ils ne cessent de revenir à ma vue" (*Journal,* p. 1310). With its insistence on the importance of a visual imagination,[9] this example of synesthesia is one of the many references to poetry and painting found in the *Journal*. The poet must learn to *see* the images presented by memory or reality: "Voir est tout pour moi. Un seul coup d'oeil me révèle un pays et je crois deviner, sur le visage, une âme" (*Journal*, p. 883). The ideal artist or "âme contemplative," we may recall, is the man with the gift of triple vision who sees and "sees again" past, present, and future realities in depth. And the poet himself, is finally, according to Vigny, a kind of "voyant" endowed with prophetic insight, capable of perceiving truths hidden behind the surfaces of things, of intuiting order and meaning where only disorder and contradictions are apparent. In a "comparaison poétique" of 1824, he illustrates this vision with the image of a voyager on a dark mountain in Iceland who suddenly discovers the sun: "ainsi le poète voit un soleil, un monde sublime et jette des cris d'extase sur ce monde délivré, tandis que les hommes sont plongés dans la nuit" (*Journal*, p. 880). This prophetic vision was, of course, attributed by most of the romantic poets to themselves without undue modesty, and Vigny, like Hugo, does not hesitate: "Jamais je ne me suis trompé au premier coup d'oeil sur ce qu'a dû être un événement, une conversation, un mot. J'exerce toute ma vie cette faculté sur l'avenir et jamais jusqu'ici je ne me suis trompé en prévoyant ce que deviendrait un homme" (*Journal*, p. 901). It is equally clear that for the romantic mind it is the artist who assigns value to things and who reveals the signification of the world's signs, and that this power is a primary function of the creative self.

Vigny compares the composition of a poem to the painter's craft, suggesting the steps involved in completing a picture that Baudelaire described concerning Constantin Guys.[10] The essential preliminary sketch ("esquisse en prose") is put aside to permit the creative dimension of time to play its role in the realization of the design. This is followed by the final and rather rapid work of painting the canvas in oil:

Les compositions comme les miennes sont d'une extrême difficulté. Depuis longtemps j'avais le sentiment de la conception de ce poème dans la tête, mais le dessin ne me satisfaisait pas. En voyageant et en passant à Tours j'ai écrit dans une auberge, au mois de décembre, une esquisse en prose dont le mouvement était bien jeté. Je l'ai crayonnée et je l'ai oubliée en portefeuille. Un jour à Londres je l'ai regardée comme un peintre regarde l'esquisse d'un autre peintre, et, la jugeant comme oeuvre d'art, je l'ai approuvée et me suis donné l'autorisation de peindre le tableau. Hier ici j'ai pris la toile et je l'ai peinte en deux jours. C'est une bonne manière de faire. (*Journal,* pp. 1118–19).

The importance of the preliminary sketch ("crayonnée et . . . oubliée") suggests the method of a Delacroix but more significantly recalls Diderot's concept of the "modèle," or inner form, that the artist (poet, actor, or painter as he presents him in the *Paradoxe sur le comédien*[11]) first produces as a result of the contact between his private world and that of nature. Instead of simply imitating a classical model or recognized form, he exercises his originality precisely in the invention of this preliminary model, which he later improves upon partly by conforming to an established artistic tradition. This concept of the artist's original model, first developed in detail in Diderot's writings on aesthetics, is an important justification for the nineteenth-century romantic belief in the value of individual creativity and the power of the autonomous creative mind.

Vigny describes the secrets of his "manière de produire" in a text that suggests Diderot even more surely, since he compares the conception of the preliminary model to the first mold of a statue, a comparison recurring frequently in the *Paradoxe:* "Je conçois tout à coup un plan, je perfectionne longuement le moule de la statue, je l'oublie et quand je me mets à l'oeuvre après de longs repos, je ne laisse pas refroidir la lave un moment. C'est après de longs intervalles que j'écris, et je reste plusieurs mois de suite occupé de ma vie, sans lire ni écrire" (*Journal,* p. 1028). Again, the original model is put aside in order that time will permit the artist's conception to take final form unconsciously or unknowingly in his mind. The value of time as a creative force transforming experience and emotion into a ground for art is, however, a function of Vigny's disillusionment with the present as well as an aesthetic device: "Jamais mon esprit n'est plus libre que quand l'oeuvre que je fais n'a nul rapport avec ma situation présente. Et j'ai toujours eu un tel effroi du présent et du réel dans ma vie que je n'ai jamais représenté par l'art une émotion douloureuse ou ravissante dans le temps même que je l'éprouvais" (*Journal,* p. 903).

Vigny thus clearly conceives of the creation of a work of art as a four-part process from inspiration to communication. It commences with the mysterious impulse from the world of dream or memory, the world of the unconscious self, to produce the central idea or matrix. Then follows the most important period of the creative act, the inventive work of the imagination that creates the preliminary sketch or model, and discovers the fable or symbol that composes the design of the work, thus giving form to the idea. The third part, the one about which Vigny writes the least (and which perhaps interests twentieth-century critics the most), is the elaboration into literary language or the signifiers, after the necessary passage of time, of the final product. The idea, or signified, finally becomes a poem clothed in verse, the fable invented by the imagination is enriched with precise details of setting and custom and is transformed into a short story or novel. The sketch has become an oil painting, or to use Vigny's favorite image, the crystal container or form has been polished to give off the purest light, completing the cycle by illuminating the reader and communicating the pleasure of beauty as well as the significance of the idea: "Oui, la poésie est une volupté, mais une volupté couvrant la pensée et la rendant lumineuse par l'éclat de son cristal préservateur qui lui permettra de vivre éternellement et d'éclairer sans fin" (Journal, pp. 1139–40).

II

Alfred de Vigny: The *Consultations* of the Docteur Noir—*Stello* and *Les Destinées*—from Alienation to Renascence

C. S. Lewis, Jung, and others have analyzed the movement of the romantic consciousness in the experience of poetry as a desire to create through harmonious, symbolic language the image of a world that would be whole, that is coherent, ordered, and beautiful. An essential rhythm of the poet's quest for wholeness can be seen in terms of the archetypal pattern of rebirth: the movement from alienation in a fragmented world to renascence in a meaningful one. Romantic poems themselves manifest in their themes and structure a sense of evolution and spiritual discovery, such as that of *The Ancient Mariner* or the *Prelude* of Wordsworth.[1] Legends, myths, and poems containing the rebirth archetype frequently exhibit a tripartite structure similar to that found in the initiatory rites and ceremonies of many peoples. A spiritual death or a refusal of the world, defined as fatally imperfect and static, is followed by contact during a time of isolation and alienation with a source of spiritual meaning and beauty (such as new knowledge of the profound life of nature, love, or God). This discovery leads to a renewal of being or a renascence on a higher plane of existence, characterized by an experience of integration and unity.

Images of dying and resurrected mythical half-gods, Titans like Prometheus, often served the romantic poets to illustrate their themes of disenchantment with society, spiritual alienation, and, finally, necessary revolt and change, even revolution. The theme of "la révolte sainte," for example, was actualized in Hugo's *Le Satyre* and *La Fin de Satan;* Michelet presented history as inevitable progress resulting from the dialectical struggle of man's liberty and genius against the fatalities of time. These works corroborate the thesis of critics[2] who see the romantic vision in terms of a rejection of the world as a mechanical, static chain of being in favor of a world in the state of perpetual "becomingness," an organic process of evolution in which man, nature, and God are parts of a meaningful whole.

Vigny's prose, often dealing with much the same content as that of his romantic contemporaries, has suggested to readers the presence of contradictory ideas and a prideful retreat to the ivory tower. His verse has created disappointment due to some awkwardness in his poetic language. Sympathetic critics, on the other hand have examined his poetic practices, the Icarian aspect of his concept of the poet, and his moral and religious ideas.[3] Germain's excellent *L'Imagination d'Alfred de Vigny* provided us with an indispensable and thorough analysis of the ways in which Vigny imagines the world of objects and sensations, offering a sensitive psychological portrait of his complex creative personality. Except for Germain's study, Vigny criticism remains fragmented, and we are left with the uneasy impression that his work is confused or disunified. This weakness is even attributed to the possibility that although he claimed to be a philosophical poet, Vigny was more "poète" than "philosophe."

It is precisely his concept of the poet and of poetry itself that seems to me to be at the heart of his work and of his experience as a writer. A closer reading of the texts concerned with the poet figure (specifically *Stello* and "La Maison du berger," as well as the autobiographical *Journal d'un poète*) reveals, I believe, a recurrent structural pattern very similar to the dialectical or oppositional structure of many poems by Hugo, and inherent in Michelet's view of history. It is precisely this pattern that gives unity and coherence to Vigny's writing. Expressed in these works is a strong confidence in the act of poetry, capable of leading to a second life, which makes Vigny perhaps the major French exponent of the romantic poem as a process of spiritual discovery. Not only are poets and poetry the major subject of much of his work (an early example of highly self-conscious literature), but he chose to represent in his own world the needs of other unappreciated poets and, through an obstinate defense of poetry, the need for poetic idealism in an increasingly materialistic society. His misunderstood efforts in parliament and through the Académie Française in favor of subsidizing young artists were part of a strong commitment to the social value of poetry.

There is very definitely a change in perspective between the publication of *Stello* (1830) and that of "La Maison du berger" (1844) concerning the poet and the creative process. Even Germain fails to take this development into account when he considers to be conclusive Vigny's presentation of the artistic personality as dualistic and permanently divided into Docteur Noir and Stello, animus–intellect and anima–dreamer.

It is quite clear that in *Stello* Vigny presents the poet as the scapegoat of society. Like a Prometheus chained to the rock, he is devoured by the sense of his own uselessness and forced to renounce what Henry James called the sacred fount of life, to take refuge in the ivory tower in order to find spiritual nourishment through solitude. It becomes evident, however, that in "La Maison du berger" we are presented with the liberation and the regeneration of the poet, a Prometheus unbound, inspired by love and a new confidence in his own genius, prepared to create and participate in the life of man: "J'aime la majesté des souffrances humaines" (*Oeuvres*, 1:181).

In this chapter, I will attempt to account for this transformation, while placing Vigny within the romantic cultural frame of reference. His representations of the poet and his experience manifest a variant of the same paradigm we will study in Hugo's *William Shakespeare:* from sacrificial victim of society's power to shepherd of men, from alienation and spiritual death to rebirth. The poet-Prometheus has been freed and his creative force renewed.

Not enough attention has been paid to the interesting variety of narrative techniques employed by Vigny in the writing of *Stello,* to the complexity of point of view, and especially to the dialectical structure underlying its composition. The work has the form of a dialogue or "consultation," actually an early example of a psychoanalytical session between doctor and patient, a form that Vigny repeats in *Daphné* and that he projected for other, incompleted works. Within the outer dialogue between the Docteur Noir, realist, rationalist, and cynic (also poet and repressed sentimentalist), and the poet-dreamer, Stello, there are three "récits" presenting the opposition between power and poetry in three different societies and in increasing complexity. The final *récit* actually presents four different kinds of "poet" from the viewpoint of the Docteur Noir, who himself "sees" poetically. A series of binary oppositions or antitheses governs the dialogue and the *récits* contained within it, giving each part dramatic tension, suggesting the movement and struggle of ideas, and finally producing the tragic consequences for poets and for poetry. The binary oppositions result, not in a new synthesis, but rather in the domination of thesis over antithesis, of power over poetry, and of solitude and a refusal over participation and communion. Gilbert, Chatterton, and André Chénier become tragic victims of the monarchical, parliamentarian, and democratic governments respectively presented in the three *récits*. Stello learns from the telling of the stories and his dialogue with the doctor that "la solitude est sainte," and that the poet must remain isolated and alienated if he is to survive.

What might be termed the romantic aspects of the narrative have been mentioned by critics, such as the Hugoesque antithesis of the grotesque and the sublime in character and situation (e.g., the materialistic Lord Mayor and the spiritual Chatterton, the horrors of St. Lazare and the stoic resignation of the aristocrats during the terror). Important elements of the text such as the use of local color and of historical setting and a mixture of styles and even genres quite contrary to classical design have been singled out. It should be stressed that each *récit* has its characteristic tone, or rather tones, since, for example, the Doctor changes his language and style as he describes in the first *récit* the frivolity of the court of Louis XV and the pathetic suicide of Gilbert. He consciously adopts the tone and style of the period he is presenting and imitates the language of the actors of the scene, becoming cryptic and witty when speaking of Louis XV, pedantic during the presentation of London's Lord Mayor, and gravely poetic concerning the Terror.

Point of view is complex and innovative. In the *récits* it is obviously the doctor-narrator who focuses on reality for his auditor and for the reader. The dialogue presents a double or rather a triple, point of view; the doctor's voice seems reliable about society, but nevertheless we are told by the narrator-persona of Vigny that the dreamer Stello is always superior to the reasoner. And yet Stello is presented as a "malade" almost driven mad by spleen. In fact, the narrator-persona remains detached, and through a use of ironic distance refuses a simple identification with either voice in the dialogue, or either part of the creative personality. It is perhaps this irony that made the text so disconcerting to its early readers, but that now gives it a modern cast.[4] The first-person narrator does not accord his sympathy to either the coldly cynical doctor or the sometimes foolish dreamer. Nevertheless, François Germain's analysis of the dialogue as a representation of the divisions within the creative personality of Vigny is penetrating and convincing, and a reading of the *Journal* reveals the importance Vigny attached to the reflection of his own personality in his imaginary characters.

In 1832, while speaking of his unhappy childhood, he explains the need he felt to repress his emotional nature:—"Une sensibilité extrême, refoulée dès l'enfance par les maîtres et à l'armée par les officiers supérieurs, demeura enfermée dans le coin le plus secret du coeur.—Le monde ne vit plus pour jamais que les idées, résultat du travail prompt et exact de l'intelligence.—Le Docteur Noir seul parut en moi, Stello se cacha" (*Journal*, p. 960). The anima side of his personality was thus contained under an iron mask and permanently controlled through extreme efforts of willpower: "J'étais né doué d'une sensibilité féminine. Jusqu'à quinze ans je pleurais, je versais des fleuves de larmes par amitié, par sympathie, pour une froideur de ma mère, un chagrin d'un ami, je me prenais à tout et partout j'étais repoussé. Je me refermais comme une sensitive" (*Journal*, p. 986).

He admits the continual presence of the two selves—the animus– "moi philosophique" and the anima–"moi dramatique"—and their alternating influence on his actions and his writing: "Je crois donc dire que j'ai cru démêler en moi deux êtres bien distincts l'un de l'autre, le moi dramatique, qui vit avec activité et violence, éprouve avec douleur ou enivrement, agit avec énergie ou persévérance, et le moi philosophique, qui se sépare journellement de l'autre moi, le dédaigne, le juge, le critique, l'analyse, le regarde passer et rit ou pleure de ses faux pas comme ferait un ange gardien" (*Journal*, p. 1032).

In June of 1844 he defines and generalizes the significance of the two personalities: "Le Docteur Noir est le côté humain et réel de tout; Stello a voulu voir ce qui devrait être, ce qu'il est beau d'espérer et de croire, de souhaiter pour l'avenir: c'est le côté divin" (*Journal*, p. 1218). According to Germain, the doctor (intellect-will-animus) finally purges the dreamer Stello (sentiment-anima) of the child's nightmare world within him through an exorcism by terror. His technique is to use the poison of bitter truth against the poison of despair, thus enabling him to understand his situation clearly, and hopefully to induce him to create his poetry without illusions.

It is not at all necessary to move from the text to its author in order to see the dialogue in terms of the dialectic between the sacred fount of life (Docteur Noir) and the ivory tower (Stello): as a conflict between the search for the sources of creativity in the realities of the outside world and the discovery of meaning and beauty within the personality of the artist himself. The stated thesis of the book counsels only the latter course for art ("l'imagination ne vit que d'émotions spontanées") (*Stello*, p. 801), and yet it is the Doctor who has lived the experiences of the dying poets, produced the "stories," and interpreted their significance. We are even told that he has his own malady, that of protecting young poets; and that he is given to poetic expression himself. He apostrophizes Death during Gilbert's agony and transforms his sensations of the scene of Chénier's execution into a series of poetic images of destiny and time: the cannon's wheel is compared to "la roue mythologique de la fortune" (*Stello*, p. 781), and the clock on the Hôtel de Ville appears as a large "lune de sang" (*Stello*, p. 775) marked with magic hours.

Vigny appreciates the paradoxical nature of truth almost as much as Diderot does, and in fact the complex interaction of personalities found in Stello recalls *Le Neveu de Rameau,* another "novel" treating the problems of creativity. Just as in that work there are at least two contrasting personalities within "moi" (the philosopher) and within the nephew ("lui"), Vigny suggests this second level of doubling in the Doctor and Stello. Voices of ego and alter ego speak through both men. In the final *récit* he even develops a multiplicity of poetic personalities; Stello and the Doctor are "poètes" but so are the brothers Chénier, and Robespierre and Saint-Just in their fashion.

The theme of the divided self, the splitting off of the creative personality, has been attributed by existentialist criticism to the problem of the alienated artist in search of a public to whom he can address himself. Sartre's early analysis of this phenomenon in *Qu'est-ce que la littérature?* is certainly corroborated by the situation of Stello. Stello is anguished primarily because he desires to write a political tract for a specific party and discovers his contribution is not desired, and that the nineteenth-century bourgeois public has only contempt for poets. In other words, he suffers and thus requires the services of the psychiatrist-doctor precisely because he cannot engage his talent in a social commitment. His problem is therefore the opposite of that of an Icarus; he has no public with which to communicate. At least since Rousseau (especially in his autobiographical works such as *Rousseau, juge de Jean-Jacques,* 1776), artists have expressed their inability to accept the conditions of society through a curious doubling of the personality. Since their desires for freedom and beauty are in manifest contradiction with the dictates of "reason"—which readily grasps the necessary limitations and imperfections of society's conventions and laws in order to survive—individual revolt takes the form of a divided self in an alienated personality.

Of course Vigny's example of the double personality (the Doctor and Stello) has other literary antecedents: Quixote and Panza, Faust and Mephistopheles, as well as the nephew (a "raté," or failure, rather than a "poète maudit") and the philosopher. Vigny quite often suggests the satanic aspects of the doctor's cynicism, his despair and omnipresence; Stello, like Faust, dreams of prophecy in poetry and power over men through knowledge.

In spite of these interesting points of reference, the real significance of the dialogue can best be decoded from the complex system of relations and contrasts in the text. Vigny is preoccupied even more with the problem of creativity itself than with the situation of the artist in the world. He questions to what extent imagination (the center of creative activity) depends on direct contact with things and on experience with others in order to begin to function. He considers, on the other hand, that it may develop like an autonomous complex through the purity of spontaneous emotions in the spirit and memory of the individual artist. The inner life of sentiment and the outer life governed by reason, dreams and reality, solitude versus solidarity, idealism and objective observation—these are the sets of oppositions that best characterize Stello and the Doctor. At the most profound level the couple represents the struggle within the artist himself between his idea, which here takes the form of the knowledge acquired by the Docteur Noir, and his fusing and shaping imagination, his desires and dreams, in this case the contrary aspirations of Stello, the poet.

In other words the dialogue takes place within the mind of the artist, as an integral part of the creative process: "La perpétuelle lutte du Poète est celle qu'il livre à son idée. Si l'idée triomphe du Poète et le passionne trop, il est sa dupe et tombe dans la mise en action de cette idée et s'y perd. Si le Poète est plus fort que l'idée, il la pétrit, la forme et la met en oeuvre. Elle devient ce qu'il a voulu, un monument" (*Journal,* p. 1071).

Stello's beliefs about the nature of poetry, which are not criticized by the doctor, constitute a clear statement of what we can term the romantic myth of poetry. In his credo he proclaims faith in the poet as the inspired guide of humanity, whose nature or God-given gift of poetic creation is a mysterious, sacred act of interpretation through imagination of the hidden meanings and secret unity of the world. He believes in his destiny, in the importance of love and enthusiasm as sources of creativity, and in the poet's mission to preserve necessary ideals in society. He senses in himself a strong creative power ("puissance secrète") and links poetry to prophecy. These familiar aspects of the romantic attitude toward poetry afford Stello the happiness of what Germain terms the inner paradise, a satisfying awareness of the value of his vocation and his own worth. Even more interesting, however, than this early example of the romantic consecration of the writer is Vigny's own mythmaking.

One of his most important techniques in poetry and prose is the transformation of the facts of observation, feeling, or idea into a fable that contains and expresses meaning in all its complexity, richness, and ambiguity. Myth for Vigny (although he uses the term *fable*), is truth condensed, a superior form of language corresponding to the diamond, crystal, or treasure chest, all material images he repeats to suggest the need for the writer to concentrate, purify, and illuminate his thought through the discovery of the proper form that is mythic structure. Vigny's often-repeated preference for the truth of art over the truth of factual reality can be best understood through his creative use of myth. For him myth both conceals and reveals the most profound aspirations, needs, and unconscious desires, hidden on the surface of man's experience. The myth of Samson, for example, becomes the expression not only of the superior man's eternal cry of distress or of disillusionment with woman's treachery but suggests the secret knowledge that love itself is an illusion that man must learn to live without: "Donc, ce que j'ai voulu, Seigneur, n'existe pas!" (*Oeuvres,* 1:194).

In *Stello,* it seems to me, Vigny has forged a myth for his time, transforming the actual lives of his historical characters and giving new forms to the theme of the "poète maudit" or "raté" already to be found in preromantic literature. The stories told by the Doctor in order to cure Stello of his ambition to act in society present three variations on the legend or myth of the scapegoat. In all current forms (eighteenth and early nineteenth century) of governmental organization (monarchic, parliamentarian, democratic-revolutionary), the poet becomes a victim or martyr and dies a real or symbolic spiritual death. The scapegoat, however, has the stature of a half-god or Titan. The mediocre Gilbert and the weak Chatterton are likened to Promethean beings; Chatterton's eyes are compared to "deux flammes comme Prométhée les dut puiser au soleil" (*Stello,* p. 656).

The structure of each story is identical; the opposition between power and poetry, the materialistic gods of the present versus the spiritualistic rebels who look to the future, produces a tragic confrontation leading to sacrifice in the form of suicide or execution. Through metaphor and mythological allusion, Vigny has elevated the three stories, as well as the theme of the sacrificial victim, to the level of a myth containing a cruel and ambiguous truth about the poet and society. The poet-seer, as Stello has presented him, with the approbation of the rational Docteur Noir, has been and will always be the victim of society because power always negates art. The artist is the natural enemy of authority, since by definition his critical, prophetic, and independent spirit is oriented to the future or the past, whereas the representatives of authority concentrate on maintaining the order of the present. The spiritualistic poet is thus always useless and even dangerous in a materialistic society. The scapegoat myth in the three stories conceals an even harsher truth: social order is seen as destructive of all manifestations of profound individuality: reverie, genius, spirituality. The very sources of artistic creativity are destroyed through the conformity and tyranny of social power. Representative governments seem to foster mediocrity, while revolutionary, totalitarian societies tyrannize the artist; we have only to think of the situation of the writer in America, forced to popularize in order to succeed, or that of a Solzenitzyn hounded into exile, to grasp the relevancy of Vigny's legends.

In short, the conclusions drawn by Stello and the Doctor in the chapter "Tristesse et pitié" develop the fundamentally antisocial or even anarchical significance of the text; all contemporary forms of social order are attacked as illogical, totalitarian, materialistic, and unjust. Vigny's narrators express the despair accompanying their loss of illusion when faced with the fatality of social order, which systematically excludes and destroys the very sources of art. From this perspective the book anticipates the disillusionment of a Musset confronted with the collapse of traditional values in the *Confessions d'un enfant du siècle* (1834); but more philosophical in nature and modern in its anarchistic tendencies, it suggests the paradoxes of *Civilization and Its Discontents* (1930). In fact in his *Journal* Vigny prophetically suggests the major elements of that Freudian discourse: "Dans l'individu est reconnu l'ennemi né de la Société s'il ne se contrefait ou ne se réforme avec effort. Donc la Société est contraire aux penchants naturels de l'homme, mais l'espèce se détruit sans la société. Il faut donc pour la conserver renouveler sans cesse cet essai. Mais cet essai ne peut être que mauvais puisqu'il s'oppose toujours (dans un but de conservation) à notre nature qui tend sans cesse à la destruction" (*Journal*, p. 1196).

Vigny's thesis (because *Stello* is also a "roman à thèse") quite simply is that if the poet tries to offer his special knowledge to society, he will be condemned to a physical or at least a spiritual martyrdom. This idea is the message contained in the fable of the sacrifice of the half-god of poetic genius that gives each *récit* its structure and meaning: Prometheus is chained to the rock for having desired to give men the fire of knowledge and in so doing having rebelled against the authority of the gods.

The third *récit,* concerning André Chénier, his brother Marie-Joseph Chénier, Robespierre, and Saint-Just—an ill-fated quartet of writers and politicians—is the most complex and the most moving to the reader. Vigny succeeds in suggesting the tragic grandeur of the last days of the Terror without excessive pathos or grandiloquence. The Docteur Noir recollects the scene with a mixture of horror and fascination that is translated into some of the finest of Vigny's poetic prose. What interests us here, however, is Vigny's analysis of the poet in a revolutionary society. He presents André Chénier as a great artist who is conscious of the visionary aspect of his poetry, a somber, angry hero of revolt who has dared to write against the tyranny of the regime in the name of liberty, and who now stoically awaits his execution. Vigny has apparently transformed his character completely, in accord with his flexible concept of the use of history in art,[5] to make of him a symbol of the ideal writer. In contrast to André Chénier is Robespierre, the antipoet, representative of totalitarian power who has, nonetheless, the imaginative gift of prophecy (he foresees Napoleon's empire) and who had written verses when young. He is sick with paranoia, and is an assassin, but above all his character illustrates the corruption of ideals in the hands of power. For not only does he oppose Chénier's brand of idealism, but he himself is an uncompromising idealist without human compassion or pity, with no sense of the need for moderation and indulgence. His idealism has rapidly become a tool for oppression.

This danger to poetry (i.e., to the preservation of ideals and ideas through poetic symbol and fable), which is always perverted when it serves society, is developed in more detail through the second group of antagonists, Saint-Just and Marie-Joseph Chénier. Saint-Just is a poet who has given himself to power; his maxims are presented as the naive, Rousseauistic poetry of a sincere young moralist who has attained prominence without having known life outside of books. His pitiless innocence, his refusal of all compromise, and his desire to live by absolute principles alone are transposed into the simple and tyrannical laws of his *Institutions,* which Robespierre sees as inspired legislation. In other words, he is a kind of Stello without the lessons of human experience provided by the Docteur Noir. Solitude and purity without contact with humanity could thus produce a negative poetry of death; and we are back to the original problem of the proper balance between the inner and the outer life, between solitude and solidarity in the creative personality.

As perverted poets Robespierre and Saint-Just are even more dangerous than as opponents of poetry, for they have transformed poetic discourse into an agent of repression and destruction. The final member of the quartet, Marie-Joseph Chénier, a man of literary talent, has compromised himself as a writer by consenting to lead an active, political life. It is easy to detect in this portrait of the weak and ineffective brother of André Chénier the same kind of reproach addressed by Vigny in his journal to poets like his contemporary Lamartine. Artistic talent in the service of politics leads only to a diminution of art and a compromise of principle.

Four poets and four different kinds of poetic discourse are presented, but only the genius André Chénier is sacrificed. The text "Un soir d'été" is one of the most beautiful ever written by Vigny. He dispenses with rhetoric in order to oblige the reader to share his horror before the absurd and tragic loss of human greatness: "Après le trente-troisième cri, je vis l'habit gris tout debout. Cette fois je résolus d'honorer le courage de son génie en ayant le courage de voir toute sa mort: je me levai. La tête roula, et ce qu'il avait là s'enfuit avec le sang" (*Stello,* p. 773).

The system of relationships in the poetic paradigm is complex and the points of view on poetry multiple. Stello's purity is reflected in that of Saint-Just; the Docteur Noir's experience is echoed in Robespierre's knowledge of men. The brothers Chénier signify the degradation of a compromise with society (Marie-Joseph) and the sacrifice of the true artist who tries to commit his idealism to the needs of society (André).

The fictional Docteur Noir himself eloquently opposes the position of a real writer, Joseph de Maistre, who attempted to justify massacre in the name of Christian expiation; he speaks for life against all those who would excuse political murder and any sacrifice of humanity in the name of power and the authority of the state. His pessimistic analysis of the psychology of revolution (the reign of mediocre men who remain in power only through the elimination of all enemies) does not concern us here, except for the interesting and very modern parallel he draws between the mind of the revolutionary assassin and that of the "splénétique," or melancholy artist-dreamer. Both are sick with disgust and disillusionment in a corrupt society whose values they cannot accept. Both are dominated by the death wish and live in anger, fear, and "spleen," which the revolutionary tries to sublimate by taking vengeance on others, and which leads the poet to contemplate suicide. The "émotion continue de l'assassinat" of a Robespierre is thus related to the "rêve maladif" of

Stello in yet another cross-relationship on the complex paradigm of poets and their characteristics to be found in this novel.

Germain has analyzed with particular thoroughness the conclusions of *Stello,* the "cure" effected by the Doctor and his ideas concerning poetry.[6] For my purposes it should be stressed that the Doctor proclaims his ordinance in a set of maxims solemn as an ancient oracle, in effect becoming a poet once again, speaking through a discourse of image and myth to present his code for the young artist. Through a series of examples from the past including that of Homer and Plato's poet excluded from the Republic, the Doctor elevates his concept to that of a universal myth—the poet is not only the eternal martyr but the saint of society, since his mission is to preserve the necessary ideals of the group, to guide its inner, spiritual life. Perpetual ostracism and solitude must be the accepted lot of the artist, who is essential to every society; for it is he who helps men fight the tide of the material, rational, and animal needs that constantly reduces and diminishes the quality of human experience. His work is eminently and finally that of a civilizing force.

Vigny's high conception of art is certainly seen in this mystique of poetry that both Stello and the Doctor celebrate in the concluding chapters. All direct action or political activity by the poet is, however, impossible. The application of his ideals to society's needs is left to others—the parliament, for example, should subsidize the impoverished artist. In yet another curious and subtle textual parallel, the Doctor continues to represent and support society's order and power (the true function, after all, of a doctor), since his discourse composed of maxims and historical allusions—not unlike the legislation of Saint-Just—is used to perpetuate the *exclusion* of the poet from an active political life. From the perspective of the author, however, Vigny has clearly fulfilled his own function by indicating to society its need for the idealism of poetry, and the danger to poets from the hostility of those in power. Through the writing of *Stello* Vigny has actually realized the conception of art that has evolved through the dialogue of the doctor and the poet.

A very serious problem nevertheless remains: Without active participation by the artist in the life of his time, how does the idealistic work of art reach and move its public? The response is both "romantic" and modern. Considered superior to religion itself as a spiritual guide (because it remains pure and abstracted from quotidian life), the work of the poet produces a communion among men that can lead them to act. Poetry elevates the spirit of its readers through the feelings it touches ("pitié"); it is therefore addressed to man's emotional nature and in turn engenders emotion. Parallel to Sartre's concept of the work of art as part of a quest for freedom, appealing to the reader's need to overcome his own sense of contingency, Vigny's ideal work of art presents emotions that must cause "une profonde et même une douloureuse impression" (Stello, p. 583) on its often unthinking and unfeeling readers. Art works are then symbols of emotion that act in turn on the emotions of the reader, thus helping to create an increased awareness of reality or images of new realities.

Vigny approximates the concept of Jung, who thought that the authentic work of art helps to restore the psychic balance of a group, a society, or even an epoch,[7] because it furnishes the necessary images of conscious and unconscious levels of experience that the society has been repressing, but that it needs for wholeness. Vigny's society, becoming increasingly materialistic and industrialized, is losing its sense of individual spiritual values; Hugo and Nerval certainly responded to this situation through their efforts at religious syncretism, renewing images of God and the irrational world in works like *Aurélia* and *La Fin de Satan*. Vigny perhaps more than any other romantic sees the hope for the preservation of individual values in those of poetry. The work of art thus helps the group rediscover realities it has repressed or denied, by presenting it with symbols that can transform its image of things and of itself.

Finally, and ironically, the very misfortune of the poet becomes a source of his happiness; through his work he has the hope of transcending time and conquering the fatality of death. The work preserves the essence of his personality, and although the poet is sacrificed in life, like the half-gods of the legends, he lives again for the future. Anticipating the "Bénédiction" of Baudelaire, Vigny concludes *Stello* with this paradox, insisting that the poet is a guide for the future of mankind; he works for his posterity and that of society: "Votre royaume n'est pas de ce monde sur lequel vos yeux sont ouverts, mais de celui qui sera quand vos yeux seront fermés" (*Stello*, p. 803).

In the present, however, there remains the unalterable opposition, the tragic antithesis between the fatality of power and the vulnerability of the poet.

In 1830, then, Vigny imagines the poet to be the tragic victim of an unjust order that threatens his idealism and to which he is sacrificed, just as in the ancient legends expiation and atonement necessitated the death of heroes in the name of a mysterious order of gods and nature. Most critics have, nevertheless, pointed to significant changes in idea and attitude from *Stello* to the *Poèmes philosophiques,* also entitled *Les Destinées* (1864); Castex spoke of the progression in Vigny's thought from a fundamentally tragic pessimism toward a humanistic optimism.[8] However, the sometimes contradictory themes of the poems have been disconcerting to many readers (praise of science, for example, in "La Bouteille à la mer" and its apparent condemnation in "La Maison du berger"). The problem stems again from too much concern with the intellectual content of the poetry instead of a careful examination of the structure of its themes and images. "La Maison du berger" (1842), which I propose to discuss in detail, was conceived by Vigny as a prologue to the *Destinées,* to be followed by a poem entitled "Réponse d'Eva," which was never completed. Much more than an introduction, in fact his poetic masterpiece, it contains the major themes and structural patterns to be repeated in various ways throughout the *Destinées.* It is significantly the one text in which the reader can observe the workings of the imagination of the poet-narrator as he gives poetic form to the experience of discovery he has undergone, a work therefore to be compared with similar texts in English romantic poetry that reveal the mind of the poet structuring the world and thereby uncovering and discovering itself.

"La Maison du berger" is also a poem about poetry, but most importantly it is a poem that *is* the romantic experience of poetry: a form given to an experience of inner discovery, spiritual change, or evolution; language that expresses the movement from the poet's situation of alienation to his integration in a new and higher order of being and knowing.

Like *Stello* most of the fables and myths of the *Destinées* contain stories that suggest a sacrifice, and are constructed according to antitheses or binary oppositions that permit no synthesis, only a tragic resolution forcing the acceptance of cruel but vital human truths. Already in the *Poèmes antiques et modernes* youthful love was sacrificed in a corrupt world ("Les Amants de Montmorency," "Le Déluge"), innocence was abandoned in "Eloa," and the need for human solidarity remained unsatisfied in "Moïse."

The poems of *Les Destinées,* however, are much more uniformly dominated by sacrifice and the presence of cruel and consoling myths ("mythes cruels" or "mythes consolants"). In the series of "mythes cruels" there is "La Colère de Samson," whose myth contains the message that man must sacrifice his ideal of human love to the bitter reality of his solitude and the perpetual war between the sexes. Man learns in "Les Destinées" the need to abandon his idea of personal freedom; Christianity with its emphasis on grace and predestination has brought only the illusion of liberty and represents no more than a modern version of ancient fatality. At the heart of the poet's disillusionment is the sacrifice of Christ ("Le Mont des Oliviers") with the concomitant realization that man must depend on himself alone, that he is abandoned in an irrational world. When man confronts woman and his own destiny as a being of will desiring freedom and spiritual certainty; that is, when his ideals (love, free will, belief in a spiritual universe) are confronted with the fatalities of experience (Samson and Delilah, human will and the fates, Christ and God), the outcome is tragic and the human ideal is lost.[9]

The need to abandon these ideals and illusions, the "cruel" truths contained in the myths, are accompanied, however, with a positive affirmation. In each case the poet-narrator has made an intellectual and personal discovery: the stoic need to affirm his own strength, to purify his mind of illusion, to develop the inner resources of his personality, his own particular "genius." In other words the myths are contradictory and ambivalent; their truths are at once iconoclastic and destructive, and yet affirmative and even consoling. They imply the sacrifice of an important ideal but affirm the power of man's spirit:

> Arbitre libre et fier des actes de sa vie,
> Si notre coeur s'entr'ouvre au parfum des vertus,
> S'il s'embrase à l'amour, s'il s'élève au génie,
> Que l'ombre des Destins, Seigneur, n'oppose plus
> A nos belles ardeurs une immuable entrave,
> A nos efforts sans fin des coups inattendus![10]

Herein lies, it seems to me, the real explanation for Vigny's constant fascination with myth and his important role as a romantic mythologizer. He finds in myth, first of all, an extension of poetic language. Like symbol, it is, for him, a crystallization of ideas, a permanent form in which to distill his own personal experience. Like symbol, it permits him to suggest more than can be explained rationally—above all the ambiguous, paradoxical, and contradictory truths that result from the poet's intuition, the world of his imagination and memory. Myths permit Vigny to pass from the limitations of the *moi* to Everyman; they become for him the revelations of the meaning of collective experience, symbolic interpretations of essential human situations that correspond to the deepest aspirations, desires, and fears of men of his generation and of mankind. Being part of a long tradition, they can be interpreted in diverse ways; therefore, they demand the response of the reader at the level of his individual experience. Like diamonds or crystals they give off light and meaning but contain mystery, are multilayered and difficult to penetrate. For Vigny, in the last analysis, myths are the creations of the imagination of poets and thinkers that contain (conceal and reveal) metaphysical, spiritual, or moral truths surpassing rational and scientific knowledge. Vigny's poetry certainly confirms René Wellek's statement: "All the great romantic poets are mythopoeic, are symbolists whose practice must be understood in terms of their attempt to give a total mythic interpretation of the world to which the poet holds the key." [11]

The consoling myths of *Les Destinées* are characterized first by their modernity, if not their originality: "La Flûte," "La Bouteille à la mer," "L'Esprit pur," and "La Maison du berger" contain stories about the present and images from contemporary experience, even though the underlying myths be ancient ones. In this instance they simply resemble poems of the "modern" section of Vigny's first collection. Far more important, however, is a different and new thematic structure. The work of the creative person, artist, or scientist, the creations of the human spirit are now seen as the means to extend and actually overcome the rational, material, and temporal limitations of existence. Instead of a tragic impasse resulting from the confrontation between man's aspirations and the fatalities of the world, a new synthesis results from this conflict, producing renewed confidence in man's creative power and his power to transform the world.

"La Flûte" evokes the power and permanence of the world of ideas through a Platonic contrast with the weakness of the flesh, thus encouraging and consoling the young *raté* who resembles Stello:

> Du corps et non de l'âme accusons l'indigence.
> Des organes mauvais servent l'intelligence
> Ils touchent, en tordant et tourmentant leur noeud,
> Ce qu'ils peuvent atteindre et non ce qu'elle veut.
> En traducteurs grossiers de quelque auteur céleste
> Ils parlent. Elle chante et désire le reste.
>   . . . . .
> Votre souffle était juste et votre chant est faux.[12]

"L'Esprit pur" extols the products of human genius capable of endowing their creator with immortality and identifies creativity as the divine element in man:

> Ton règne est arrivé, PUR ESPRIT, roi du monde!
> . . . Aujourd'hui, c'est l'ECRIT,
> L'ECRIT UNIVERSEL, parfois impérissable,
> Que tu graves au marbre ou traces sur le sable,
> Colombe au bec d'airain! VISIBLE SAINT-ESPRIT![13]

"La Bouteille à la mer" presents an allegory of the acceptance and comprehension of a work of art by its readers in terms of the partial conquest of the destructive fatality of the ocean through the knowledge of a sea captain's charts. The Captain dies in the storm ("Son sacrifice est fait"), but he is destined to have a second life in the immortality of his science:

> Il sourit en songeant que ce fragile verre
> Portera sa pensée et son nom jusqu'au port,
> Que d'une île inconnue il agrandit la terre,
> Qu'il marque un nouvel astre et le confie au sort,
> Que Dieu peut bien permettre à des eaux insensées
> De perdre des vaisseaux, mais non pas des pensées,
> Et qu'avec un flacon il a vaincu la mort.[14]

Thus, the element missing, in *Stello* and in the pessimistic poems of *Les Destinées* (those in the series of cruel myths), is belief in the power of the created work itself and in the divine nature of creativity:

For Vigny man has now become his own god, and his works are proof of his divinity.

Indeed, "La Maison du berger" presents the complete spiritual itinerary of the poet-narrator as he relates an experience of inner discovery; an experience with life and poetry from which he emerges renewed, regenerated, as if reborn. Liberated from alienation, his period of spiritual death, he is newly confident in his own genius and the value and power of art. He discovers himself and is ready to create, to attempt to write in the name of mankind. The rebirth of the poet (for that is the central theme of the poem), aided by the love of Eva, ideal woman and muse, recalls the situation of Prometheus and Asia in Shelley's poem *Prometheus Unbound*. In fact, "La Maison" is Vigny's version of the Prometheus legend, as well as a retelling of the part of the story of Adam and Eve in which man is saved from the sin of narcissism through the regenerating force of woman's love.

The poem is constructed in dialectical form; in each of its three parts there is a series of antitheses, or contradictions, whose conflict produces a new synthesis. The movement of themes and images corresponds to the flux of ideas in the poet-narrator's mind and here signifies change, growth, and renewal.

Part 1 might best be called spleen and evasion or invitation to a voyage, suggesting the themes of Baudelaire's masterwork; part 2, the discovery of an aesthetic; and part 3, the poet's metaphysics. The poem begins the way *Stello* ends, with the poet expressing his isolation when faced with the fatalities of the modern world, and his despair when confronted with the tragic limitations of the human condition. Instead of Stello, the figure of a pure but an incommunicable light, the poet is now a shepherd involved with life, and the poem is addressed to a mysterious Eva, who seems to have replaced the Docteur Noir. Images of weight, suffering, and slavery dominate the first stanzas, evoking Napoleon's exile and Prometheus's enchainment to his rock; "âme enchaînée," "plaie immortelle," "rocs fatals," "aigle blessé," reinforce the effect of alienation and spiritual death that the poet feels in this "monde fatal, écrasant et glacé" (MB, p. 173).[15]

Instead of the destructive nature of political power that dominated the text of *Stello,* the materialism and technology of modern civilization now menace the very sources of poetry. The city and science (with their product and sign the railroad) signify fatality here, and are placed in opposition to nature (a source of consolation and spiritual value) and reverie (the impetus to poetic creation), which together evoke the possible happiness of escape with Eva. The interplay of themes and ideas, the conflict between the static fatality of the city, and the sentimental appeal of nature—these produce, however, in the central symbol of the work (the "maison du berger") the idea of a new life in the shepherd's caravan. Neither limited to city or country nor dominated by the excesses of modern technology, the poet and his lover will travel through country and countryside into contact with the life of various peoples and will collect impressions for poetry. The shepherd dreams of becoming a guide for men.

The themes and images of the poetic structure are linked according to a logic suggesting the inner working of the poet's imagination. The theme of science, which imposes ever-new limits on man's freedom by eliminating chance and the unknown, and by forcing conformity—"La science / Trace autour de la terre un chemin triste et droit" (MB, p. 176)—leads directly to a meditation on its antithesis, reverie, a metonym for the poetic world of imagination, beauty, and mystery, the very center of his spiritual life. The danger of science and modern technology is precisely that they could destroy the sources of poetry: reverie before the beauty of nature, imagination's contact with the mystery of experience. Part 2 thus develops as a long debate on the meaning and value of poetry whose very essence is threatened in modern society.

If the "thesis" in this section is now the possibility of political life and action, it is opposed by the "antithesis" of pure poetry and thought, or the meditative life. The same set of binary oppositions that were found in *Stello* become the basis this time for a new synthesis about the role of the poet in society and the value of poetry. The true poet neither participates actively in political life nor isolates himself in holy solitude; he becomes, however warily, the guide or shepherd of humanity:

> Diamant sans rival, que tes feux illuminent
> Les pas lents et tardifs de l'humaine Raison!
> Il faut, pour voir de loin les peuples qui cheminent,
> Que le Berger t'enchâsse au toit de sa Maison.
>
> (MB, p. 178)

It is in part 2 of the "Maison" that Vigny most profoundly develops his concept of the meaning and role of poetry and resolves the seemingly insoluble paradoxes of *Stello*. The familiar images of the diamond, mirror, pearl, and monument are used to convey Vigny's sense of the function of poetic forms; the symbols and myths must operate to concentrate and purify the "profondes pensées" of the artist. The poem thus becomes a durable condensation of the spirit or light of the individual poet, but also preserves the highest ideals of his civilization from the destruction of time:

> Ce fin miroir solide, étincelant et dur,
> Reste des nations mortes, durable pierre
> Qu'on trouve sous ses pieds lorsque dans la poussière
> On cherche les cités sans en voir un seul mur.
>
> (MB, p. 178)

Poetry is considered to be superior to reason, which functions by dividing and separating phenomena, since it is capable of grasping the highest synthetic truths through intuition and imagination: indeed, the poet through his revelations of the spiritual sense of life becomes the intuitive, moral guide of human progress:

> Le jour n'est pas levé.—Nous en sommes encore
> Au premier rayon blanc qui précède l'aurore
> Et dessine la terre aux bords de l'horizon.
>
> (MB, p. 178)

The creative spirit of the poet represents for Vigny a kind of divinity in man, and through the exercise of this faculty in the poetic act man participates positively in the divine element of the universe:

> Mais notre esprit rapide en mouvements abonde:
> Ouvrons tout l'arsenal de ses puissants ressorts.
> L'Invisible est réel. Les âmes ont leur monde
> Où sont accumulés d'impalpables trésors.
>
> (MB, p. 179)

A religion of human genius has clearly replaced traditional Christianity for Vigny; he remains an idealist whose need for transcendence is now satisfied by the works of the "pure Spirit."[16]

There are consequently three ways in which poetry can transcend the fatalities of life: first, the work brings immortality to the poet himself; second, its form condenses and reveals the spiritual life of man, preserving his ideals against the danger of the collapse of temporary forms of civilization; and finally, through its intuition of supreme truths it becomes the highest means to knowledge capable of guiding man to a better future.

If we return for a moment to the ordinance of the Docteur Noir at the end of *Stello,* the change in vision is striking. The Doctor had recommended to the young poet the necessary and sacred solitude of the ivory tower—the poet of "La Maison" is liberated and reborn through the love of Eva. Imagination, he said, thrives only on the spontaneous emotions of the artist—the poet now seeks to know and love "tout dans les choses créées" and during a long voyage with Eva will learn to admire "la majesté des souffrances humaines."

According to the Doctor his mission was to produce works, useful in their very uselessness; his situation was to be damned in the eyes of those in power, and to live without hope a destiny of pain and doubt. Instead, the poet of the "Maison" is confident that poetry may become the spiritual leader of science and reason, and he displays measured optimism concerning the future for himself and society.

The long period of stagnation, alienation and sterility experienced by the poet in part 1 of "La Maison" ends through contact with a new spiritual element, the very force of his own creative self, which produces new affirmation and strength in part 2. This force is, of course, poetry itself, and it is incarnated in the dream of love for Eva. The rebirth of the poet, his "poetic" health, is thus achieved in part 3 of "La Maison" through reunion with the woman, a projection of his anima in the redemptive figure, Eva. She now replaces Christ in the poet's world, saving him from death and helping him return to wholeness.

For Germain the ordinance of the Doctor implied the necessary division or separation of the two parts of the poet's personality. In order to survive the animus—*volonté*—must repress the feminine anima—*rêverie*. The poet must in effect refuse life, or at least use his willpower to cure himself of the "rêve maladif" of communication and participation. In other words he must accept sterility in the name of purity, curtail the effects of reverie (the very source of poetry), and concentrate solely on his craft.

The sacrifice of the feminine part of the poetic personality—the anima, or *rêverie*—which is the lesson of *Stello* in the last analysis, could only lead to a spiritual death. It is revived, however, in "La Maison" in the form of an overwhelming need for love as a necessary condition of creativity. In the context of the conflict of ideas throughout the entire poem feminine symbols can be seen to dominate the consciousness and creative imagination of the poet-narrator. Woman takes the form of nature, a goddess, a "voyageuse indolente" (MB, p. 181), Diana, vestal virgin and priestess; she incarnates reverie, the poet's muse, and most significantly poetry itself: "O toi des vrais penseurs impérissable amour!" (MB, p. 178). Spiritualized and yet profoundly human,[17] the mysterious Eva of part 3 becomes the redemptive figure whose love makes it possible for the poet to find again his sense of wholeness. She not only symbolizes poetry, "L'enthousiasme pur dans une voix suave" (MB, p. 179), but also the fragility and impermanence of man and the possible grandeur of human suffering. Her delicate sensitivity, compassion, and deep understanding of human values—"C'est à toi qu'il convient d'ouïr les grandes plaintes / Que l'humanité triste exhale sourdement" (MB, p. 180)—are the necessary complement to the poet's intelligence and will; indeed, these qualities are the source of all creativity, and their assimilation makes feasible the poet's reintegration in the world of men and nature:

> Eva, j'aimerai tout dans les choses créées
> Je les contemplerai dans ton regard rêveur
> Qui partout répandra ses flammes colorées,
> Son repos gracieux, sa magique saveur;
> Sur mon coeur déchiré viens poser ta main pure,
> Ne me laisse jamais seul avec la Nature,
> Car je la connais trop pour n'en pas avoir peur.
>
> (MB, p. 180)

The artist's empathetic penetration of the world of things and man, and his possible identification with it, was denied to Stello. This attribute—considered by writers as close to Vigny but as diverse as Diderot, Balzac, and Baudelaire to be essential to the creative process—is now granted to the poet of "La Maison du berger" as a function of the ability to love.

The dialectic of part 3 is expressed in terms of antithesis between the goddess of Nature—hostile, indifferent, and eternal—and the fragile, impermanent, human woman. Nature moves (*roule*) with the indifference of the railway trains of part 1; woman loves, suffers, and knows the perishable but privileged beauty of the passing moment, of that which is always menaced by death, but alone has human value. The poet concludes from this contrast that what counts for man in his impermanence and contingency is giving meaning to a world that has none without him. The very fragility of woman makes him love men again and seek to illuminate the sense of human suffering against the beautiful but insensitive backdrop of nature:

> Viens du paisible seuil de la maison roulante
> Voir ceux qui sont passés et ceux qui passeront.
> Tous les tableaux humains qu'un Esprit pur m'apporte
> S'animeront pour toi, quand devant notre porte
> Les grands pays muets longuement s'étendront.
>
> (MB, pp. 181–82)

Eva thus figures the regenerative principle of love that brings the poet back to the sources of being, a charitable love, or agape, which is a means of access to knowledge and spiritual elevation, and the necessary impetus to creativity. The last stanzas develop the image of the poet as a modern Prometheus[18] freed and reborn through the strength of love and confidence in the power of poetry. He enters a new life of knowing and becoming, with the possibility of renewing his genius and reconciling himself with nature and man.

The poem itself is therefore an experience of rebirth in that the writing of it permits the poet-narrator to rediscover the ties that exist between the alienated self and the world of others and things; as the poet develops the language to express the world of coherence and beauty that his imagination discerns, a second life begins for him, and a new reality born of his images, symbols, and myths is created.

Vigny himself expressed this paradox of the archetypal rebirth pattern, which illuminates the sacrificial death of the poet in *Stello* and his subsequent renascence in *Les Destinées,* when he wrote the following lines. They are addressed to Antoni Deschamps, one of the many unfortunate young poets who were suffering from incomprehension and poverty, and who were beginning to consider Vigny, the successful playwright and poet, as the primary contemporary defender of poets and the cause of poetry:

J'ai souffert d'abord et gémi avec vous et j'ai admiré la beauté de vos sentiments, autant au moins que la beauté de vos vers; je l'admirais et je m'attristais avec vous, mais quand je me suis reculé de ce grand tableau de votre âme et quand je l'ai considéré avec des yeux plus sereins et moins troubles, je me suis senti heureux comme d'une seconde naissance qui vous aurait été donnée.

Croyez-moi, mon ami, vous voilà guéri. La Poésie qui vous avait perdu vous a sauvé. Vous conserverez toute la vie sur le front la trace du tonnerre, mais ce ne sera qu'une cicatrice, et votre âme est restée intacte sous ce front blessé.[19]

III

Alfred de Vigny:
The *Consultations* of the Docteur Noir—
Daphné and the Power of Symbols

Vigny's novel *Daphné,* written in 1837 but unpublished during his lifetime and still neglected, is nevertheless essential to a profound comprehension of his intellectual and artistic development. A historical novel about the Emperor Julian (361–63), it merits analysis as another example of the romantic use of history to illuminate contemporary events. Although it is primarily a novel of ideas, it offers a rich tapestry of characters and voices, scenes of nineteenth-century Paris juxtaposed with fourth-century Antioch, and a complex symbolic network that prefigures Vigny's use of myth and symbol in the *Poèmes philosophiques.* In addition to considering the metaphysical questions raised by Julian the Apostate's renunciation of Christianity, the novel develops the theme of the artist, and his role in society, and focuses specifically on the power of sign and symbol, the "crystal préservateur,"[1] in relation to the idea it contains.

Daphné must be read as a preamble to *Les Destinées,* for it is the culmination of Vigny's study of the possibility of the poet's action in society. Julian the Apostate, a poet, soldier, and nobleman, unites in one figure three victims of society's contempt. The *Journal d'un poète* reveals Vigny's lifelong preoccupation with the historical figure of Julian and his desire to complete a series of works entitled consultations to follow the model of *Stello.* The very last entry in his journal (September 23, 1863) contains a plan for the *Deuxième Consultation;*

the list of literary projects concerning Julian before and after 1837 is extensive. *Stello* (1831), which concludes that action is impossible for the poet; *Grandeur et servitude militaire* (1835), with its portrait of the immorality of blind obedience to society's rules; and *Daphné,* portraying the error of action through religious reform, constitute a trilogy of novels united thematically and structurally. After the completion of *Daphné,* Vigny, officially at least,[2] accepted the advice of his Docteur Noir, devoting himself exclusively to poetry and definitively renouncing the temptation to become directly involved in political or social action.

The novel of *Daphné* has a frame that links it formally to *Stello.* The introductory chapters and the conclusion of *Daphné* contain a dialogue between Stello, the poet "enthousiaste," and his enemy / friend the Docteur Noir. Stello is once again tempted to act in society; he dreams of influencing the masses of men through his religious spirit, his purified moral vision. The main body of the text was originally designed to contain three *récits* offered by the doctor to dissuade the poet from any social commitment. Exactly parallel in structure to its predecessor *Stello,* this novel was to present the stories of Melancthon, Rousseau, and Lamennais, all religious reformers who, according to Vigny, succeeded only in weakening belief in the spiritual truths they sought to defend. Vigny finally chose to concentrate the doctor's lesson in only one *récit,* the story of Julian, which offers the conclusion that religious action is impossible and indeed destructive when undertaken by a man of artistic and poetic sensibility. The multitude is incapable of understanding the elevated spiritual vision of the artist, deforms his truth once it is translated into concrete forms, and makes of him its scapegoat. The two consultations thus answer negatively and conclusively the desire for action; the *récits* they contain illustrate its inevitable failure.

Vigny's own *Poèmes philosophiques* or *Les Destinées* therefore are in a very literal fashion the poems of his fictional *Daphné,* written under the influence of the Platonist and Stoic philosopher Libanius, who counsels Julian and doubles for the Docteur Noir. These are "poésie pure," the purest possible expression of the moral and religious spirit or conscience of the poet, through diamond-hard and crystallike images and symbols, uncontaminated by sensuous matter, materialistic values, and degraded language, i.e., the sophistry and opportunism of political discourse. A mandate to write the poetry of the "esprit pur" is the therapeutical result of the two consultations, an almost liturgical and certainly cathartic function of the "confessions" of Stello.

Before beginning an analysis of the text itself, there are two additional connections between fiction and reality that should be elucidated. Georges Bonnefoy, in his *La Pensée religieuse et morale d'Alfred de Vigny* (1944), has studied in detail both the striking parallel between Julian's life and Vigny's own spiritual itinerary and the correspondence Vigny perceived between the disorder of the Roman Empire in the fourth century and that of France, specifically in the decade following the collapse of the Bourbon monarchy and the July Revolution of 1830. Any reader of the *Journal* is impressed by the repeated allusions to Julian the Apostate, from the mention of the tragedy about the emperor he wrote at the age of eighteen and later destroyed, to the following admission, dated May 18, 1833: "Je ne puis vaincre la sympathie que j'ai toujours eue pour Julien l'Apostat. Si la métempsycose existe, j'ai été cet homme. C'est l'homme dont le rôle, la vie, le caractère m'eussent le mieux convenu dans l'histoire" (*Journal*, p. 988).

In a long chapter entitled "Les Deux consultations du Docteur Noir," Bonnefoy compares the treatment of Julian the Apostate's character in *Daphné* to Vigny's own struggles with Christianity. Vigny's correspondence, the *Journal,* and other published works reveal three stages in his spiritual life that are indeed similar to those of the historical figure. Julian's intense, mystical faith in Christ, the enthusiasm of his childhood that endowed him with moments of poetic ecstasy, was abruptly ended through the impact of the teaching of the bishop Arius. The Arian rejection of Christian dogma, especially Christ's divinity, in favor of a more rational, humanistic version of Christianity, destroyed Julian's faith, and is compared by Vigny to the liberalized approach to Catholicism of Lamennais, or Strauss (in his *Vie de Jésus*) and the influence of presocialist reformers such as Saint-Simon and Fourier.

Rationalist and humanitarian critiques of supernatural elements in Christianity after 1830 seem to have completed the work of Enlightenment philosophy, and made impossible for Vigny further belief in Christian doctrine. Julian's official restoration of the pagan gods is seen by Vigny as an attempt to give an acceptable form, through the signs and symbols of polytheism, to an exalted, Platonic version of divinity superior to the "corrupted" forms and doctrine of Christianity. The importance of Hellenic ideals or atticism in Vigny's later work, his effort to replace the Christian concept of divinity with the Platonic notion of abstract eternal ideas, and his desire to equate the creative spirit of man—the "esprit pur" of superior intellect and imagination—with the divine element in the universe represent his final wisdom. This understanding was painstakingly acquired through a series of personal religious crises and a careful study of diverse metaphysical systems including Buddhist philosophy.

Vigny's version of Julian's spiritual life can thus be seen as a paradigm for his own—the sincere Christian faith of his youth, followed by the rejection of Christian doctrine resulting from rationalist criticism, and finally the espousal of a refined version of Platonism, or the ideal of atticism. Vigny defines his concept in the *Journal*: "L'Atticisme est l'amour de toute beauté. La beauté de la pensée a pour fin la poésie la plus parfaite qui est le plus grand effort de la pensée conservée par les langues. La beauté des actions a pour fin les marques de grandeur, de dignité et d'honneur qui rendent la vie d'un homme digne de mémoire" (*Journal*, p. 1277).

The frame of the novel also develops the historical parallelism that gives to *Daphné* a unified spatial as well as temporal point of view. Paris after 1830 is observed by Stello and the Doctor; indeed, their promenade through the city is the structural link of the story sequences narrated. Paris in the disorder following the collapse of Napoleon and the monarchy seems threatened by barbarianism from within, just as Antioch, the Christian center of the Roman Empire, was threatened by Huns and Vandals from without. The poet and his doctor witness the mindless destruction of precious books following the sacking of the archbishop's library on February 14, 1831; they attest to the restless boredom of the crowd along the Seine ("Foule" is the title of chapter 1), and they sense the threat of yet another dangerous upheaval. The "people," according to the narrator and his observers, have lost their religious faith, and their moral values have consequently been undermined. Again, the current thinkers and reformers who, like Lamennais, defend Christianity by humanizing it, make the error of emptying it of its true spirituality and idealism, thus destroying its moral imperative. As Dostoyevski would later write: without a belief in immortality there is no morality. The frame sets the stage for the narration of the invasion of Antioch by the barbarians, which will conclude the story of Julian; the sacking of the archbishopric is an index of the destruction of the temple of Daphné, the spiritual treasure house of polytheism.

Fear of revolution, distrust of the proletariat, and scorn for the liberal reformer compose the very conservative ideology that Vigny's narrator conveys. Paradoxically, the weakening of orthodox Catholicism, in which Vigny himself no longer believed, is, in the novel, a sign of the decadence of current French civilization and, more profoundly, a sign of the loss of a truly spiritual definition of man that had been preserved through philosophy and religion from ancient Greece to modern times. Antioch and the destruction of the temple of Daphné become historical symbols of the devaluation and degradation of Western spiritual values.

Vigny's fascination, almost obsession, with the figure of Julian certainly appears as the projection of a profound desire. Julian realizes in one person the ideal of a purified moral conscience, an "esprit pur," and a man of vast political power. He is the poet-king, Marcus-Aurelius made emperor, or Prometheus, as he is twice referred to in the text. He acts although he is a poet; he attacks Christianity (thus satisfying Vigny's dissatisfaction with the Church); he restores the spiritual life of the past (reforming monasteries and establishing schools); and he defends his work with the austere morality and sense of duty of the noble soldier resigned to die for his ideal.

But of course he fails; like Prometheus, the mythical figure central to romantic thought, he is punished for his effort to aid humanity. He is thus perhaps the most complete fictional creation of Vigny, since he translates both the ambition to act (which Vigny must learn to abandon) and a recognition of its futility and inutility (from which Vigny, in his refusal of involvement, gains reassurance). Julian the Apostate corresponds to a basic need in Vigny's personality; in this fantasy he projects both his desire to act and his desire to believe that action for him is impossible and destructive.

In terms of religious thought Bonnefoy concludes that Vigny has expressed in *Daphné* yet another paradox: "sa haine et répulsion personnelle du Christianisme, en même temps la reconnaissance presque forcée de sa nécessité."[3] Indeed, Julian's failure does signal the success of Christian symbolism to preserve the highest moral and spiritual values. Bonnefoy's conclusion about the paradoxical message of the story of Daphné can serve as a useful introduction to an analysis of the function of the fable of Julian, the text's symbolic code, and the theory of symbolism, which provides a unifying theme in the novel.

The links between the *Poèmes philosophiques* and the story of Julian on the level of Vigny's literary theory and personal biography have already been suggested. The connection is a deeper one, however, since the fable of Julian and the symbolism of the city of Daphné function in the text according to the same organizing principles as the myths and images of *Les Destinées*.

Julian's legend is another in the series of historical fables or myths that Vigny uses to symbolize a complex, contradictory, and paradoxical truth, a spiritual meaning that could not be expressed discursively; it requires the clarity, richness, and durability of the crystal image to illuminate and preserve it. Like Moses, the poets of *Stello* (Gilbert, Chatterton, Chénier) and the figures of *Les Destinées* (Christ, Samson, and the sea captain of "La Bouteille à la mer"), Julian belongs to the aristocracy of intelligence and spirit who are sacrificed in the name of an idea. His sacrifice, as is the case with the others, signifies the loss of an ideal, but concomitantly the affirmation of a new value. Christ's death in "Le Mont des oliviers," for example, signals the end of belief in the immanence of the Christian God, but also the affirmation of the ideal of human fraternity. The fable of Julian's life is structured on a series of binary oppositions, a thesis and antithesis whose conflict does not produce the synthesis of the optimistic poems in *Les Destinées*. These poems, discussed in the previous chapter, offered a vision of positive change resulting from the victory of man's creative spirit over the "fatalities" of the world ("La Maison du berger," "La Bouteille à la mer," "L'Esprit pur").

Julian's desire, his project, is the preservation of the spiritual treasure of polytheism, the pure idea of divinity, through the pagan symbols of the ancient pantheon of gods. His effort is opposed by the dynamic growth of the popular new Christian religion. Adopted by the barbarians, Romans, and Syrians, Christianity appealed to the senses through its miracles and objects of veneration, its promise of a rich afterlife, and its belief in a man who is God. The synthesis resulting from this opposition requires the death and sacrifice of Julian, victim of the historical fatality of an irrepressible religious movement, and produces the transfer of man's spiritual treasure from paganism to Christianity.

This action in the form of a dialectical conflict is presented through various *récits* told by friends of Julian during a banquet meeting at the home of Libanius. The Socratic session provides an opportunity for the expression of multiple points of view, including that of the narrator, a Jewish merchant whose position gives him a measure of objective distance from the events. Libanius affords the explanation of the "resolution" of the struggle, however, in a conversation with Julian himself, who has come to consult the "Docteur Noir" of Antioch.

Libanius develops a theory of signs and symbols that needs only a shift in terminology to suggest a modern semiological perspective. Julian was doomed to fail in his work, according to the philosopher, since he did not understand that the symbols and doctrines of paganism had been emptied out of all meaning or potential for signification. The spiritual truths of the temple of Daphné (i.e., belief in the Idea of an eternally creative God, an ideal moral life of stoic purity and simplicity, and the harmony of beautiful forms), these ideas or "signifieds" could no longer be appropriately conveyed by signifiers such as the sun–god and other pagan deities encumbered with irrational legends of petty intervention in human affairs. The Christian signs, however, were still full with potential meaning, especially for the masses, rich with a sensuous kind of beauty and capable of representing the spiritual ideas that must be preserved. Although Libanius is a Platonist who cannot believe in Christian doctrine, he understands that only Christian ideology and the empire of its signs can prevent the Western world from declining into barbarism. Even though its signs are composed of signifieds that are illusions (miracles, angels, the personal afterlife, and other irrational phenomena), the spiritual realities for which they stand are the essential ideas that alone give value to man's existence.

The climactic moment in the novel is the lesson Libanius gives concerning the relationship between symbol and idea. This metaliterary text must be seen in the context of a continuing meditation on symbolism that spans Vigny's production, and makes *Daphné* almost a book about the function of symbols in art and society. Libanius exemplifies his theory with the image of an Egyptian mummy preserved by a thick crystal container. Although the specific doctrines of its religion are dead, the essential, spiritual ideal of the ancient religion represented by the immortal body of the dead god has been preserved through time by the purity and durability of the crystal that encloses and protects it. The crystal, in the case of the Egyptian mummy, is the appropriate symbol; Libanius compares it to religious dogma strong enough to protect moral and spiritual truths against the corrosion of history.

Again, Julian's error is seen in the context of poetry; his "poetic" appreciation of divine truths, that is, his moments of ecstatic insight when he sensed the divine essence of Creation, were authentic. However his choices of the ancient intermediary gods and solar deities to convey ideas of destiny, universal force, etc.—symbols in which he himself did not believe—exemplified inferior poetry, and illustrated once more the incapacity of the poet to act in the political or religious domain. He tried to impose a poeticized, personal vision on humanity, but failed to grasp the importance of the right choice of symbols; like a poet (Stello) he was too absorbed in his inner world to realize the need to convince the barbarians of the truth of his visions. In fact they would have been incapable of comprehending them. Libanius, like Vigny himself, concludes that there must always be a separation between the moral conscience of the strong and that of the weak; the weak in mind and spirit will always need concrete signs and even sensuous images in order to accept moral ideas. The idealistic poet is ill-suited to influence the multitude; he should seek to maintain the elevation of his inspiration, and write authentic poetry expressing the intensity and profundity of his experience in a language that needs as little symbolism as possible. Or, since all ideas must be expressed through a language of signs, he must choose the signs with a minimum of physicality, of material and sensual connotation.

Thus the real meanings of Julian's legend and *Daphné* itself become clear. Julian symbolizes the failure to recognize the power of the appropriate symbols to convey meaning, as well as the incapacity of poets to act. The people need forms that can foster their belief, according to Libanius; the Christian barbarians can perhaps best preserve the spiritual inheritance of humanity through their new signs and doctrines.

The image of Daphné becomes rich with multiple significance and is the unifying center of a complex symbolic network. Like the archbishop's library in the novel's contemporary frame, the books of Alexandria, and the preserving crystal of the mummy's tomb, the actual temple of Daphné represents the symbol that protects and preserves a storehouse of spiritual truth, in this case a source of Hellenic moral, aesthetic, and spiritual knowledge. It is the beautiful and appropriate sign (aesthetically harmonious and pure) of the essential mysteries it contains. It thus signifies the necessity of containing the ideal in its most complementary form.

As a suburb of Antioch, the city of Daphné figures as a refuge of atticism, a beautiful oasis of Greek philosophy and religion. Its destruction by the Christian barbarians at the end of Julian's story suggests a parallel with Paris, contemporary storehouse of the values of Western philosophy, the city of enlightenment, now endangered.

Daphné is of course a mythic figure as well, particularly appropriate as a symbol of Julian's quest, since she was the desired lover of Apollo the sun-god, whose worship Julian reinstates. The temple of Daphné is also a source of love, a feminine symbol of the poet's quest for the redemptive woman, a romantic image that suggests Nerval's Aurélia, who intercedes in his search through dream and myth for assurances of man's immortality.

Daphné is thus a symbol of the need for appropriate symbolism; as a city it is a cultural sign, and as a myth it contains the tragic truth of the impossibility of transforming an elusive spiritual ideal into an accessible reality—Apollo's loss of Daphné metamorphosed into a laurel tree corresponds to Julian's inability to give form to his mystical vision. Although *Daphné* is a short novel, it offers a singular richness and density surpassing even *Stello*. On the level of narrative discourse the points of view are multiple, giving expression to the complexity of conflicting ideologies. The omniscient, impersonal narrator introduces the frame and concludes the novel with a vision of history and a lesson on human thought, the dangers of incarnating pure ideas in action or false symbols. Dialogue between the Docteur Noir and Stello dominates the frame of *Daphné*. Each one in turn becomes the narrator of several "récits;" Stello relates the story of Abailard and

Héloïse, and characters like the lovesick student Trivulce[4] (an ironic double of Stello) relate their own stories.

The main section of the novel takes the form of four letters sent from the Jewish merchant Joseph Jechaiah, who is visiting Antioch, to his friend in Alexandria; his perspective is that of a sympathetic witness to the last days of Julian's reign. His presence and objectivity lend to this narration a measure of authenticity, whereas his religious stance permits him a certain distance and impartiality vis-à-vis the violent opposition between pagans and Christians.

The letter form is particularly appropriate for the reporting of the extraordinary events, the description of the rare beauty of Daphné and the recording of the conversation of Libanius and his followers; Jechaiah's voice conveys his calm appreciation of ideas expressed, his wonder and irony, to the silent correspondent who stands in for the reader. Embedded in his letters, moreover, are *récits* recounted by Libanius, Jean, and Basile, who thus become narrators in the third degree; a letter from Paul de Larissa relates Julian's death on the battlefield. Anecdotes of Julian's childhood and his political activities are told in flashback form during the Socratic seance that prepares the reader for Julian's dramatic arrival at Daphné, and his own defense of his actions, his request for counsel.

The multiplicity of narrative voices and *récits* corresponds to a pattern of figures and characters who symbolize a variety of philosophical and moral attitudes, united by their reactions to religious "enthousiasme." Those who express a direct emotional, even mystical, perception of the divine or eternal ideas, the enthusiasts, include, first of all, Stello himself, the pure poet. He is mirrored by Abailard, the theologian and lover who was victimized by both the public and the religious tribunal, and by the anguished student Trivulce, sick with an impossible love for the image of the mythological Daphné. The story of Trivulce thus forms a direct link between the frame and the main novel. Contrasted with these figures in the frame are the nun (who leads Stello to the room of the sick student in the "pays latin") suggesting simple faith and charity without philosophy or idealism, and the rationalist Docteur Noir. Once again, as in the novel *Stello,* he is the realist, the pragmatic ego, conscience, or animus to the sensitive anima of his poetic counterpart.

In the main part of the novel the same oppositions define the actors:

Julian is the poet and mystic who chooses to embody his ideas in political action; his friend and disciple Paul de Larissa dies a martyr's death due to his total devotion to polytheism (he is lapidated by the Christian barbarians). Christ must be included because, although he does not appear in the novel, he is often compared to Julian (the Antichrist), since he also attempted to raise the ignorant multitude to a superior level of spiritual experience and was mocked for his effort. In the rationalist camp Libanius the Platonist and Stoic dominates the novel, and is characterized as an ancient Docteur Noir with, however, a sincere philosophical belief in the pure idea of an eternal Creator. His disciples Jean Chrysostome and Jean de Basile have resolved the conflict between metaphysical thought and social action in their society: the first by embracing Christianity as Libanius recommends, the second by remaining a pagan and a Platonist, withdrawn from society like his mentor.

Thus, the actors and the actions in the text are all a function of the opposition between idea and action that is a structuring principle in many of Vigny's works. When the poet or enthusiast acts, he transgresses the law of pure expression in art with negative or tragic consequences. Bonnefoy affirms with some justification that this novel enacts Vigny's most profound idea, "la tentation de l'idée pure, au lieu de s'exprimer purement dans une oeuvre d'art est de l'exprimer grossièrement dans l'action et de s'y perdre."[5]

The actions in the text are determined not only by the simple opposition between paganism and Christianity, or the barbarian menace to an aristocratic spirituality ("la conscience des faibles" and "la conscience des forts"), but by that between action and contemplation. The real protagonist of the novel is Libanius, who does not act, but contemplates the eternal essences of Daphné, combining in one person the enthusiasm of Stello and the stoic resignation of the Docteur Noir.

During the philosophical discussion that forms the central part of the text, Libanius frequently uses artistic metaphors to explain his views. Images from art compose the symbolic code of the novel, and the theme of the creative process gives it unity and significance.

After Julian's arrival at the home of Libanius, a long discussion ensues on art and style in which Libanius compares Julian's political task to that of a sculptor faced with a block of marble to chisel and form.

He compares the "people" to be educated to the marble, and the "pensée politique" to the creative genius of the sculptor; style is likened to the particular beauty of the statue calculated to seduce the spectator without deceiving him: "car saisir le pouvoir et l'exercer, ce n'est encore là que le premier pas du statuaire qui saisit son ciseau de fer et son marteau de bois et se place devant le marbre. Le bloc est l'assemblée grossière des hommes dont la forme ne change que sous les coups des grands statuaires. Or, pour concevoir cette forme que tu voulais donner à ce marbre énorme, où aurais-tu pris ta pensée première, sinon dans ce génie poétique né en toi?" (*D*, p. 832). Libanius through his very classical aesthetic is expressing Vigny's own concept of creative activity, often elaborated in the *Journal d'un poète;* the artist must begin with the pure idea and search for the complementary symbol or myth, the preserving crystal of form in which to incarnate it. Libanius admits that Julian had discovered a significant idea but failed in his work as sculptor, since the shapes he gave to his stone were outmoded, no longer beautiful, and unconvincing to the uninitiated.

The central image of the art of Egyptian mummification has already been discussed as a symbol of the preservation of religious essences. Related images such as the books (the treasure of Alexandria) and the manuscripts of the archbishop destroyed by vandalism recur through the novel. In an early chapter (chap. 4) entitled "Le Christ et l'Antéchrist" two statues in the room of the student Trivulce prefigure the action to follow in the main novel and contain indices of the enigma of Julian's life. One is the statue of the mutilated Christ— its realistic details convey both his humanity and a loss of faith in Christianity; the other is a statue of the young emperor Julian:

ses yeux étaient levés au ciel comme par une révolte indomptable. . . . Son manteau impérial découvrait un sein nu; au-dessous de son coeur était enfoncé un javelot qu'il arrachait de la main gauche, tandis que sa main droite étendue était pleine de son sang puisé dans cette blessure et qu'il paraissait offrir en libation à la terre, ou jeter au ciel avec reproche, ou montrer au Christ suspendu sur le bois sacré, en lui disant quelque chose.

Deux signes donnaient un caractère étrange à cette statue mystérieuse: l'extrémité du javelot qui lui perçait la poitrine portait, au lieu de plumes, la forme d'une croix, et l'Empereur avait à sa ceinture un rouleau de papyrus sur lequel on lisait ce seul mot: Daphné. (*D*, pp. 789–90)

The javelin, the cross, and the papyrus point to the three elements of his personality and the source of his tragedy—the soldier, the religious reformer, and poet, the victim of Christianity and his own failed genius. The most important artistic image is that of the refuge of Daphné and its temple: its spiritual storehouse is compared to an elixir of life; its moral truth to the axis of the world, the "sève de la terre" (*D*, p. 841).

The narrator sets the stage for the philosophical discussion with Libanius through the same technique Vigny uses in his "poèmes philosophiques." He presents a brief description of the natural decor, first the approaches to the temple and then its harmonious gardens, with carefully chosen symbolic details, prefiguring and containing the human drama that is to follow. The symbolic details of the Garden of Gethsemane, for example, announce Christ's death in "Le Mont des Oliviers" in a fashion similar to this:

La chaleur ne se faisait plus sentir sous ces grandes ombres, et les palmes ne cessant jamais de battre l'air comme de larges mains, l'air faisait passer autour de moi les odeurs délicieuses des plantes et les parfums du lotus. De temps en temps seulement, lorsque le vent de l'occident envoyé par la mer venait à faire ployer tous les palmiers à la fois, les rayons rouges du soleil se plongeaient dans l'ombre, comme des épées de feu, et leur passagère ardeur rendait plus délicieuses la fraîcheur et l'ombre qui n'étaient troublées et traversées ainsi que par de rares éclairs. (*D*, p. 798)

Julian's arrival is preceded by the following description, an excellent example of atticism in Vigny's style:

La nuit était en ce moment si muette que nous pouvions distinguer le bruit léger des sources de Daphné. Toutes les étoiles éclairaient le ciel par de si larges feux qu'il nous semblait que nous étions placés au milieu d'elles. Je voyais à travers les colonnes du portique les lauriers du bois sacré s'entrelacer en berceaux et se balancer ainsi que les cyprès, les cèdres et les arbres indiens sous le vent frais qui venait de la mer voisine. Les parfums de l'aloès, du santal et du lys des eaux pénétraient nos cheveux, nos épaules et nos bras de leurs fraîches odeurs, et nous les sentions apportées par les gouttes invisibles de la rosée nocturne. (*D*, pp. 824–25)

In both these passages the welcome peace of night's darkness (and death) is contrasted with the bright fire of sunset ("des épées de feu") and the stars. As a desired refuge from the passions and agitation of an active life, Daphné offers the philosophical consolation of serene beauty, harmonious proportions, and calm sensuality. The delicious odors of aloes, sandalwood, and lily, all associated with purification of the body and spirit, suggest the renewal of life at Daphné. The lotus can symbolize nascent life, revelation, and various forms of evolution; the laurel and palm evoke victory and fecundity, while the cedar and the Indian trees represent Christian incorruptibility and Eastern resignation, as well as the universality of Daphné's spiritual lesson. The laurel and palm are of course, sacred to Apollo, God of intellect, prophecy, and the arts and enemy of barbarism. His unattainable loved one, Daphné, immortalized by the laurel tree, suggests that the richest life is that of the soul after death. The presence of the cypress, the promise of the lotus, and the dominance of night reveal Daphné as a "ville des morts" (*D,* p. 801). Its springs, the sacred wood with its branches intermingled protectively, and the ever-present neighboring sea promise a source of spiritual rebirth.

The carefully balanced descriptions of Daphné's beauty correspond to Vigny's Hellenic idealism and illustrate his concept of the "crystal" symbol that contains the pure idea. Thematically as well as stylistically, however, the text often suggests other nineteenth-century treatments of Eastern or oriental fictional worlds, particularly *Salammbô*. As in Flaubert's novel about Carthage, the conflict between the barbarians and the materialistic, emasculated inhabitants of Antioch results in the destruction of a civilization, one also dominated by a feminine principle; the secrets of the temple of Daphné are permanently lost, just as the theft of the sacred veil of the goddess of Tanit in *Salammbô* prefigures the final destruction of Carthage.

Vigny's impersonal descriptions of the oriental splendor of Julian's army and the corrupt sensuality of the people of Antioch anticipate those of Flaubert in colorful evocations of rich, decadent grandeur. The following description of the army's elephants would not be out of place in *Salammbô:* "Après eux passèrent six cents éléphants, qui portaient les tentes et des vivres pour l'armée dans le désert. Cent autres éléphants couverts de longues housses de pourpre et couronnés d'algue marine étaient conduits par de beaux enfants vêtus de lin qui les guidaient de la voix et avec une baguette d'or. Ces animaux devaient être sacrifiés le lendemain au bord de la mer et, par ordre de l'Empereur, immolés à Neptune," (*D,* pp. 795–96).

The final chapter, "Fin de Daphné," presents the narrator's vision of history by situating the fall of Julian's empire in a larger cultural context: "Tout est consommé—Ils regardèrent la statue de Julien. A ses pieds était Luther, et plus bas Voltaire qui riait" (D, p. 857). Vigny's narrator thus suggests a counterrevolutionary view of the need to conserve established religious values in traditional signs and symbols in order to maintain morality in the people, the "conscience des faibles."

Stello and the doctor have just witnessed the sacking of the church in Paris and recognize its resemblance to the destruction of the temple of Daphné. Julian, Luther, Voltaire, and—although he is not mentioned in the novel—Lamennais (often criticized in the *Journal*) have contributed to the progressive weakening of the belief in the spiritual values of Christianity: Julian through his inability to adapt Christian symbols to his exalted vision; the others through their attacks on orthodox dogma and thought.

Paradoxically, the historical parallel that underscores the rapport Vigny discovers between his situation as an artist in 1837 and that of the Emperor Julian is the menace of new religions, increasing materialism, and barbarity. Vigny, as a reluctant defender of orthodox Christianity against those who would humanize and socialize it, resembles Julian the defender of the finest values of Hellenism against the barbaric Christian hordes.

The essential idea for Vigny is that the life of the "esprit pur," the integrity of the spiritual and intellectual heritage that is man's greatest value, must be preserved. Man's essence as a creative thinker, whose nature is spiritual, must be perpetuated even if it can be done only through the support of an ideology he cannot accept, but whose symbols still have the power to foster belief.

As I have tried to illustrate, however, the novel is more than conservative propaganda for church and monarchy; it is finally a text about ideas and how to write them. Ideas, the half-gods of our dreams, as Vigny's narrator claims, must be molded, sculpted in forms of language and art that do not betray their original purity, rendered durable, compelling, and capable of communicating their unique illumination.

IV

Victor Hugo: *William Shakespeare* and the Romantic Paradigm of Creativity

Dans l'ombre immense du Caucase
Depuis des siècles, en rêvant,
Conduit par les hommes d'extase,
Le genre humain marche en avant;
Il marche sur la terre; il passe,
Il va, dans la nuit, dans l'espace,
Dans l'infini, dans le borné,
Dans l'azur, dans l'onde irritée,
A la lueur de Prométhée,
Le libérateur enchaîné!

"Les Mages" (*Les Contemplations,* livre 6)

Published in 1864 when he was living in exile, *William Shakespeare* became Victor Hugo's major statement on the role in society of the creative person—or as the nineteenth century preferred to label him, the genius. Ostensibly an introduction to his son's translation of Shakespeare's plays into French, this lengthy text is actually an elaborate consecration of the romantic myth of the artist that Hugo and others had developed and propagated for forty years. A privileged interpreter of the sacred for humanity, the artist has become the seer who discovers signs of the ideal order of the universe through the apparent disorder of changing phenomena.

The work includes a brief account of Shakespeare's life, some rather astute analyses of certain aspects of the plays, and even an attempt at placing Shakespeare's life and works in a specific sociocultural context. On a second level, Hugo provides an aesthetic, a view of genre development, and a concomitant philosophy of history more complex than that of his Preface to *Cromwell*. The work manifests, however, the same optimistic progressivism, based on a tripart evolutionary development from antiquity to the Renaissance, and finally to the modern age of revolution.

On the deepest level, it seems to be an act of self-justification, in any case an apology for belief in no less than the great artist as God's representative in human history, "l'oeuvre des génies est du surhumain sortant de l'homme."[1] Shakespeare is presented as the exemplary model for the pattern Hugo discerns in the creative life of Western man, and which informs every aspect of the book's organization and thought. The table of contents itself presents the deep structure underlying Hugo's vision in its simplest form; it divides the work neatly into three parts: Shakespeare's life and genius limited by historical exigencies; second, the eclipse of his work after his death through its deformation by critics; and finally, a renewal in the new and more profound comprehension of his theater and poetry by a universal and popular audience—an effect that translations such as Hugo's are designed to promote.

The pattern is easily recognizable as a variant of the universal, archetypal rebirth myth that structures many individual romantic works of art (such as Alfred de Vigny's "La Maison du berger"). It underlies the romantic view of history and even romantic philosophy. Interpreted according to Morse Peckham's categories,[2] it translates as an evolution in thinking about the universe occurring toward the end of the eighteenth century. Instead of comprehending the world as a completed and unproductive static mechanism, man began to view it as a creative, dynamic, and organic force in which man and nature are integrated harmoniously.

In terms of literature and writing in particular, the presence of the rebirth archetype signals a cultural concept of creativity that Hugo expounds in *William Shakespeare* and that can now be considered a romantic paradigm. Eighteenth-century writing, dominated by conventional forms and excessive emphasis on rational discourse, arrives at a kind of spiritual death (corresponding to the exhaustion of monarchical society). After a descent into Hell, a period of searching and alienation, writing enters into contact with a new spiritual element— the sources of poetry, intuition and imagination, the springs of Freud's primary processes of cognition (this second period corresponds to the turbulence of the Revolution of 1789, the tragic grandeur and collapse of Napoleonism). Finally, writing reaches the stage of a rebirth. It becomes a "moyen de connaissance" (means to knowledge), indeed the revelation of divine order through disorder, the use of poetic language to symbolize the ideal and to metaphorize the link between man, nature, and God. This stage covers the development of romanticism itself after 1830, when the artist assumes his function as social and political guide, when romanticism and liberalism, as Hugo states, have become one and the same. This same development is carefully chronicled by Bénichou in his *Sacre de l'écrivain*[3] from the historical and literary perspective of early nineteenth-century concepts of the writer's function: Hugo sees it in mythical terms, as the latest manifestation of the essential pattern of artistic creativity in the Western world.

The persona of Hugo, the narrator of *William Shakespeare,* engages in a curious dialogue with the ghost of the great dramatist, thus perpetuating a long tradition of fruitful communication, exchange, and transmission of values among artists; Dante, of course, spoke to Virgil, and Shakespeare's plays, according to Hugo, manifest a meaningful dialogue or intertextual rapport with Aeschylus.

A lengthy preliminary portion of the text is devoted to Hugo's version of the legend of Aeschylus's life and works. Its effect on today's reader is at first that of a curious series of reflected images (or "mise en abîme," as French critics term it), for Aeschylus is treated as the prototypical poet-prophet whose own "story" is an enactment of the archetypal pattern Hugo, and the romantics in general, discovers in the myth of Prometheus. The myth of Prometheus, of course, was given dramatic form by Aeschylus himself. In Hugo's view Aeschylus was the all-inclusive genius, compared to the limited bourgeois mind of Socrates. Aeschylus's works contain the spiritual dimension and the civilizing force that Hugo considers the primary signs of genius; he introduced the common people into his plays, and in *Prometheus Bound* gave form to the highest expression of man's creative spirit. According to Hugo, Prometheus, the man of progress, transmitted the creative power of fire from the gods to suffering humanity and endured a living death for his act, only to be reborn in the work of future creators, specifically in the life of Christ, whom he seemed to announce. Aeschylus is therefore the originator of the fundamental "typical" image of the creative artist (Hugo explains that the greatest artists create the representative types of their age—such as Hamlet for the Renaissance, and the nineteenth-century figure who was yet to be invented). Aeschylus himself suffered exile and a symbolic spiritual death in the loss of his works in the burning of the library of Alexandria. In the view of Hugo and many other romantic thinkers, he was "reborn" in the Renaissance, however, and specifically in Shakespeare, whom he prefigures just as Prometheus suggests Christ.

Thus, Hugo identifies the essential creative figure with that of Prometheus before studying the specific qualities of Shakespeare's art and those of the creative process in general. A definite historical continuity is projected by the narrator for whom the "story" of Aeschylus, presented in the three-part sequence of the archetypal rebirth pattern, explains the deepest meaning of the life of a Western artist. The lost work of Aeschylus, *The Apotheosis of Orpheus,* anticipates in Hugo's view the dialogue between Dante and Virgil and even that between Hugo and Shakespeare. For Hugo's book is an apotheosis of Shakespeare that nonetheless projects the need for a contemporary poet-prophet. Hugo looks forward to the artist (perhaps himself) who can give a profound expression to the revolutionary world of the nineteenth century, still awaiting its representation in figures as profoundly "typical" as Prometheus and Hamlet, who symbolized the crises of the ancient world in transition and the anxiety of the shift from medieval values to Renaissance society.

Present everywhere in *William Shakespeare* is the voice and persona of Hugo, the "subject" whose experience gives the study a personal, elegiac tone. Hugo's own premature exile is characterized by a kind of spiritual death, because it meant the loss of political and personal ideals. This exile is a time, however, during which the creative nature of suffering and even death is active and is already leading to a renascence through a profound understanding of God's order, and a commitment to humanitarian and socialist reform. Hugo's own life as he recreates it therefore exhibits the same pattern that he discerns in

Prometheus, Aeschylus, and Shakespeare. He writes of them in the traditional metaphors of the exiled artist—his island, like Rousseau's, is his prison, but a welcome shelter, for it provides him with the opportunity to explore his inner self and past experiences. The island-prison is actually a metaphor for his imagination, which paradoxically deepens and expands through its very restrictions,[4] becoming a primary source of creativity.

In *Les Contemplations,* as Susanne Nash[5] has argued convincingly, Hugo transposed the elements of his creative experience, the creative process itself, into the six sections of his poetic masterpiece, thus imposing a unity beyond that of mere biographical data. Centered on the death of Léopoldine and the suffering it caused, *Les Contemplations* exhibits once again the rebirth pattern, as books 5 and 6, "En marche" and "Au bord de l'infini," develop the profound spiritual initiation resulting from the poetic and human experience that Hugo has undergone.

William Shakespeare is also a text about the creative process but in a historical, critical, and mythical mode. Through the life and works of Shakespeare, themselves illuminated and structured by the legend of Aeschylus and the myth of Prometheus, Hugo as critic offers a model of creativity divided into the three aspects of its process: origins and motivation, the elaboration of the work of art, and finally the relationship between artist, artwork, and the public or society for which the work is destined and whose conditions may determine it.

L'heure du changement d'âge est venue. Nous assistons, sous la pleine clarté de l'idéal, à la majestueuse jonction du beau avec l'utile. Aucun génie actuel ou possible ne vous dépassera, vieux génies, vous égaler est toute l'ambition permise; mais, pour vous égaler, il faut pourvoir aux besoins de son temps comme vous avez pourvu aux nécessités du vôtre. Les écrivains fils de la Révolution ont une tâche sainte. O Homère, il faut que leur épopée pleure, o Hérodote, il faut que leur histoire proteste, o Juvénal, il faut que leur satire détrône, o Shakespeare, il faut que leur *tu seras toi* soit dit au peuple, o Eschyle, il faut que leur Prométhée foudroie Jupiter, o Job, il faut que leur fumier féconde, o Dante, il faut que leur enfer s'éteigne, o Isaïe, ta Babylone s'écroule, il faut que la lueur s'éclaire! Ils font ce que vous avez fait; ils contemplent directement la création, ils observent directement l'humanité; ils n'acceptent pour clarté dirigeante aucun rayon réfracté, pas même le vôtre. Ainsi que vous, ils ont pour seul point de départ, en dehors d'eux, l'être universel, en eux, leur âme; ils ont pour source de leur oeuvre la source unique, celle d'où coule la nature et celle d'où coule l'art, l'infini. Comme le déclarait il y a quarante ans tout à l'heure [Preface to *Cromwell*] celui qui écrit ces lignes: *Les poètes et les écrivains du dix-neuvième siècle n'ont ni maîtres ni modèles.* Non, dans tout cet art vaste et sublime de tous les peuples, dans toutes ces créations grandioses de toutes les époques, non, pas même toi, Eschyle, pas même toi, Dante, pas même toi, Shakespeare, non, ils n'ont ni modèles ni maîtres. Et pourquoi n'ont-ils ni maîtres ni modèles! C'est parce qu'ils ont un modèle, l'Homme, et parce qu'ils ont un maître, Dieu. (*W.S.*, pp. 309–10)

This exalted poetic credo could easily serve as a résumé of the entire book, a condensaton of Hugo's major concepts presenting his model of creativity essentially unchanged since the early declaration of romantic writing in the thirties. It is above all the description of a central myth of romantic literature, which reveals both its power and its weaknesses. Hugo's idealism seems never to waver; his confidence in the efficacy of the artist's function and the power of language are not questioned, although Flaubert and even Hugo's contemporaries, Musset and Gautier, have already parodied them. A romantic faith in the divine origin of creativity and its eventual role in the amelioration of human suffering is affirmed with oratorical conviction, even though the revolution of 1848 had proved the inability of romantic socialists to direct the government or to control the self-interest of the bourgeoisie. Lamartine, the poet-president of the Republic of 1848 was the very incarnation of this romantic myth of the artist as visionary and guide. Elected by opposing factions as an acceptable moderate, he was manifestly incapable of choosing between the demands of liberal or conservative forces, and consequently his brand of political idealism failed tragically.

Hugo's concept of the origins of creativity repeats the ancient notion of artistic talent or genius as the gift of God which the bearer is inspired to develop. Like Diderot, he also sees genius as the product of nature or even chance, noting, however, that certain ideas and forms seem to be transmitted mysteriously by great artists from generation to generation. Much of what Hugo says could easily serve as an illustration to the study by Kris and Kurz entitled *Legend, Myth, and Magic in the Image of the Artist*,[6] which describes the motifs recurring in biographies of artists and studies of creativity. They devised a prestructuralist classification of the themes and ideas that have become constants in all presentations of artistic life since the earliest accounts. These constants, although almost independent of any provable factor, seem necessary to structure the artist's life in a manner convincing to the public—e.g., the artist is almost always presented as a child prodigy; the painter's images are often considered to have magic qualities. Creative ability as a gift of God or nature is seen by Kris and Kurz to be a persistent motif in Greek and Renaissance biographies. Hugo's contribution is indeed more original when he attempts to describe the faculties and qualities that comprise artistic creativity. He makes no attempt to examine its origins in the modern psychological sense—as, for example, through the transformation of childhood fantasies or the sublimation of powerful instincts and drives. However, he does see, much like Balzac, the creative person as endowed with an unusually intense quantity of energy, specifically the special ability to unite in himself disparate, contrary qualities.

The truly creative person is recognized, according to Hugo, by his unusual capacity to combine "les facultés les plus lointaines" (*W.S.*, p. 161) within himself and in his discoveries about the world outside him. Pascal's double interest in mathematics and psychology, analysis and synthesis, his idea of "les deux infinis" culminating in a special vision of cosmic and human reality is cited as an example of the great artist's capacity to produce a double vision, a "réflexion double" (*W.S.*, p. 162). This concept is central to Hugo's view because it permits him to link together, in his customary desire for a totalizing philosophy, his vision of the universe, his interpretation of the role of the artist, and his confidence in language as a direct revelation of truth.

The special ability to recognize the double nature of reality and translate it into rhetorical, poetic devices like antitheses makes of the artist or poet the chosen interpreter of the seeming contrast between the apparent disorder in the universe and the profound order that lies beyond and through it: an order discernible in the signs and symbols of nature. Antithesis therefore corresponds to the deepest truth about reality, and its "words" reveal the secrets of "things," since it defines nature itself. It is, of course, only one of the linguistic devices that translate philosophical truth for Hugo, but it represents the necessary beginning; before understanding the ultimate harmony between man, nature, and God, the artist must see and name the elements of multiplicity and dissonance that he observes everywhere.

Although a "thematic constant" or mythical motif, Hugo's view of the artist as God's chosen interpreter is enriched and clarified by his theory of the actual process by which the artist creates. He discusses the techniques and faculties involved in the elaboration of the work: "Dieu crée dans l'intuition; l'homme crée dans l'inspiration, compliquée d'observation cette création seconde, qui n'est autre chose que l'action divine faite par l'homme, c'est ce qu'on nomme le génie" (*W.S.*, p. 178). The great artist is defined by his capacity to comprehend and translate into his medium universal mystery and the unknown, the ideal and the beautiful, which Hugo defines as the "quantité d'infini" (*W.S.*, p. 85), the spiritual essence to which he gives form in his work. The goal and the true motivation of the artist is thus to translate the absolute into the relative worlds of sound, paint, and language; and he is especially prepared for this task through the powers of observation, imagination, and vision with which he has been endowed. The great artist very simply incorporates "toute la somme d'absolu réalisable à l'homme" (*W.S.*, p. 67); he participates in the divine through his creative power, imitating only the perpetual creativity of God in his expanding universe. He is himself a microcosm of nature, and his mind is a metonym for the entire human spirit. God therefore is "intérieur à l'homme" (*W.S.*, p. 178), which is the real meaning of the commonplace—inspiration.

In discussing the qualities of Shakespeare's genius, Hugo does offer a kind of poetics, or a set of principles underlying the production of a work of art. "Il y a deux poètes, le poète du caprice et le poète de la logique; et il y a un troisième poète, composé de l'un et de l'autre, les corrigeant l'un par l'autre, les complétant l'un par l'autre, et les résumant dans une entité plus haute" (*W.S.*, p. 258). In yet another formulaic condensation of his thought, Hugo here expresses the very essence of his conception of the creative process. The finest artist combines "caprice" and "logic," or rather he transforms them into the elements of a higher creative order. Caprice certainly stands for the forms of fantasy, reverie, and the dreamworld that become the sources of imagination's play; logic or rational processes such as analysis, conceptualization, and abstraction are the thinker's province. The "third poet" combines concept and form, image and idea, into a new reality that realizes or reveals an underlying spiritual truth.

The well-known poem "Pasteurs et troupeaux" from book 5 of *Les Contemplations* can serve as an exemplary model of Hugo's theory in practice through poetry. The poet's direct observations of the pastoral scene in Jersey lead to the discoveries of a seemingly curious or capricious resemblance between the young shepherdess with her flock and the promontory rock standing before the waves on the beach. This link between the worlds of man and nature is based on visual harmonies the poet discerns between the color of bits of fleece left on shrubbery and the foam of the waves dancing in the sunlight:

> Ses agneaux, dans le pré plein de fleurs qui l'encense,
> Bondissent, et chacun, au soleil s'empourprant,
> Laisse aux buissons, à qui la bise le reprend,
> Un peu de la toison, comme un flocon d'écume.[7]

A four-part homology—foam is to fleece as promontory is to shepherdess—results from the poet's observation, transformed by his imagination into a poetic simile.

The poet's solitary promenade and his chance encounter with the shepherdess, his perception of a connection between foam and fleece are the result of "caprice." The theological idea of divine Providence providing an ultimate source of meaning and design to all concrete phenomena is an accepted tenet of the "poète de la logique." The "third poet" then transforms the perceived (observed and imagined) relationship, revealing order in the world of nature, where chaos and decay seemed dominant, into a symbol of the universal presence of divine Providence; the "pâtre promontoire" is the benign shepherd of the sea, just as the young girl guides her flock. The shepherds and flocks of man and nature in turn become annunciatory signs of the greater Shepherd and His universal flock.

Hugo's formula of the three poets succinctly states the conclusions about the creative process reached by Silvano Arieti in his recent and valuable psychoanalytic study of creativity, *Creativity, the Magic Synthesis:*

The *primary process,* for Freud, is a way in which the psyche functions, especially the unconscious part of the psyche. It prevails in dreams and some mental illnesses, especially psychoses. The primary process operates quite differently from the secondary process, which is the way of functioning of the mind when it is awake and uses common logic. Primary process mechanisms reappear in the creative process also, in strange, intricate combinations with secondary process mechanisms and in syntheses that, although unpredictable, are nevertheless susceptible of psychological interpretation. It is from appropriate matching with secondary process mechanisms that these primitive forms of cognition, generally confined to abnormal conditions or to unconscious processes, become innovating powers. . . . I have proposed the expression *tertiary process* to designate this special combination of primary and secondary process mechanisms.[8]

The "third poet," or tertiary process, successfully fuses the work of the irrational poetic faculties with the rational, categorizing, conceptualizing mind into a new creation:

> The primary process offers the artist the imagination—that is, the faculty of presentation which provides the basic matter, as well as a loose form of organization such as the emergence of similarities, suggestions, and partial representations. The secondary process provides the screening and elimination of many suggestions and partial representations, whether in verbal, pictorial, or other forms. The tertiary process ultimately comes into being as a "click," or match, between the primary and secondary processes, which brings about an accepted emerging representation. Eureka! The new unity is created.[9]

The essential faculty producing this new unity is, for Hugo and Arieti, the work of imagination, the truly creative faculty that transforms the facts of observation into a new vision, observed reality into the intuition of a higher order. The great Hugo scholar Jean-Bertrand Barrère suggests that nowhere has Hugo stated this concept with greater clarity than in the *Post-scriptum de ma vie* in a text entitled *Contemplation suprême*. Barrère quotes the text and comments that Hugo defined the three stages of poetic knowledge by linking them with their objects in the world outside the poet: "'Peu à peu l'horizon s'élève, et la méditation devient contemplation; puis, il se trouble, et la contemplation devient vision.' Ils correspondent à trois formes de l'activité spirituelle, '*observation, imagination, intuition,*' ayant pour objet respectif 'humanité, nature, surnaturalisme.'"[10]

Imagination is thus placed at the center of the creative activity, for it is above all the synthesizing faculty. Precisely for Hugo, it is the faculty that gives form in language to the discoveries the poet makes about nature and man. Rather than being truly original, however, the work of the imagination reveals the already existing, underlying spiritual harmony of things through words.

In his discussions about the elaboration of a work of art, Hugo consistently uses organic and dynamic images from nature to explain the function of creative faculties and even linguistic and rhetorical devices. The poet's life is compared to the complex structure of an oak tree, now a romantic commonplace; reverie, which is an inner source of images, is defined as "un regard qui a cette propriété de tant regarder l'ombre qu'il en fait sortir la clarté" (*W.S.*, p. 144). Tropes and figures in Hugo's imagery are part of the rich garden where fantasy, compared to arabesque in architecture, embellishes the earth in thick layers of vegetation. The poet's mind is quite simply a microcosm of nature; consequently, the formation of metaphor is essentially the revelation of similarities of form and meaning existing in reality, unperceived by the uninitiated mind—metaphors that become in turn symbolic of a spiritual essence. The ideal is thus made manifest in the real through the mediation of the poet's language; the metaphoric identity, for example, of promontory and shepherdess evokes symbolically the existence of God, the Divine Pastor.

The organic and dynamic link between the poet's imagination and the world of nature has often been commented upon, and is certainly at the heart of Hugo's romantic aesthetic; in *William Shakespeare,* however, equal emphasis is placed upon the necessary relationship between the poet and the group he addresses, or "humanité" itself as he indicates in the *Post-scriptum.* The artist's work is shaped by the collective consciousness; he creates types or "exemplaire de l'homme" (*W.S.*, p. 179) that offer to the group a new self-portrait, containing its deepest aspirations, needs, and anxieties as well as its current form of idealism. These representative human types, e.g., Prometheus and Hamlet, endure longer than individuals precisely because they contain a "quantité d'éternité" (*W.S.*, p. 181); they result from the unique collaboration of the individual artist and the vast collective conscience that dominates him like a mysterious natural force, but which he transcends through his deep knowledge of its identity and his ability to express it.

Through this understanding of the complex relationship between the work of art and the audience to which it is addressed, Hugo develops his most original insights in *William Shakespeare.* He anticipates Jung's concept of the role of the visionary, not only in his emphasis on the great artist as a prophet or seer capable of intuiting spiritual truth but in his comprehension of the artist's role as healer who helps to restore the psychic balance of his group.[11] In Hugo's view the exemplary types created by the dramatist or the revelations of the poet compensate for the lack of spiritual dimension, specific moral and psychological gaps in the life of the artist's society. The artist's work is thus eminently civilizing, and he replaces the political leader as hero or guide in Hugo's vision of history. The new Prometheus of the revolutionary century, he inspires, directs, and molds humanity through his work. He offers not only an idealistic view of life, as Vigny prescribed, but also a practical commitment.

In concrete terms he declares that the artist must cure the bourgeoisie by restoring to this class, dominated by goods and money, a sense of spiritual values; moreover, he must literally create the common people as an intelligent group. Revolution in his time means "la France sublimée" (*W.S.*, p. 308), and the artist's role is to promote the transformation of a materialistic society according to his utopian vision.

Reading *William Shakespeare* illuminates Sartre's very negative stance regarding the romantic and realist writers' concepts of their function. In *Qu'est-ce que la littérature?* he claims without much evidence that Hugo was an exception and praises him as the only truly popular writer in the nineteenth century. Hugo does indeed develop a veritable mystique of the people in this text, anticipating important aspects of Sartre's thought in a mythical rather than an existential mode. Quite contrary to Vigny's conclusions, writing for Hugo means "engagement" (commitment) in a profound sense: "il faut qu'il soit populace" (*W.S.*, p. 233). The writer must hear the language, "voix," of the people, and in turn teach them the language of generosity, law, and especially freedom. Sartre in *Qu'est-ce que la littérature* speaks of the bourgeois writer's need literally to change his social class, to address himself to a virtual public, the public for whom the act of writing is a justified claim of its social rights. To write is thus to name and to limit, to uncover the flaws of the world and demand change.[12]

A true literature of the people is now needed, Hugo similarly claims. Their rich sensibility can be elevated and moved to action, through emotion provoked by contact with the beautiful. Shakespeare's art was a people's art, and socialist writers who proclaim the need for universal education are currently working to "transformer la foule en peuple" (*W.S.*, p. 239).

To write also means to proclaim liberty, since for Hugo freedom is inscribed in the essential spiritual order that the poet-prophet attempts to reveal behind the apparent disorder of societies. The artist's goal is doubly humanitarian, both political and moral, practical and ideal. Poetic language is no barrier to commitment (as it is for Sartre), because it is in his deepest nature that the poet's comprehension of the people and their needs is to be found. The conventions of poetic discourse are a vehicle to express this understanding and not an end in themselves.

Once again we return to the archetypal patterns with which we began, completing our review of Hugo's projection of the model of creativity. The artist must himself return to the source of being; during his time of spiritual sterility (brought about by the incomprehension of critics and bourgeois readers), it is precisely an espousal of the suffering and "death" of the people that can redeem him, that makes his rebirth as a writer at a higher level possible. In *Les Contemplations* personal suffering after the death of Léopoldine was the source of a new richness of insight and poetic growth. Here the people are the matrix ("le grand flanc," "la matrice universelle" [*W.S.*, p. 249]) in which the artist can be nourished. Only through an awareness that his own personal suffering and alienation are identical with that of the poor classes can he fully realize his potential. Physical and moral suffering as a necessary experience effecting a deepening of understanding and feelings is symbolized by Job and John of Patmos in *Les Contemplations* and *William Shakespeare*. In the latter text, however, Hugo develops the concept of communion with the people's misery as the point of contact with a new spiritual element—the redemptive power of human suffering, capable of freeing the artist from his isolation and death, and leading to renewal.

Prometheus's liberation from his chains thus follows the experience of sterility and alienation, and produces the need to "construire le peuple" (*W.S.*, p. 237), to act as a civilizing force through a purified vision of his ideals, and through a precise commitment to the needs of the people. Death has played its paradoxical, mythical role: "la mort est une force," "tout y est germe" (*W.S.*, p. 280); in biblical imagery Hugo celebrates its power to transform and renew. In part 3, appropriately entitled "Après la mort," he celebrates the nineteenth century as one of death and rebirth. The year 1793 marked the end of a world, a decisive crisis in history that produced from its ashes the new revolutionary century, a society whose renascence the writers, "les organes d'un recommencement" (*W.S.*, p. 305), must foster in a spiritual dimension.

The artist's life and work are therefore purified by a passage through death. Shakespeare was the victim of puritanical censorship and lack of support by the royal court; his work was mutilated by critics and destroyed as it was rewritten by lesser minds. His plays were rediscovered, however, in the eighteenth century and finally their full genius was recognized; according to Hugo his works eventually transformed the very spirit of England: first, by giving form to the historical crisis marking the end of the medieval world, and second, by defining the national character in its richness and complexity. Governments protect and buy second-rate writers; truly great writers die, misunderstood or disdained, diminished by critic-readers who produce an eclipse about them. This spiritual void is temporary, in Hugo's view, and even salutary. Indeed, it represents the paradoxical second step in the rite of passage, for these same writers are reborn in new societies. The French Revolution placed Voltaire and Rousseau in the pantheon; the English are at last constructing monuments to Shakespeare.

Hugo's view of the well-known mission of the artist reaches its most complex formulation in *William Shakespeare*: "La majestueuse jonction du beau avec l'utile" (*W.S.*, p. 309). For him there is no contradiction between a work of art and social progress, since great art has always been produced in opposition to despotism.[13] Although the artist's goal is to "rêver l'utopie" (*W.S.*, p. 253), his imaginative power gives him insight at the practical, concrete level of political and social life that makes a commitment necessary: "pour combattre les violences et les impostures, oui, pour réhabiliter les lapidés et les accablés, oui, pour conclure logiquement et marcher droit, oui, pour consoler, pour secourir, pour relever, pour encourager, pour enseigner, oui, pour panser en attendant qu'on guérisse, oui, pour transformer la charité en fraternité" (*W.S.*, p. 309).

He advocates revolt, unending protest against concrete expressions of world tyranny through art that has become action. History, he claims, must also be rewritten, for it is the record of the creators of civilization, the dynasty of genius and not the story of kings and battles. Historical progress is a text to which each great creator adds a phrase to express the divine idea—fraternity—more completely. The elevation of the human spirit, not material goods, is the sign of civilization; therefore, the function of art is literally to make civilization progress. Hugo's visionaries represent the lineage of the divine order made manifest in history along the human chain of being. In Promethean imagery, the creator, or "cet homme solaire" (*W.S.*, p. 143), sent from God's world to illuminate this one, must "compléter un univers par l'autre, verser sur le moins de l'un le trop de l'autre, accroître ici la liberté, là la science, là l'idéal, communiquer aux inférieurs des patrons de la beauté supérieure, échanger les effluves, apporter le feu central à la planète, mettre en harmonie les divers mondes d'un même système, hâter ceux qui sont en retard, croiser les créations" (*W.S.*, p. 142–43).

The role of the greatest artist is to "résumer les crises décisives de l'humanité" (*W.S.*, p. 66), to synthesize the work of revolution in his time. Hugo maintains his linear, three-part vision of history as unlimited progress, and suggests that after Aeschylus and Shakespeare, antiquity and the Renaissance, the revolutionary century is awaiting its major exponent. Hugo criticizes Goethe's conservatism and claims that in spite of its reputation his work lacks the requisite universality; no mention is made of Faust, already treated by Balzac and other romantic writers as a representative myth or exemplary type of modern man. Marx is never alluded to, although Hugo distinguishes his own brand of idealistic socialism from materialist or determinist philosohies that tend to de-emphasize political liberty, and could easily lead to new forms of despotism.

In any case, the new writer-prophet for the nineteenth century that Hugo invokes in *William Shakespeare* will resemble the seer, or "voyant," he describes; the artist who meditates on the reality of universal order through the present disorder, who has the courage to explore the abyss of the unknown and thus stretch his imagination into a vision of spiritual truth. The following text from *William Shakespeare* is dominated by images of the ocean figuring the abyss, and the promontory of Patmos symbolizing the rich inner world of the creator that transcends it. It recalls "A la fenêtre pendant la nuit" from *Les Contemplations,* in which Hugo's persona describes his own state of poetic voyance. The reader cannot avoid the conclusion, artfully prepared by Hugo, that he himself is the new Prometheus.

> Tout homme a en lui son Pathmos. Il est libre d'aller ou de ne point aller sur cet effrayant promontoire de la pensée d'où l'on aperçoit les ténèbres. S'il n'y va point, il reste dans la vie ordinaire, dans la foi ordinaire ou dans le doute ordinaire; et c'est bien. Pour le repos intérieur, c'est évidemment le mieux. S'il va sur cette cime, il est pris. Les profondes vagues du prodige lui ont apparu. Nul ne voit impunément cet océan-là. Désormais il sera le penseur dilaté, agrandi, mais flottant; c'est-à-dire le songeur. Il touchera par un point au poète, et par l'autre au prophète. Une certaine quantité de lui appartient maintenant à l'ombre. L'illimité entre dans sa vie, dans sa conscience, dans sa vertu, dans sa philosophie. Il devient extraordinaire aux autres hommes, ayant une mesure différente de la leur. Il a des devoirs qu'ils n'ont pas. Il vit dans la prière diffuse, se rattachant, chose étrange, à une certitude indéterminée qu'il appelle Dieu. Il distingue dans ce crépuscule assez de la vie antérieure et assez de la vie ultérieure pour saisir ces deux bouts de fil sombre et y renouer son âme. Qui a bu boira, qui a songé songera. Il s'obstine à cet abîme attirant, à ce sondage de l'inexploré, à ce désintéressement de la terre et de la vie, à cette entrée dans le défendu, à cet effort pour tâter l'impalpable, à ce regard sur l'invisible, il y vient, il y retourne, il s'y accoude, il s'y penche, il y fait un pas, puis deux, et c'est ainsi qu'on pénètre dans l'impénétrable, et c'est ainsi qu'on s'en va dans les élargissements sans bornes de la méditation infinie. (*W.S.*, p. 141)

Observation and contemplation through a confrontation with the unknown ultimately lead to vision. For Hugo this is the highest form of knowledge the artist can achieve, quite literally an interpenetration of his nature and the absolute. The third and last stage in his development, that of the visionary, is both a renascence and a fulfillment of his destiny.

Hugo provides in *William Shakespeare* a romantic model of the creative process in terms of the artist as seer. His pattern of growth and change is structured by a passage from sterility and death to renewal, through contact with a deep spiritual reality. A more profound comprehension of nature and man's place in the universe, to be translated into the languages of the arts, results from his absorption in the suffering of humanity.

Thus the progression of the creative process (observation-imagination-vision), the story of individual artists' lives (Aeschylus, Shakespeare, Hugo), and the history of literature itself (neoclassicism to romanticism) are informed by Hugo with the same underlying sequence or adaptation of an archetypal rebirth pattern that can be seen as a fundamental romantic paradigm.

V

Honoré de Balzac and the Mechanisms of Creative Energy: *Louis Lambert* and the Impossibility of Sublimation

Le mouvement, en raison de la résistance, produit une combinaison qui est la vie; dès que l'un ou l'autre est plus fort, la vie cesse.

(Louis Lambert)

Balzac wrote many novels and stories that present artist figures, ranging from the successful genius Daniel d'Arthez[1] to the mediocre but successful painter of the bourgeoisie Pierre Grassou. The admirable d'Arthez seems to represent an ideal model of the great writer who persists in his work, although he is misunderstood and impoverished, until his honesty and genius are finally recognized and rewarded. Most of the other painters, musicians, and writers, however, certainly do manifest the patterns of failure that have been studied rather frequently.[2] Victims, like Lucien de Rubempré, of society's degraded values or their own lack of willpower, or even of the pressures of thought and creativity on their physical natures, Balzac's artists lead tragic lives. Success or failure of the creative enterprise is nevertheless not the real issue in these works; Balzac is primarily concerned with the complex mechanisms of the creative process. In the *Etudes philosophiques* he poses the metaphysical questions underpinning the artist's attempt to penetrate the secret of creation itself; Frenhofer,[3] for example, would rival God in his Promethean desire to create life through art. Other works deal with the antithesis or conflicts between technique and theory,[4] "life" and "art," the "usure de la pensée," defined as the process by which the very activity of creating destroys the creator.

Louis Lambert (1832–33) and *La Recherche de l'absolu* (1834) are the most profound and characteristic of these studies of creativity. In the former, we find a theoretical basis of the creative process analyzed with great subtlety; in the latter, an effort to translate theory into practice through science. There are many thematic and structural parallels between the two books; both contain the romantic conflict between love and the artist's work, both have ambiguous endings forcing the reader to decide whether Louis and Balthazar are mad or truly men of genius. More significantly, both figures are visionaries who seek the absolute—which is defined philosophically as the highest, most elevated form of thought, or as energy condensed into a pure fusion of spirit and matter. Louis finds the absolute of religious truth through the cultivation of his inner life to the exclusion of the outer, physical being; Balthazar seeks it through chemistry, the outer life developed from the level of abstractual thought to what Balzac calls "spécialité," or imaginative speculation about the secret of God's creation—the very essence of life itself.

Before we examine these works, it is important to see that Balzac also adhered essentially to the model of the artist that Hugo and many other romantics accepted. The truly creative person is a seer capable of revealing the underlying causes, principles, and spiritual laws of the universe that concrete phenomena contain and conceal.[5]

Balzac's preface to the first edition of *La Peau de chagrin* (1831) is an extraordinary document, an "essai psychologique" in which he scrutinizes the creative process while maintaining the romantic myth of the artist as "voyant" and creativity as a mysterious gift from God. Although recognizing the importance of technique and form he is primarily concerned with the origins of creativity and defines the artist's "seconde vue"[6] as a special intuitive power and inner vision. His emphasis is on the primary process or irrational faculties of the mind that give the artist his unique ability:

C'est une sorte de seconde vue qui leur permet de définir la vérité dans toutes les situations possibles; ou, mieux encore, je ne sais quelle puissance qui les transporte là ou ils doivent, où ils veulent être. Ils inventent le vrai, par analogie, ou voient l'objet à décrire, soit que l'objet vienne à eux, soit qu'ils aillent eux-mêmes à l'objet. . . . Il va, en esprit, à travers les espaces, aussi facilement que les choses, jadis observées, renaissent fidèlement en lui, belles de la grâce ou terribles de l'horreur primitive qui l'avaient saisi. Il a réellement vu le monde, ou son âme le lui a révélé intuitivement.[7]

Mimesis or observation of exterior reality are quite secondary to this visionary capacity. In fact Balzac sees the dream as a form of creative activity in a "natural state." He already compares the play of creative imagination to the work of the unconscious self, and in this text anticipates the Freudian link between the mechanisms of dreamwork and those of the work of art:

Les hommes ont-ils le pouvoir de faire venir l'univers dans leur cerveau, ou leur cerveau est-il un talisman avec lequel ils abolissent les lois du temps et de l'espace? . . . La science hésitera longtemps à choisir entre ces deux mystères également inexplicables. Toujours est-il constant que l'inspiration déroule au poète des transfigurations sans nombre et semblables aux magiques fantasmagories de nos rêves. Un rêve est peut-être le jeu naturel de cette singulière puissance, quand elle reste inoccupée![8]

Louis Lambert (1832), written one year after this preface, is essentially the portrait of an artist as a young genius dominated by the faculties of the primary process and by a rich inner life that makes of him a visionary and speculative philosopher. In this fictional world Balzac represents the complex mechanisms in creativity at work, the psychological conflicts in the man behind the romantic myth of the artist as seer. Balzac the realist gives us a detailed and uncompromisingly lucid portrait of the artist whose genius depends on his capacity to explore the riches of his unconscious self, to test the validity of his intuition and the constructs of his analogical imagination.

The text is divided into three parts providing multiple points of view and utilizing a variety of narrative techniques. Part 1 presents the childhood of the genius through the experience of the narrator, who shared Louis's unfortunate existence in the school for boys; the second part is devoted to letters written by Lambert, disclosing the conflict within him between his inner, creative self and his desire for love and finally marriage with Pauline; part 3 consists of the resolution of Louis's drama, related by his uncle to the first narrator, and of the remaining fragments of Louis's philosophy of willpower, which were preserved by Pauline and then recorded by the narrator. This

tripartite architectural division develops temporally the essential opposition in Louis between his creative spiritual life, or inner being,
and the demands of the outer life, the physical, material necessities of
his being in the world.

In a sense the couple, narrator and Louis, "the poet and Pythago-
ras," as they were designated by their classmates, can be seen as two
halves of the same person. As is the case with Stello and the Docteur
Noir, or Lui and Moi in *Le Neveu de Rameau,* Louis—the dreamer, or
the irrational man, misunderstood and repressed by society (in this
text the college that resembles a prison)—is complemented by the alter ego, the realist narrator.

Capable of action and materialist in his philosophy, the narrator is
animus to his partner's intuitive, spiritualist, and "feminine" anima.
The narrator's function is much more crucial than mere storyteller or
witness, since it is he who gives permanent form to Louis's "pensées,"
thus preserving these fragments from destruction. Indeed, the same
rebirth pattern underlying Hugo's version of Shakespeare is operative
here: Louis's only finished work, his youthful "Traité de la volonté"
is destroyed by the college fathers, who sell the paper upon which it
is written to the local grocer. His work thus mutilated is saved for
posterity by the narrator, who reconstructs Lambert's main intellectual arguments and gives them a new form. The novel is therefore
the story of an artist's life followed by excerpts of his thought, re-
created by his friend, or alter ego; or should we say rather that the
elaboration of the work is accomplished by the second poet, the rational thinker who puts order in the visions of the dreamer, consequently completing the act of creation.

In any case, ego and alter ego, the dreamer and the rationalist, represent the anxiety of a divided personality in an overcivilized and excessively materialistic society in which the artist as a whole person
cannot find expression; he lives a fragmented and incomplete existence. Biographers and other critics[9] have discovered in this work the
most autobiographical of Balzac's novels, and in the figures of Louis
and the narrator they have discerned a projection of the anxiety of
duality and conflict that Balzac seems to have experienced himself.

Remaining strictly within the text, however, it is clear that Lambert
and the narrator symbolize the basic oppositions in Balzac's theory of

creativity: the conflict between the spiritual and the material, the quest for ideas and the striving toward the ideal versus the pull of desire, nature, and social realities.

This antithesis stated simply between forms of spirituality and materialism thus dominates characterization and the structure of the narration and, finally, is at the heart of Louis's intellectual development. The mechanisms of the creative process studied by Balzac take the form of a dialectic that on a philosophical level suggests the problematics of the Hegelian interaction of spirit and matter.

In the first section of the novel the narrator retrospectively presents two of the three phases of Louis's creative evolution. The third phase had remained unknown to him until his chance encounter with Lambert's uncle years later. The precocious intellectual activity of the thirteen-year-old prodigy is ascribed to a physical debilitation and to the unusual perfection of his mental apparatus. In any case his inner life is described as excessive and demanding, a veritable "débauche," or orgy, of ideas that he absorbs and that absorb his energy.

The first stage of intense intellectual activity is succeeded by a passage to a self-reflective level; he begins to study the function of the mind itself, "après avoir tout abstrait"[10] he tries to learn the secret of thought. At this second stage he has passed from things to their expression, from substance to principles and laws. From the intellectual level of random perception and cognition linked to sensation, the thinker passes to the abstract and finally, at the third stage, to what Lambert, and Balzac in other theoretical writings, term "la spécialité" (LL, p. 598). Beyond classification and philosophical systematization the thinker now becomes capable of grasping the totality of experience; he speculates intuitively on the hidden spiritual domain of origins and the causes governing man's evolution. The unique domain of this visionary philosopher is to "voir tout et d'un seul coup" (LL, p. 598), and the faculties always associated with "spécialité" are intuition, imagination, and analogical thinking.

And yet Lambert the visionary is a failed philosopher; in fact, the reasons for his failure constitute the originality of Balzac's modification of the romantic model of creativity. In spite of Louis's enormous intellectual growth, which we will trace in detail, he never succeeds in resolving the radical opposition between matter and spirit that he initially posits, and he proves incapable of giving permanent concrete form to his intuitions of truth. The narrator does indeed suggest that had Lambert lived, he might have developed his search for a unitary system on a sound scientific basis. The link between *Louis Lambert* and *La Recherche de l'absolu* is thereby made manifest; it is, of course, Balthazar (protagonist of *La Recherche de l'absolu*) who will search for the absolute, the spiritual essence of matter through the science of chemistry, thus attempting to forge a new creation by transforming the real with the secret discovered in the mind. Balthazar, like Balzac himself, will adopt a monistic philosophy, reconciling spiritualism and materialism, and will define man as endowed with a given quantity of energy (or willpower) that he transforms into thought (or spirit).

Lambert resembles Nodier's visionary madman, the pathetic Jean-François les bas-bleus,[11] far more than he does a writer like Nerval, who succeeds in transforming his own "spécialité" into an artwork. *Aurélia* presents a total worldview through myth and religious syncretism in which Nerval's spiritualist intuitions of immortality are given form in language and character, just as Blake's visions become plastic.

Louis's failure to create—the reader senses that his visions could have made another book—can be illuminated by his own theories as well as by his personal experience. Once again, the development of Lambert's thought is given a three-part pattern by the narrator. Under the influence of his reading of Swedenborg, Louis accepts the dualistic concept of two distinct beings in man, the inner and the outer self. His goal is to strive toward "la perfection de l'être intérieur" (*LL,* p. 534), which requires that the soul or spirit, in the act of purifying itself, separate itself from the needs of the body. The seer who develops his inner resources, fundamentally the faculties of the primary process, approaches the elevated status of a Swedenborgian angel, much like the future Séraphita, central figure in Balzac's mystical novel.

As evidence of the extraordinary power of the inner self, Louis cites the dream experience. According to him, it reveals the faculty of the mind to travel in time and space, to free itself from the confines of the body, and even to penetrate matter. He calls for a new science of dreams, recalling the German romantics as well as Nodier, and one of his own dreams becomes the initial impetus to create. His only work, the "Traité de la volonté," has its source in a dream (just as Balzac will later claim that the unifying concept of the entire *Comédie humaine* occurred to him as if in a dream).

In dream activity can indeed be seen the first signs of Louis's genius. He dreams of a landscape with a château that he has never known; a few days later the schoolboys are taken to this very place on a rare excursion. The unconscious product of intuition, prophecy, or perhaps the reconstruction through analogy with landscapes whose pictures he had stored in his prodigious memory, this astounding dream experience convinces the young artist that he carries within him an active source of knowledge and beauty. His inner being contains a mysterious agent capable of transforming sensory impressions more powerful than his rational processes. He speaks of his unusual ability to draw from memory, "ce riche dépôt, une foule d'images admirables de réalité, de fraîcheur, desquelles il se nourrissait pendant la durée de ses limpides contemplations. . . . Soudain je rentre en moi-même, et j'y trouve une chambre noire où les accidents de la nature viennent se reproduire sous une forme plus pure que la forme sous laquelle ils sont d'abord apparus à mes sens extérieurs" (*LL*, p. 510).

He stops short of inventing the Freudian unconscious, or id, but this experience becomes the turning point of his philosophy. He moves now from a strictly dualistic system to attempt a unitary explanation of man's condition that Balthazar will later pursue in science, and Balzac in his own fictional masterwork. The narrator exposes in detail Lambert's philosophy of willpower; the development of this theory had almost used up Lambert's creative energy, "son âme se dévorait elle-même" (*LL*, p. 549).

Although prompted by the dream experience to believe in the power of the inner self to act autonomously, the actual origin of Louis's research is a childhood memory. Again, a poetic comparison becomes the source of an entire system of thought, a method that the narrator compares to that of Cuvier, who was able to reconstruct the history of natural phenomena based on a fragment; a mere piece of bone becomes the source for an explanation of an entire species. Louis recalls the sparks of electricity caused by the brush in his young mother's beautiful hair; he develops an analogy between this persistent childhood image and ideas that, like sparks, are the products of human will. The kernel of his thought is that ideas are dynamic, organic forces resembling electricity, which emanate from the human source of energy, "la volonté." He is almost convinced of "la matérialité de la pensée" (*LL*, p. 552) but never really accepts the logical, necessary consequence that spirit and matter are therefore essentially identical in nature.

Louis, at this stage, replaces Swedenborg's notion of the angel in man with the concept of "l'être intérieur actionnel"; this "être innommé, voyant, agissant" (*LL*, p. 544) is contrasted with the self who acts directly in the world ("réaction"); the former is not determined by purely natural causes or environment, it retains its autonomy. Creative ideas thus clearly have their source in a kind of unconscious self, a vital and vast network of sensations, memories, and imaginative constructions. He studies their origin and mechanisms and again compares them analogically to natural systems; ideas are to the inner self as perfume is to flowers and children to their parents. Dynamic and organic, brilliant ideas grow from this mysterious and uncontrolled source:

Souvent au milieu du calme et du silence, me disait-il, lorsque nos facultés intérieures sont endormies, quand nous nous abandonnons à la douceur du repos, qu'il s'étend des espèces de ténèbres en nous, et que nous tombons dans la contemplation des choses extérieures, tout à coup une idée s'élance, passe avec la rapidité de l'éclair à travers les espaces infinis dont la perception nous est donnée par notre vue intérieure. Cette idée brillante, surgie comme un feu follet, s'éteint sans retour: existence éphémère, pareille à celle de ces enfants qui font connaître aux parents une joie et un chagrin sans bornes; espèce de fleur mort-née dans les champs de la pensée. Parfois l'idée, au lieu de jaillir avec force et de mourir sans consistance, commence à poindre, se balance dans les limbes inconnus des organes où elle prend naissance; elle nous use par un long enfantement, se développe, devient féconde, grandit au dehors dans la grâce de la jeunesse et parée de tous les attributs d'une longue vie. (*LL*, p. 547)

Some perish instantly, others are transformed into forms that have the capacity to alter even the material world. Creative energy thus is linked to an electric fluid, whose most refined form is thought; destructive as well as positive, however, it can consume the thinker who expends his energy too rapidly. This theme is of course developed in a much more thorough way in *La Peau de chagrin* and especially in *La Recherche de l'absolu*.

Like Prometheus for Hugo, Christ for Lambert is the exemplar of his system. He is the one who truly perfected his "être intérieur" and finally rendered thought visible as the verb became action and flesh. His "guérisons magnétiques" (magnetic or hypnotic healing) (*LL*, p. 555) are seen as proof of the power of thought to transform the material world. Interestingly enough, *Jesus-Christ en Flandre* is also the only text in the *Etudes philosophiques* in which the power of ideas is presented without its destructive component; the strength of faith in the Christian idea itself saves the passengers from drowning in shipwreck.

In spite of his new philosophy of energy and the creative power of thought, Louis Lambert eventually refuses to confront the realities of society and physical love. In the third phase of his development he retreats to the Swedenborgian dualist position, totally renouncing material life in favor of a mystic's refuge in the inner life. Essentially, he gives up the conflict or dialectical movement between the active, spiritual force of ideas and the resistant world of matter, flesh, and forms that alone makes a creative work possible in Balzac's eyes: "Le mouvement, en raison de la résistance, produit une combinaison qui est la vie, dès que l'un ou l'autre est plus fort, la vie cesse" (*LL*, p. 601).

No synthesis has emerged from the opposition between spiritualism and materialism that had determined the intense intellectual activity of his adolescence; no creative resolution followed his deep understanding of the potential force of "la pensée" in the world:

> Son oeuvre portait les marques de la lutte que se livraient dans cette belle âme ces deux grands principes, le Spiritualisme, le Matérialisme, autour desquels ont tourné tant de beaux génies, sans qu'aucun d'eux ait osé les fondre en un seul. D'abord spiritualiste pur, Louis avait été conduit invinciblement à reconnaître la matérialité de la pensée. Battu par les faits de l'analyse au moment où son coeur lui faisait encore regarder avec amour les nuages épars dans les cieux de Swedenborg, il ne se trouvait pas encore de force à produire un système unitaire, compact, fondu d'un seul jet. De là, venaient quelques contradictions empreintes jusque dans l'esquisse que je trace de ses premiers essais. (*LL*, p. 552)

In Balzac's fictive universe it remains for Balthazar to attempt to force the material world to reveal its spiritual secret. Indeed, the narrator suggests that Lambert had almost exhausted himself through his exclusive concentration on the production of pure ideas. In a like manner, Frenhofer in *Le Chef-d'oeuvre inconnu* and Gambara find their ability to paint and compose music ruined by the excessive theorizing that had absorbed the totality of their creative energy.

The climax and conclusion of this life of the artist are not witnessed by the narrator; Louis recounts his own story in his letters, describing disillusionment with contemporary Parisian life and the final development of his thought. His letter dated "Paris 1819" marks the end of his youth; in terms borrowed from Rousseau[12] and anticipating Vigny's Stello, he states the impossibility of creative people surviving in a society that opposes them instead of uniting them in a common goal. Claiming to have made a long study of this society dominated by material acquisition, he concludes that no political system can be justified; history has meant only degeneration, and the modern city offers images of misery that transform the artist's imagination into a negative faculty. Like Stello, he advocates governmental subsidy for the artist, who seems now to be no more than society's scapegoat. This pessimistic view of the artist's situation, it should be remarked, differs radically from Balzac's own official stance in the Avant-Propos to the *Comédie humaine* (1842), where even conformity to the goals of church and monarchy are deemed necessary by the self-appointed author-secretary of society.

Lambert's profound disenchantment (which makes of him another in the line of alienated romantic antiheroes, spiritual descendants of Saint-Preux) helps to explain his refusal to act. This rejection of the world is, in turn, vindicated by the development of his final wisdom.

Obviously a projection of Balzac's own speculation, Lambert develops an analogy from contemporary biology, zoology, and pseudo-science to rationalize his return to the Swedenborgian view of man's spiritual development. In Paris he had studied what he terms "l'unité de la composition zoologique" (*LL,* p. 566) and had hypothesized that the transformations in animal species due to material or environmental forces are analogous to the moral and spiritual progression of man. The metempsychosis or "transformations successives" (*LL,* p. 570) of humanity toward God that Swedenborg delineates in the record of his visions suggest a parallel evolution.

Beginning once more with the intuition of an analogy or similarity between two different orders, he deduces an entire system, thus combining the poetry of the primary process of cognition and the logic of the secondary. The chain of being[13] in nature along which the same animal matter is transformed indicates the possibility of a similar chain extending from man to God and consequently revealing an essentially divine order. Lambert suggests that the resemblances between animality and humankind should form the basis for future scientific study. It is of course, this very analogy that Balzac develops in the Avant-Propos, claiming to have encountered it like a chimera.[14] As a result he places the study of social species formed and deformed by their various milieus at the center of his own philosophy and creative work.

Lambert announces the superiority of Swedenborg's thought and gives up his attempts at further reconciliation of the materialist-spiritualist opposition. The concept of man's gradual metamorphosis from a lower, physical state to a higher, spiritual one seems to resolve the contradictions he had observed; it offers a unified view of man's condition, a close analogy with the study of the animal kingdom, and the possibility of human development through successive stages without real conflict and according to a preordained plan.

Man's moral and spiritual progression consequently requires the perfection of the "être intérieur" and the concomitant denial of the demands of the body; society's present state of corruption could only prohibit this moral growth. Lambert concludes that although he is endowed with creative potential, he would have to combat society in order to give his ideas communicable form; his underdeveloped "outer" self, his frail physical body, could not withstand action, and his rich inner life would be destroyed.

As evidence of society's threat to his genius, he develops an argument found from Rousseau's *Rêveries* to Nerval's *Aurélia*. In a moving and lucid letter he analyzes moments of romantic despair when he doubts his own ability; he speaks of mental fatigue due to "travaux inutiles" (*LL*, p. 579), of his doubts about his religious beliefs and of his "fatale imagination" (*LL*, p. 575). Near folly, he suffers from the burden of his creative force because it seems to construct only chimeras, empty dreams, and fantasies. The influence of the "génie raisonneur" (*LL*, p. 579), or the demon of society's negative rationalism, persistently undermines the consoling constructions of his imagination. Arieti's "third poet" does not intervene to maintain the equilibrium between creative imagination and analytical reason necessary to give form to a creative work. Louis cannot reconcile in an intellectually satisfying manner the Swedenborgian mystical visions of man's afterlife and the hard facts of contemporary biology and physics for which natural and mechanical laws suffice to explain our condition.

Rousseau and Nerval[15] both analyzed similar moments when the atheistic conclusions of eighteenth-century materialist philosophy led them to question their spiritual affirmations and to experience the *néant* (nothingness) of their own existence. In such moments when he feels abandoned by the creative force within him, Lambert expresses a desire for death and senses acutely the pressure of madness:

> En ces moments, du moins je le crois, se dresse devant moi je ne sais quel génie raisonneur qui me fait voir le néant au fond des plus certaines richesses. Ce démon impitoyable fauche toutes les fleurs, ricane des sentiments les plus doux, en me disant: "Eh! bien, après?" Il flétrit la plus belle oeuvre en m'en montrant le principe, et me dévoile le mécanisme des choses en m'en cachant les résultats harmonieux. En ces moments terribles où le mauvais ange s'empare de mon être, où la lumière divine s'obscurcit en mon âme sans que j'en sache la cause, je reste triste et je souffre, je voudrais être sourd et muet, je souhaite la mort en y voyant un repos. (*LL,* p. 579)

In fact, one can assume that in these letters Lambert is examining the inner conflicts caused by the creative process itself. The imaginative side or the impetus to create, which he compares to an inner force he can scarcely control (the autonomous complex in Jung's terminology or Arieti's first poet) is in conflict with his critical reason and his body's sensual desire. Instead of producing truth through creative work, as promised in Hugo's model of the integration of the primary and secondary processes of cognition, Lambert arrives at despair. His experience is a negative version of the romantic visionary paradigm; the "three" poets are in disorder, since he is unable to control the paralyzing duality fragmenting his personality. Even his confidence in the power of language[16] is finally undermined when he discovers: "ne suis-je pas forcé d'employer des mots humains trop faibles pour rendre des sensations divines" (*LL,* p. 583).

In phrases recalling Rousseau, his "âme expansive est refoulée sur elle-même" (*LL,* p. 576), he reflects on the special rhythm of his creative impulse; the initial energetic force with which he penetrates reality through thought is followed by a deception, a withdrawal into his inner self: "D'intimes élans de force, quelques rares et secrets témoignages d'une lucidité particulière, me disent parfois que je puis beaucoup. J'enveloppe alors le monde par ma pensée, je le pétris, je le façonne, je le pénètre, je le comprends ou crois le comprendre; mais soudain je me réveille seul, et me trouve dans une nuit profonde, tout chétif; j'oublie les lueurs que je viens d'entrevoir, je suis privé de secours, et surtout sans un coeur où je puisse me réfugier!" (*LL*, p. 576).

Like René and other disenchanted romantic figures, he is obscurely aware that his ideals are unattainable, and that his efforts to give concrete form to spiritual intuitions are perhaps no more than illusions. The circular rhythm Starobinski[17] discerns in Rousseau's efforts to extend himself from soul-center to circumference is directly parallel to Lambert's creative efforts; his attempts to move from his inner world to the world of meaningful communication with others is inevitably followed by despair and retreat into an inner prison. This same rhythm of longing and deception was given linguistic shape in the romantic phrases of Chateaubriand's prose[18]—a brusque élan followed by a long falling off, inscribing stylistically the realization of the impossibility of reconciling dreams and reality.

The conflicts within Lambert are intensified and finally resolved through the problematics of love and sexuality. Indeed, the final portion of the novel offers a fictional introduction to the theory of sublimation that anticipates Freudian concepts in a rather surprising fashion.

Louis's love for Pauline de Villenoix is at first presented as another variation of the romantic "impossible" love theme, a love between two unfortunate social outcasts, idealized beyond any possibility of realization in marriage. Their love is an "abîme" (*LL*, p. 572), a refuge or death-in-life: "Oui, je voudrais dérober à la nature entière un bonheur que nous sommes seuls à comprendre, seuls à sentir, et qui est tellement immense que je m'y jette pour y mourir. (*LL*, p. 587).

Musset's repeated antithesis between "love" and "art," a romantic cliché that is the subject of "Les Nuits" and other works, is also invoked in Louis's troubled apprehension that the idea of love might easily absorb the energy necessary to devote to philosophy or art. This same opposition is found in the story of Balthazar and Joséphine, and is crucial to the resolution of *Le Chef-d'oeuvre inconnu* when the young Poussin is obliged to choose between his love for Gillette and his desire to learn the secrets of Frenhofer's art.

Love is first described as the perfect idea of spiritual union, the Swedenborgian purity of two angelic natures united in immortal harmony. As in many other romantic scenarios, familial and social obstacles to their union seem only to maintain the intense beauty of their relationship; and love outside of marriage seems superior to its banal absorption in daily life. Balzac's concern, however, for the physiological and concrete side of human experience again transforms this modern version of Tristan and Isolde into a drama of desire and impotence with curious parallels to Stendhal's *Armance* (1827). Financial and family obstacles are eventually removed, marriage becomes possible; but Louis appears to go mad the day before the ceremony, and is saved from his attempt at self-castration by his uncle, who relates the final events of Louis's life to the narrator.

Lambert's letters reveal an increasing obsession with sexual desire. The same tension recurs between spiritualism and materialism, whose opposing poles dominate the text. Lambert, who had lived a life of chastity, is now "altéré de ces félicités inconnues" (*LL*, p. 586); from an "âme-soeur," Pauline will offer him the concrete pleasures of the "possession d'une femme aimée" (*LL*, p. 586). Desire imagined and finally expressible assumes the force of a "délire," "j'étais dans un de ces moments de folie où l'on médite un meurtre pour posséder une femme" (*LL*, p. 586).

As in so many of Balzac's *Etudes philosophiques* the conclusion presents an enigma for the reader to penetrate. Although the narrator offers his explanation, he suggests the complexity of causes and laws behind human events, and he forces the reader to decide for himself. Is Frenhofer truly an innovative genius—inventing abstract painting—or just a madman? In the case of Lambert, various interpretations are proposed by the text; yet others suggest themselves legitimately to a modern reader.

The narrator stresses above all the consistency of Lambert's life. Through a complete denial of the physical and its demands, he has now acceded to a purely contemplative plane of existence. Refusing the world ouside, he can concentrate on the perfection of his "être intérieur," and indeed the final images of Louis are those of a true mystic speaking in spiritual or philosophical aphorisms that only Pauline, who still loves and cares for him, can understand. In a sense, he has freed himself from the life of the body, and Pauline, who does not consider him mad, claims that he exhibits an astonishing "vélocité de vision mentale" (*LL*, p. 595) as he advances in "les espaces de la pensée" (*LL*, p. 595). He has at last attained the superior Swedenborgian state of the visionary, or man-become-angel, and the final pages of the novel are devoted to his special insights on substance, spirit, and thought itself.

A curious ambiguity, however, hinges on the castration attempt. Did he try to mutilate his body because "il se crut impuissant" (*LL*, p. 590), as the uncle declares—afraid of being impotent for the very physical love he had begun to desire—or in order to gain access to a superior level of being, as the narrator maintains? In any case the life of the spirit seems to have annihilated that of the body; the extreme development of his inner faculties, according to the narrator, had made the slightest excitement a danger. Not only was spiritual love a rival to his creativity, but physical love was simply too strong for his weakened state.

Unlike Balthazar, who, as we shall see, succeeds in transforming his sexual energy into creative work, Louis Lambert simply refuses sublimation. Aware that his increasing desire would use up his energies and, consequently, his gift, or "génie" as he terms it, for intuition of spiritual truth, he denies his sexuality and preserves his visionary power. The "first" poet or primary process survives alone, but he is incapable of giving form to his knowledge. The energy necessary for the work of creativity, which requires the ability to find a new goal or substitutive form through art or philosophy for the goal of the sexual drive is denied to Lambert. The shaping power of the tertiary process or "third" poet is lost, and what remains are the fragmentary insights without logic or cohesion of the mystic or madman. One of these insights quoted by the narrator near the end of the text could serve as a conclusion to Lambert's life, but also as Balzac's most characteristic statement in the *Etudes philosophiques* of the working mechanism of the creative process: "Le Mouvement est le produit d'une force engendrée par la Parole et par une résistance qui est la Matière. Sans la résistance, le Mouvement aurait été sans résultat, son action eût été infinie" (*LL*, p. 601). The action of Lambert's word plays itself out in the domain of the infinite or the purely mental and spiritual; it meets no resistance because he has refused to engage in the struggle with forms, the matter of life; it therefore remains a pure but sterile movement. Lambert's failure is a failure to create or perhaps, more precisely, a failure to sublimate.[19]

The reasons or causes for this failure, as Balzac would say, are perhaps explicable through the psychoanalytical concept of the pre-Oedipal stage of behavior. The narrator gives us many traces for the construction of such an interpretation; Louis writes to Pauline of his anxiety before the anticipated marriage: "Je mettrai peut-être sur ta chère tête un fardeau plus pesant que ma tendresse ne sera douce à ton coeur. S'il existe en moi quelque puissance inexorable à laquelle j'obéis, si je dois maudire quand tu joindras les mains pour prier, si quelque triste pensée me domine lorsque je voudrai me mettre à tes pieds pour jouer avec toi comme un enfant, ne seras-tu pas jalouse de cet exigeant et fantasque génie?" (*LL,* p. 580). He poses again the possible conflict between his tyrannical creative force and the love he feels for Pauline, but the most significant detail is "pour jouer avec toi comme un enfant."

Louis Lambert has never really developed into a man; the narrator repeatedly refers to his frail body, and his only written work was done by the crucial age of thirteen. Psychologically he seems to be arrested in a pre-Oedipal stage that according to the terms of Lacanian psychology results in seeking refuge in the world of "l'imaginaire." Louis never leaves this level to experience the "symbolique" rivalry and subsequent identification with the father: the capacity to struggle and work in the real world dominated by "la loi du père." He has no love or hatred for the "fathers" of the school; he ignores them until they destroy his only creative effort at the end of his natural boyhood, thus denying his maturity. It is Madame de Staël herself, a strong and "phallic" mother, who discovers the young boy genius and pays for his schooling. Pauline, who replaces her, becomes his protectress and keeper, capable of comprehending even his complex thought processes when the intermediary steps are omitted in his speech. Her very name suggests the strength of religious rule and masculine order, and she proudly exclaims to the narrator: "N'est-il pas tout à moi! Depuis trois ans, à deux reprises, je l'ai possédé pendant quelques jours" (*LL,* p. 595).

He can only dimly recall his real mother; his memory of her was, however, the source of his first and only writing. He has remained a child, and the increasing development of sexual desire in him brings with it a growing dread of sexuality and an unconscious fear of castration. As long as his sentiment for Pauline remains on the level of romantic impossibility and idealism, he can maintain the double illusion of love and mysticism. Physical desire forces him into a fear of sexuality that denies the imaginary identity between Louis and Pauline, who is, after all, an incarnation of the phallic mother whose resemblance to himself is a consolation.

To castrate himself is therefore the only way to remain a child, to avoid a sexual confrontation with the other, and to perpetuate his spiritual union with Pauline. It is also the source of his refusal to fashion and shape forms and words into a creative product, his inability to work with the matter of things that resists change, as Balzac expresses it. Lambert chooses the contemplative world of his visions and remains in the narcissistic world of the imaginary.

VI

Honoré de Balzac and the Mechanisms of Creative Energy: *La Recherche de l'absolu* and the Myth of Faust

Balzac's use of myth in the *Etudes philosophiques,* written mainly be-tween 1830 and 1835, was examined first by Albert Béguin in his *Balzac visionnaire* (1946). In this valuable study, he presented the many examples of mythical patterns and figures found in these nov-els: Christ and Satan, Don Juan, the androgyne, visionary figures and Promethean rebels. For Béguin, the presence of these patterns in the narrative structures transforms the *Etudes philosophiques* into symbolic accounts of the confrontation between man and the super-natural. For the most part, however, Balzac is presenting the drama of human genius: nineteenth century "titans" with an extraordinary will to power and knowledge who struggle against the limits of rea-son, time, and matter, seemingly imposed on man by the gods. Promethean revolt against the supernatural order, in the name of man's potential development, would thus appear to be the archetypal pattern underlying these myths.

The figure of Faust can be discerned in *L'Elixir de longue vie* and in the pact between Satan and Faust in *Melmoth réconcilié:* it is present in the relationships between Rastignac and Vautrin in *Le Père Goriot,* and in Lucien and Vautrin in *Illusions perdues.* Faust is best seen in *La Recherche de l'absolu* (1834), which offers Balzac's most complex and subtle study of the man of genius, actually by this time a romantic cultural myth itself. Balthazar Claës personifies the highest form of human endeavor—"la spécialité," thought developed to its fullest expression—and illuminates the resulting conflicts between genius and society. A Flemish Faust-turned-chemist and pater familias becomes an exemplary model of the grandeur and limitations of human potential.

This novel containing the Faust myth provides, moreover, a model of Balzac's understanding of the dynamics of creativity itself. It clarifies his "philosophical" concepts of energy, and thought, and the two principles of monism and dualism that recur as important themes, and dominate his approach to the creation of characters and action. This novel is perhaps the very keystone of his fictional universe, not only illustrating the concepts and problems central to his preoccupation as a novelist but offering an approach to narrative structure that suggests the real link between the *Etudes philosophiques* and the *Etudes de moeurs*.

La Recherche is a "drame bourgeois" like *Eugénie Grandet,* which it resembles (Balthazar and Marguerite afford a striking parallel to Grandet and his daughter); it contains, however, as Balzac suggests, a mysterious plot. It is, of course, the mythical plot of the story of Faust that gives to the domestic drama, a study of Flemish customs, its form and its various meanings. Myth is here an inextricable thread of the narrative, as it so often is even in the *Etudes de moeurs,* and its function is precise: it gives form and expression to an apparently unsolvable philosophical problem, or at least a paradoxical one. It provides Balzac a means to examine at multiple levels of experience the fundamentally contradictory forces, the essential dualism, inherent in the dynamics of all life, in which creativity and destruction are ineluctably joined. The myth embodies the inevitable conflict between the stable laws of order (which are, after all, the necessary origin or point of departure for all movement and change) and the need for disorder, the disruptive impetus to progress and renewal.

Indeed, Balzac seems primarily concerned in the *Etudes philosophiques* to study the dynamic oppositions, the heroic and often tragic struggle and conflict between order and disorder from whose inner tensions all creation and life result. "La vie résulte du jeu de deux principes opposés, quand l'un manque, l'être souffre."[1] It is this contradictory and paradoxical game that fascinates Balzac; more than the masterpiece that Frenhofer fails to create (*Le Chef-d'oeuvre inconnu*) or the absolute itself that Balthazar may or may not have discovered, Balzac's interest in these narratives is to trace the disorderly patterns of genius in opposition to the fixed laws of family and environment, or to the established limits of the worlds of art, science, and knowledge themselves. The stories reveal the destruction inherent in the very process of creation, and the cruel truth about human thought and energy: excessive exercise of the mind consumes the mind; man's vital energy is a given quota whose dissipation genius must risk in the active pursuit of new knowledge. The effort to create a reality free from the limits of time becomes an intense combat to the death with the forces of time.

Balthazar seems "sublime" to Balzac precisely because he struggles against time, which eventually, inevitably, annihilates him. Throughout the *Etudes philosophiques,* man is indeed heroic only as he attempts to overreach or transcend himself with the concomitant risk of death. It is obviously here that we find the most important thematic link between Balthazar Claës and Faust. Both figures refuse the common acceptance of the rational, material, and temporal limits of the human condition, and risk self-destruction in order to grow in knowledge and power. The figure of the disillusioned idealist with a will to truth and strength rivaling that of God himself, this paradox of a man who would be more than man, is, of course, the romantic variant of the myth of Faust which Balzac has encoded in his novel.

From the original Faustbook and Marlowe through Goethe, Spengler, Nietzsche, Mann, and others, specific themes and images recur in different guises, giving coherence to the Faustian tradition.[2] The hero's unlimited desire and despair before the inadequacy of contemporary science lead him to the edge of suicide; magic, alchemy, or even technological prowess are therefore seen as means to supreme knowledge and power. A desire for rejuvenation accompanying the frustrations of old age is viewed in the context of the hero's desperate struggle with nature and his own limitations. The hero's relations with others usually include a tragic love (which becomes a potential source of redemption), audacious attempts to dominate, and a fantastic rapport (pact or wager) with demons and other supernatural beings who initiate and tempt him into a dangerous (anti-Christian) quest.

A reader of Balzac's *Recherche* will immediately recognize the presence of all of these items in its thematic structure. It is true that Gautier, Quinet, Musset, and Nerval also treated many combinations of these themes in the thirties and forties in lyric or epic poetry, often in visionary prose works from an autobiographical perspective. Balzac, however, makes the romantic variant of the Faust myth an integral part of a complex fictional structure with a "realist" orientation: an essentially bipolar system of correlations and oppositions on all levels of the discourse. Character and its indices, actions, cultural conventions, symbol and theme, as well as the posing of enigma become signs of the mythical pattern at many different levels of meaning and experience: individual and social, philosophical, psychological, and even ontological. Underlying the personal and interpersonal conflicts of the Faustian figure of genius are the fundamental processes of human thought and creativity as Balzac understood them.

To begin with Balthazar Claës, his name alone may lead us to the secret of the myth in Balzac's work.[3] Claës (meaning "clé" or key) certainly suggests the key to the special knowledge that he is seeking. There is a telling episode in which he loses the key to his wife's chamber, totally distracted from the real world by his search for the surreal. His first name actually contains the paradox, the ambiguous truth of the life of genius according to Balzac; Balthazar-Belshazzar is at once magus and prodigal father-king. He is certainly the spiritual searcher whose name recalls the bearer of gold to the infant Christ, for he is striving to understand the mystery of God's creation. He may also evoke ironically the prodigal waster and destroyer of wealth and goods, the Old Testament Belshazzar who worshipped gold and whom God punished during an orgiastic feast. Whether Balzac intended this pun or not, it is nevertheless true that lavish feasts play an important part in the plot of *La Recherche,* and that in the midst of the final celebration of the three marriages, the restoration of the family's honor, and the father's reputation, Balthazar is suddenly struck again with the obsessive idea of the absolute (like the handwriting on the wall of Babylon), the idea that had led to the destruction of the Claës fortune several times before.

The biblical resonance and the possible connotations of the name add yet another mythical dimension to the character; the moral aspect of the temptation to overstep the bounds of moderation and the confrontation between the hero and the supernatural are suggested.

At the deepest level the ambivalence of the name points to the principle of destruction inherent in all creativity. Ironically, Balzac's Balthazar uses up his family's gold and, therefore, risks its survival in order to discover the primary "metal" from which all others are produced; real metals must be destroyed to reveal their essence.

His name also illustrates the technique by which Balzac has embedded a mythical plot in a domestic setting. It recalls the very homely expression used for family gatherings, and especially copious meals, "on va faire un Balthazar," thus combining the ideas of extraordinary exploits, religious values, and a common level of experience.

La Recherche can thus be read as Balzac's novel about genius, and Balthazar's character can best be understood as the abnormal product of his milieu, a definition of genius inherited by Balzac from Diderot and other eighteenth-century thinkers. Madeleine Fargeaud, in her remarkably thorough book on *La Recherche*,[4] studied in great detail the importance of Flemish life and customs in this work and in Balzac's oeuvre in general. For our purposes, it suffices to see that the conflict between Claës and his environment—family, group character and traditions—is not a simple binary opposition, but that the traits that compose Balthazar's genius are indeed exaggerated characteristics of those of his own people. Balzac takes great pains to characterize the Flemish with his customary emphasis on the interaction of environment and personality, and the physical and moral interdependence resulting from biological determinism. The long introductory chapters "La Maison Claës" and "Histoire d'un ménage flamand" establish as basic values the Flemish love of order and stability. The narrator emphasizes their character traits of impeccable honesty, moral severity, and tenacity, as well as a profoundly bourgeois, materialistic devotion to goods, money, and the pleasures of family life. Added to these characteristics and indices are the potential for great passion, heroism, and unusual perseverance that Balzac attributes to the historical influence of the Spanish "genes" on the Flemish national character.

Flemish "realism," then—a willing acceptance of the values of an imperfect, limited, and finite world—is opposed on all levels of the fictional discourse to the excesses of the genius who "unrealistically" permits himself to become absorbed in the world of the ideal, or idea, and who rejects the relative order of things to seek out the absolute.

This genius is, therefore, quite clearly an "unnatural" product of a specific cultural matrix; his inner conflicts, as well as those outside him, result from hereditary traits developed to the extreme level of disorder. Balzac repeats the familiar romantic nature image of the tree to illustrate the destructive effects of genius in society; its unusual growth results in the desiccation of the plants and shrubs that surround it: "Vous desséchez la terre autour de vous, comme font les grands arbres! Moi, pauvre plante, je n'ai pu m'élever assez haut, j'expire à moitié de ta vie."[5]

Balthazar's patience and incredible perseverance in his quest, demonstrated by his heroic efforts to continue in spite of repeated failure and his own physical degeneration, and his total passion for the idea of the absolute are thus traits of the combined Flemish-Spanish heredity developed into monomania. In fact, Balzac's general definition of genius centers precisely on this concept: the special capacity to devote one's total quota of vital energy or willpower to one idea or creative project.

In any case, we learn that Balthazar's forebearers had their own mania, and that an admired ancestor had risked his life in the name of freedom from Spanish dominance; a strong seed of revolt against the norms of society is firmly implanted in his nature. The very facade of the Claës house suggests symbolically the presence of an eccentric inhabitant within its walls. In addition to ornamentation signifying the weaver's craft (a weather vane in the shape of a spindle) and Christian symbols above the principal door, rainwater is expulsed from the walls of the second floor through the mouth of a fantastic sculpture of an animal. The gargoyle is a sign for the grotesque excesses of Balthazar to be found within the confines of this family, whose ancestors include both diligent craftsmen and staunch religious believers.

The system of relations between the actors of this Balzacian drama thus develops from the rich complex of Flemish characteristics the narrator has carefully delineated in the expository chapters. Balthazar's wife, Josephine, can signify love as opposed to science. The finite, imperfect world (she is lame and slightly hunchbacked) that she represents is contrasted with the infinite or absolute; the virtue of Christian piety and ignorance she typifies is opposed to the satanic, prideful knowledge her husband is seeking. She is the female-victim, abandoned and destroyed by the male genius who prefers science to woman, just as Josephine was abandoned by Napoleon in the name of his future glory.

The first half of the novel is indeed devoted to the conflict between the genius and his wife, as well as to the struggle between Balthazar and the material world whose ultimate secret he is seeking. There are many passages that are clearly focalized in Josephine's perspective, and her efforts to penetrate the enigma of her husband's behavior parallel those of the reader.

The oppositions are again more subtle than simple binary ones; Josephine, with her noble Spanish ancestry, pride, and religious fervor, is portrayed by Balzac as a "genius" of love much like Pauline in *Louis Lambert*. The conflict, therefore, is between two kinds of genius or, more accurately, two ideas that are consuming the vital energy of the protagonists: the idea of the absolute and the idea of conjugal love. We are told that love makes Josephine prophetic, able to penetrate the hidden world of cause and principles—characteristics of genius according to Balzac. Although "ignorante," she learns chemistry in order to compete with her rival. She is as excessive and monomaniacal as her husband, and her death results from the loss of his love; her existence was sustained by a single idea to which all of her energy was directed—without it she must die. Within her the conflict between love of husband and love of children is lost to the former, as she realizes on her deathbed that she had been prepared to sacrifice not only herself but her children's future to Balthazar's obsession.

The second part of the novel develops the conflict between father and daughter. In Balzac's dramatic framework the climax and denouement are thus a function of the contrast between the genius's struggle against time, and the concurrent, successful efforts of the family—represented by Marguerite—to maintain its order. The father-daughter relationship in Balzac's works has a special significance, often suggesting historical and mythical meaning. The importance of paternity—at the very center of the traditional Western view of familial, societal, and religious order—is, of course, frequently treated by Balzac; the absence or loss of father figures, father replacements, parricide, and regicide are recurring themes. *Le Père Goriot,*

with its obvious reference to Lear and his daughters and its meta-
phorical linking of father-king and God, most clearly suggests Balzac's fear for society from the weakening and loss of paternal authority. Modern post-Napoleonic Paris in *La Comédie humaine* is
a world whose degraded values (money, pleasure, and social prestige) diminish and even destroy the essential family unit; fathers like
Goriot or the Baron Hulot are its victims; substitute fathers like
Vautrin offer a new, despotic, and immoral order to those weak men
needing images of authority. In *Eugénie Grandet* the father-daughter
relationship parallels that of Balthazar and Marguerite, offering an almost grotesque variant of Claës' search. For Grandet, however, gold
has become an absolute in itself, whereas Balthazar's need for money
is but a necessary means to pursue his intellectual quest.

Marguerite is not, therefore, the victim of the Faustian figure's refusal to respect the laws of the imperfect world of human reality, as
she is in Goethe's *Faust,* or as her mother, Josephine, appears to be.
On the contrary, she is the savior of her family, the redemptive figure
who, with traditional Flemish strength and inflexible tenacity, restores the family fortune and honor (at least six times!) and maintains
respect for the father and the order he represents. Of course, it is also
Marguerite (Gretchen) who intercedes for Faust in Goethe's version
and thus redeems him in Christian terms at the end of part 2. She can
thus be understood in the larger cultural context of the romantic
imagination and its development of the archetypal figure of the redemptive woman (from Chateaubriand's "sylphide" to Nerval's Aurélia) whose love becomes a source of spiritual regeneration.

Marguerite's dilemma is between the current needs of the family,
with its time-honored traditions, and her duty to her father, who
claims to be striving for the future of humanity as he continues to
dissipate goods and money. Balzac is posing again the moral questions already enunciated by Diderot in the *Neveu de Rameau* regarding genius. Does it have the right to jeopardize the limited values of
the group in the name of the good of the species? And must the prophetic nature of genius dictate that he will always be misunderstood
in the present, contributing only to mankind's future development?
Is an evil or destructive genius (Racine in Diderot's example) nonetheless preferable to a mediocre citizen?

In my view, Marguerite's function in the text can best be elucidated through insights into the role of mediation and substitution in the logic of mythical thinking. The necessary tensions between creation and destruction in the activity of the genius, and the unavoidable conflict between the laws of order and the impetus to disorder, are the basic elements of the paradox that Faust's legend incarnates for Balzac. The myth became for him a kind of exemplary model for the structure of the dynamics of creativity. It not only gives expression to a paradoxical, ambiguous truth, it also provides a logical scheme for coming to terms with its irreconcilable elements. Far from offering unnecessary repetition of the same sequence of actions, as many critics have alleged, the two parts of the novel constitute a pattern of substitution and mediation that clarifies Balzac's approach to the problem of genius.

In her dying moments, Josephine begs Marguerite to assume the function of "médiatrice" between her father and the family. She transfers to her daughter the duty that she was unable to accomplish: daughter substitutes for mother; filial love presumably can better resist the unreasonable demands of the father than conjugal love. In fact, however, the chapters "Dévouements de la jeunesse" and "Le Père exilé" present yet another substitution. Marguerite assumes the role of the father to become head of the family and restores the family fortune; the principle of paternity passes to the daughter, the father-genius, childlike in his irrational behavior, is banished. The reader is again encouraged to think of Napoleon, whose genius had become destructive and who was also rejected by his daughter—France.

The strength of Antigone and the blind seer Oedipus is another mythical resonance evoked by the heroic efforts of Marguerite to recreate their family life. She restores the patrimony, recomposing fortune and family lands by developing farms in the forests Balthazar had tried to sell. Her efforts at reconstruction are ironically juxtaposed with the decomposition and destruction effected by her father, who would consume, in his search for the secret, all of the symbols of his family's honor. The rare tulips and forests, paintings and china, like the family gold, are no more than matter to be melted in the alchemist's crucible. Balthazar decomposes in order to create, Marguerite recomposes to maintain order.

The resistance she offers in the name of family stability to her father's rapid consumption of energy not only saves his reputation and prolongs his existence but embodies the necessary principle of opposition essential to all creative life, to the game of tension and struggle that, according to Balzac, alone produces change and discovery. The alternation in the sequence of actions in the second part of the novel between the destructive efforts of Balthazar's search and the moments of repose when he is forced to remain idle while Marguerite reestablishes the family's honor captures the very rhythm of creativity itself. The dialectical movement between the disorder produced by thought (genius) and the inferior but necessary laws of the concrete, physical world of order (familial, societal, material)—the productive conflict between traditional forms and the search for new forms—is symbolized by the struggle between father and daughter, and transformed into a domestic drama. In the last analysis, Marguerite expresses the instinctive, inherited female drive for the survival of the family; she effectively combats and controls the destructive tendencies of the male, whose creative impulse leads him beyond its boundaries.

The two parts of the novel thus give a perfectly balanced form to the dualism of the world of genius: "La Mort d'une mère" is the tragic result of the destructive effect of creative energy that met no resistance, threatening the existence of the family; "L'absolu trouvé," the final chapter, is the positive culmination of the dynamic conflict between the two orders. Alienated paternity has been reintegrated by the daughter into a healthy family structure, and the father's experiments seem near to fruition.

The book's ending is, of course, ambiguous and ironical; Balthazar, misunderstood genius or madman, dies with the secret he had perhaps discovered, a victim not only of time but of children in the town who cause his paralysis, taunting him with cries of sorcery and injuring him physically. The threat of genius to the traditional order of society is thus emphasized by the scene of these unthinking children seconded by a worker; they instinctively recognize him as a dangerous presence in their world. The theme of the townspeople's superstition, their hostile incomprehension and the children's indifference to his suffering return us at the end of Balzac's novel to the Renaissance origins of the myth and the story of Faust the magician.

The other characters of the novel function to reinforce the basic pattern of oppositions and correlations we have established through Balthazar, Josephine, and Marguerite.

The old abbé de Solis, Josephine's religious counselor, resembles her in the reality of his physical defects. He is a sincere Christian and might best be classified as the counter-Balthazar; suffering from his physical condition, he nevertheless is a kind of mystic, or "illuminé," who experiences moments of spiritual ecstasy. Balthazar is, on the contrary, as strong as the winged horse Pegasus in pursuit of his chimera, to which Balzac compares him, but satanic in his desire for knowledge. A satanic genius searching for the surreal is, therefore, contrasted with the mystical Christian suffering the imperfections of the real.

The group of Josephine, the abbot, and his nephew, Emmanuel de Solis,[6] provide Balzac with the basis for the antithesis he develops throughout the novel between Christian acceptance of the limits of the finite and Balthazar's unlimited ambition for knowledge. Balthazar's prideful quest for the power to create living matter is considered satanic by Josephine, who speaks of the cursed passion of temptation. She singles out the negative, inhuman side of science: "Décomposer n'est pas créer" (*RA*, p. 90), and insists that the force that gives inert matter movement and life can only be initiated by God. "Dieu dispose d'une puissance que tu n'auras jamais" (*RA*, p. 96). Horrified by the pact Balthazar-Faust has made with the Polish gentleman, who initiated him into the scientific research with which he is obsessed, she exclaims: "Le Tentateur peut seul avoir cet oeil jaune d'où sortait le feu de Prométhée. Oui, le démon pouvait seul t'arracher à moi. Depuis ce jour, tu n'as plus été ni père, ni époux, ni chef de famille" (*RA*, p. 93).

She also attacks the exaggerated egoism and inordinate confidence in the capacities of the individual self inherent in Balthazar's attitude, and characteristic of romantic, Faustian man: "le démon seul peut t'aider à marcher seul au milieu de ces abîmes sans issue, parmi ces ténèbres où tu n'es pas éclairé par la foi d'en haut, mais par une horrible croyance en tes facultés!" (*RA*, p. 97). Balthazar[7] confirms his satanic lack of moderation when he justifies his efforts to Marguerite in the following terms: "La nature entière nous appartiendra" (*RA*, p. 191).

These relationships and their potential meanings organized by the system of characters are given additional resonance through a rather complex network of symbols based on the antithesis animate/inanimate or nature/artifice. Emmanuel is associated with Christian roses and sunlight; Marguerite with the hardy daisy and the natural pearl. These flowers and jewels are contrasted with the tulips, a sign of the family's rather ostentatious luxury, sold by Balthazar to purchase chemical products, as well as with the false diamond that his experimentation finally produces. The irony of sacrificing and destroying real flowers and family jewels in order to produce artificial ones suggests throughout the text the idea of the antinature, antihuman destructiveness of genius.

Gold and money play an important role in the action of the novel, especially during the conflict between father and daughter. Marguerite restores the gold, symbol of the family's honor, but gold is also linked to the preoccupations of the chemist. Those ignorant of his scientific erudition accuse Balthazar of seeking the philosopher's stone, and merely perpetuating the alchemist's desire to turn baser metals into gold for personal profit. Balzac, however, develops the rapport between Balthazar's scientific quest and the serious metaphysical nature of the alchemists' ambition; his hero is aware of the philosophical complexity of the ancient tradition, and he willingly inscribes himself as their successor in his quest. Jung has, of course, drawn similar analogies between the modern Faust figures and the alchemists; he saw in the latter an expression of the "wise old man," an archetype of the exemplary intellect who dreams of revealing the essential underlying unity of all phenomena.

Gold is, then, an important symbol, a positive value when it represents family honor and even the alchemist's goal. In the form of money, however, it represents the new and degraded values of a changing society, for it has become the all-pervasive, mediating force between the characters and authentic values. Goldmann's analysis[8] of the implications of the shift from the unique "valeurs d'usage" to interchangeable "valeurs du marché" in the new capitalist society is certainly corroborated by Balzac's treatment of the role of money in Flanders: the family and science, Marguerite as well as Balthazar, depend on this necessary mediator to produce the values they consider authentic. There is an astonishing scene during which the father, obsessed with his need for money to purchase chemical equipment, becomes violent and grotesque, grasping at the gold coins glittering in the darkness, in defiance of his terrified daughter.

Enigma as a narrative technique is, of course, frequently used by the Balzacian narrator. As a means to maintain reader involvement in the text and to pose intellectual puzzles, it recurs throughout the *Comédie humaine*. Nowhere does it play, however, the central role it assumes in *La Recherche de l'absolu*. Balthazar's character remains enigmatic for at least a third of the work. At his first appearance, he emerges from the darkness, and the mystery of his behavior is gradually revealed simultaneously to Josephine and to the reader. Even when Balzac intrudes in the narrative in order to analyze the nature of genius, his narrator maintains its essential enigma; he exposes the dual personality of genius, paradoxically combining the force to create and to destroy. The ambivalent nature of genius is extended to thought itself, for ideas are also presented as destructive. By its very nature genius attacks the values of social order; the processes of thought exhaust the vital energies of the creator and often depend on deconstruction in order to discover new truth. The havoc caused by the idea of the absolute, for example, is symbolized by the empty walls of the Claës home, ravaged by the "fire" of thought that has traversed them.

The most important enigma is that of the absolute itself, and the story of the search for it is the secret just as certainly as the telling is the secret in the short fiction of Henry James.[9] The belief in a unique substance common to all phenomena both material and spiritual, the secret of the unity of the creation, is linked here by Balzac to his own theories of thought and human willpower, and finally can also be seen as a metaphor for the creation of a fictional universe.

To begin with Balthazar's intellectual quest, it is clear that the principle of the absolute, which he defines as a form of "matière éthérée," or energized matter, is the single substance at the source of all life. In his pseudoscientific research, mingled with alchemist theories and philosophical speculation, he is nonetheless attempting to isolate the substance common to both proton and neutron. Through his crude version of thermodynamics, he dreams of controlling the means by which matter is given movement, "Si je trouve la force coercitive, je pourrai créer" (*RA*, p. 97). His work illustrates Louis Lambert's concept of "spécialité," and he is, in effect, developing much of Louis's theoretical speculation into concrete experimentation.

Chapter 3, "L'Absolu," is devoted to Balthazar's elaboration of his theories. Like Louis Lambert, he defines human willpower as a certain quantity of vital energy, in reality an embodiment of the principle of the absolute, which he compares to an electric fluid. Man, "qui représente le plus haut point de l'intelligence et qui nous offre le seul appareil d'où résulte un pouvoir à demi créateur, la pensée!" (*RA*, p. 95), is thus the creature whose faculties absorb more than any other "de plus fortes portions de principe absolu" (*RA*, p. 9).

Thought is then an emanation of the will, a superior form of energy like electricity (the influence of Mesmer and other contemporary scientists and pseudoscientists is obvious here), at once a physical and spiritual substance that can create, but that also consumes itself, for it uses up the sources of vital energy or willpower given to each person. Human life, and especially that of the thinker or genius, is, therefore, quite literally a race against time, a difficult struggle to use enough vital energy to create, and yet to conserve enough energy to survive. Reduced to a simple formula, life is the struggle of being to transform energy into creation. In the effort to create himself by becoming essential in the world, to create values and forms outside of himself and capable of resisting the ravages of time, the creator accelerates the process of self-diminution. The theme of thought consuming the thinker that explains so many characters and actions in the *Comédie humaine*[10] is here given an elaborate theoretical justification; Balzac stated it succinctly in *Les Martyrs ignorés:* "La pensée est la plus violente de tous les agents de destruction, elle est le véritable ange exterminateur de l'humanité, qu'elle tue et vivifie, car elle vivifie et tue."[11]

Man's moral life is thus determined in a profound way by his biological condition; the influence of environment seems secondary to the presence in him of a specific quota of energy: "L'homme est un matras. Ainsi, selon moi, l'idiot serait celui dont le cerveau contiendrait le moins de phosphore ou tout autre produit de l'électromagnétisme; le fou, celui dont le cerveau en contiendrait trop; l'homme ordinaire, celui dont la cervelle en serait saturée à un degré convenable" (*RA*, p. 95).

Balthazar, like Lambert, attempts to reconcile the apparent dichotomy between spiritualism and materialism, and is indeed obsessed with a monistic view of the universe: "Eh! quoi de plus conforme à nos idées sur Dieu que de croire qu'il a tout fait par le moyen le plus simple? L'adoration pythagoricienne pour le UN d'où sortent tous les nombres et qui représente la matière une" (*RA*, p. 92). He recognizes that the alchemists with their emphasis on the "grand Ternaire" had made considerable progress toward the discovery of the "substance commune à toutes les créations, modifiées par une force unique, telle est la position nette et claire du problème offert par l'absolu et qui m'a semblé cherchable" (*RA*, p. 91).

In spite of this dream of monism, his scientific knowledge, and his exhaustive research, he must accept the reality of a dualistic world, a world in which ideas are both creative and destructive, in which spirit and matter appear as separate entities and life and death as irreconcilable facts. At the deepest level of the text, it is this paradox that the myth of Faust incarnates: the wish for an impossible unity that is opposed by the reality of dualism and pluralism, one versus many, the desire to be the infinite, indivisible God and the reality of a multifaceted but limited, finite man. We know that Balzac the writer was himself obsessed with the principle of unity in his fictional world, and the philosophical problem of a monistic or dualistic universe is given an elaborate treatment in several *Etudes philosophiques*. The theory of will as the union of spirit and energy is of course central to *Louis Lambert; Séraphita* presents the Swedenborg-inspired universal analogy between nature and God's world as well as the mythical union of two sexes in one.

For Balzac the novelist, this impossible unity and harmony could be attained; omnipotent God in his fictional world, he could endow it with the principle of the absolute, or the common substance of language that transforms all of his characters and situations into a meaningful whole. The inextricable links developed between character and environment and between the psychological and physiological lives of his heroes as well as the device of recurring characters from novel to novel are all aspects of the total world he attempted to create through the energy of words.[12] He tried to deny the distinction between language and things, fictions and reality, through the claims of his particular brand of mimesis, the blurring of history and imagination.

Balthazar, after all, studied chemistry under Lavoisier, and his quest is seen against the backdrop of Napoleonic France. Indeed, the parallel is often suggested between the titan Napoleon's exaggerated ambition, his fall and exile, and those of Balthazar. But this comparison quickly takes us from history to the shifting grounds of myth; Napoleon and Balthazar, in the minds of Balzac and his generation, both repeated the Promethean pattern of revolt against the limits of the established order, whether they be the concrete boundaries of nations or those of knowledge.

In conclusion, the Faustian myth in *La Recherche* gives expression to paradoxical truths about human genius, providing a model for understanding the apparent contradictions in the dynamics of creativity, human energy and thought. It suggests symbolically the essential dualism that man must learn to accept as inherent in the dynamism of all life and human creativity. The play of the opposing principles of stable order and creative disorder, existing forms and the drive toward new forms, produces the conflict necessary to all meaningful change or transcendence.

The story of Balthazar's quest not only illuminates major aspects of Balzac's philosophical speculation, it establishes a pattern of action and character that can be seen as fundamental to his fiction both in the *Etudes philosophiques* and in the *Etudes de moeurs*.

The failed genius or artist who plays such an important role in the *Etudes philosophiques* (Louis Lambert, Frenhofer, Gambara), like Balthazar, is defined by an inner tension between the obsession with the creative idea and the emotional, physical realities of his own nature. The degeneration of the man Balthazar from healthy father and husband to a childlike figure existing on the edge of madness illustrates the tragic loss of energy totally consumed by the force of an idea. On the second level, that of human relations, he finds himself in conflict, first with the other (wife or lover), whose needs he cannot satisfy, and then with the larger group (family, social milieu). The genius, always a man for Balzac, finds himself in a sexual conflict, since science, art, or philosophy require the energy the normal man could devote to love, fatherhood, or sexual passion. Balthazar quite clearly succeeds in sublimating his sexual energy; he has transformed the goal of his drive from woman to science, only to discover, however, an even more tyrannical mistress in his search for the perfection and purity of the absolute. Lambert, on the other hand, who refuses all conflict with the other, endures a fragmented existence, taking refuge in his inner world of ideas. The intellectual and moral superiority of the genius and his need for independence and material support are in direct opposition to the conventional values and virtues of the society his excesses seem to threaten.

Thus the action of these novels springs from the opposition between the determining factors of heredity and chance appearance, the hazards of the genius; the relative, mediocre world of the group and the thinker born from the group who seeks only the ideal. Finally, in metaphysical terms, the human and domestic conflict seems to symbolize the contrast between finite reality in which the genius must live and the absolute or surreal to which he aspires.

The order of creativity in the *Etudes philosophiques* implies a dangerous tension; genius may be prophetic, but it is undeniably destructive, and its energy is self-consuming. It remains, however, heroic and truly superior, in Balzac's view, to the order of stable forms that provides the raw materials from which it grows, and which it transforms into new knowledge and a new creation. The young Poussin, for example, in *Le Chef-d'oeuvre inconnu,* learns from the tragic experience of Frenhofer the need for a healthy balance between imaginative theoretical speculation and the solid craft of art with its emphasis on materials and technique. The narrator suggests through the very choice of Poussin as protagonist that he will succeed in the creation of masterworks where the fantastic old painter had failed.

In the *Etudes de moeurs* the same dynamics prevail. Characters endowed with great energy give the human comedy its thrust and its tragic grandeur; for the opposition between the forces of energy and creativity and those of a stable order, between the activists and the conservatives, continues to motivate Balzac's fiction. The major distinction lies in the values now served by the forces of energy. In the *Etudes philosophiques,* the genius figure in his quest serves the authentic values of knowledge, art, mysticism, poetry, or music (Balthazar, Frenhofer, Séraphita, Lambert, and Gambara), while in the social novels energy is found in the service of degraded values, and the quest takes place in a degraded mode. The absolute sought for is now money for Grandet, social prestige for Rastignac, and power over men for Vautrin. Lucien de Rubempré began with the ambition to be a poet, but settled for the secondary value of journalism, and eventually prostituted himself in order to survive.

Throughout the *Etudes philosophiques,* the conflict between the genius figure and the limits of his own condition is placed on a philosophical and metaphysical level; his struggle is authenticated by the narrator, who labels it heroic and even sublime. In the social works, however, the "inferior," conservative, or traditional order of society and family becomes ironically superior to the hero's quest. The Baron Hulot places his absolute in the pursuit of sexual pleasure, and his degeneration can readily symbolize the decline of an entire class since the French Revolution.[13] The will to superior knowledge characteristic of the *Etudes philosophiques* has become a will to power in the *Etudes de moeurs,* whose quest is played out in a degraded mode in a society whose values have been transformed by the mediating force of money.

In any case Balzac understood that the imaginative structures of myth may still elucidate the rituals of modern city life. The opening pages of *La Fille aux yeux d'or* offer a detailed sociological analysis of the class structure in Paris through a contemporary vision of Dante's Inferno, replete with a detailed comparison of the city's quarters to the circles of Hell. The young hero, de Marsay, is yet another clear example of the integration of the Faust myth in a domestic setting. He is compared to the illustrious searcher for the infinite, but his quest is for perfect sexual bliss. No sublimation of goals from the instinctual to the cultural, from physical passion to a passion for knowledge, occurs; the perfect woman as object for absolute pleasure, rather than the absolute of science, obsesses him. Balzac therefore presents him as a corrupted product of the hellish environment of Paris, dominated by the degraded values of "l'or et le plaisir."

The important role played by Vautrin in a series of novels adds resonance to the social permutation of the Faust myth written into *La Recherche de l'absolu.* Satanic revolt against a corrupt social contract, the desire to be a superman in order to enslave other men, energy in the service of crime to gain fortune and social prestige, are all aspects of the myth in a degraded mode. The partnerships formed between Vautrin and the weaker young men repeat the pact of Mephistopheles and Faust, and suggest the ambiguous morality of their conflict with society's order. The two distinct and often conflicting souls that Goethe's Faust felt within himself, one inclined to spiritual longing and the other directed to the baser side of nature, are again actualized in Balzac's male couples.

From Balthazar to Vautrin, the presence of the romantic variant of the Faustian myth indicates the same pattern of an impossible effort to transcend man's limited and imperfect condition; the absolute, God's secret, or a human need carried to its extreme end becomes the goal of a search that leads to inevitable conflict between the searcher and the others. The outcome of the quest is less important to Balzac than the dynamics of the struggle, always the primary matter of his fiction.

In Balzac's novels the genius, his term for the highest form of the artistic and creative temperament, makes a noble use of his vital energy, although he fails in his effort to create a reality outside the mediocrity of the real. The social seekers, who place their ideal in a baser mode, destroy themselves and corrupt others. In a sense, both are sacrificed to the absolute whose quest alone in Balzac's world gives value to existence.

VII

Théophile Gautier and the Romantic Aesthetic: The Model Parodied—"Du Beau dans l'art" and *Les Jeunes-France*

> Tout homme qui n'a pas son
> monde intérieur à traduire
> n'est pas un artiste.
>
> (*Du Beau dans l'art*)

Gautier's oeuvre is multifaceted, seemingly paradoxical in its changing aesthetic background, and most often misunderstood in its relationship to romantic literature. The stories of *Les Jeunes-France* (1833) satirize through fiction the foibles and pretentions of the young artists Gautier himself frequented, and with whom he had enthusiastically supported the innovations of Hugo's *Hernani* only two years before. His numerous articles and reviews of literature, art, and music, also unjustly neglected, constitute a unique record of decades of creative activity in France. The Preface to *Mademoiselle de Maupin* (1835) has been given privileged status, since it is supposed to defend a counterromantic concept, the much heralded and maligned art-for-art's-sake dictum. Its value, we are told, consists in its anticipation of the poetic principles of English and French symbolists, when in reality it is a virulent attack against the mediocrity and arbitrary practices of contemporary journalism.

In fact, however, Gautier never lost his great admiration for Hugo's poetic genius, and his essay "Du Beau dans l'art" (1856),[1] almost contemporary with *William Shakespeare,* represents a considerable deepening of his aesthetic philosophy, actually an interiorization of the romantic or Hugoesque model we have studied. This text is central to any understanding of Gautier's evolving attitude toward creativity; it renders coherent the apparent contradictions in his many statements about art, and even provides a "missing link" between Diderot and Baudelaire.

Formally, the essay reminds the reader of Baudelaire's great study of Constantin Guys in *Le Peintre de la vie moderne* (1863), since it is a commentary on the works of the Swiss realist painter Topffer. Rather than eulogize the artist, however, the text presents a curious dialogue; Gautier's point of departure—and this is characteristic of much of his work—is a named text. Topffer's *Réflexions et menus propos d'un peintre genevois* is the intertext, quoted and refuted, which is offered as a justification of mimetic realism in painting. Gautier represents himself as a romantic idealist who dialogues with the realist Topffer as he "deconstructs" and criticizes his essay. The role of dialogue readily suggests Diderot, but more profoundly, the central concepts of the artist's inner model and of art as a re-creation of nature link Gautier's essay with *Le Paradoxe sur le comédien.*

Gautier is little interested in the origins of creativity, and in fact counsels against useless attempts to penetrate these mysteries; he is likewise unconcerned with the third aspect of the creative process, that is the relationship of work to reader or spectator. His antipathy for any suggestion of "progress" in art or for the social commitment of the artist, enunciated again in this essay, is well known. In this respect he obviously anticipates Baudelaire and denies the Hugoesque function of the artist. He therefore concentrates his effort on the second or central problem of creativity, the elaboration of the work of art, and analyzes its process with unusual subtlety.

In a nutshell, Gautier believes that the true artist is endowed with a special intuition of ideal beauty; his role is to transform real forms into his own image of this ideal. Consequently, the artist remains a visionary, capable of intuiting absolute beauty, which seems to exist as a Neoplatonic universal, or rather as an attribute of God's world; for beauty in its essence—he declares—is God: "Le beau dans son essence absolue, c'est Dieu. Il est aussi impossible de le chercher hors de la sphère divine, qu'il est impossible de trouver hors de cette sphère le vrai et le bon absolus. Le beau n'appartient donc pas à l'ordre sensible, mais à l'ordre spirituel. Il est invariable, car il est absolu, et cela seul peut varier qui est relatif" ("Du Beau," p. 160). The work of art, the poem, music, or picture, is therefore the recreation of real words, sounds, and colors—the signs of nature—filtered through the inner world of the artist: "Si le type de la beauté existe dans son esprit à l'état d'idéal, il prend à la nature des signes, il les transforme: il y ajoute et il en ôte, selon le genre de sa pensée, de telle sorte qu'un objet qui, dans la réalité, n'exciterait aucune attention, prend de l'importance et du charme étant représenté" ("Du Beau," p. 135). The painter begins by painting his own dreamworld, where images of the ideal are manifested, and then imposes it on the outer world of forms: "C'est son âme qu'il peindra à travers une vue de forêt, de lac ou de montagne. C'est ce sentiment de beau préconçu qui inspire au sculpteur une statue, au poète une églogue, au musicien une symphonie; chacun tente de manifester avec son moyen cette rêverie, cette aspiration, ce trouble et cette inquiétude sublimes que causent au véritable artiste la prescience et le désir du beau" ("Du Beau," p. 136). Contemporary critics would agree that Gautier maintains the fallacy of originality, for the essential element of the creative process is indeed the richness of this inner world: "l'intuition, la déduction, le souvenir" ("Du Beau," p. 148) are the primary and secondary qualities through which the artist illuminates reality. Gautier criticizes Topffer and his work precisely because his realistic imitations of natural scenes are mirrors instead of lamps, to use Abram's famous terminology taken from Keats.[2]

Gautier's essay is striking, not because he continues to support the fallacy of originality (although he himself depends so much on previous texts and forms in his own creative work), but because he deviates so little from the romantic model. Instead of an emphasis on the function of the imagination that according to Hugo uncovers the profound structure of reality, Gautier clearly interiorizes the visionary faculty. His artist is not so much the one who *reveals* the essences behind the surfaces and appearances of things as the one who *creates* a new image through his special intuition. The Neoplatonic ideal of beauty exists in the form of an inner reflection that becomes the basis of the "modèle intérieur" ("Du Beau," p. 140).

In contrast to imitation, whether it be of classical models or a mimesis of natural scenes, Gautier describes the elaboration of an inner model that becomes the basis for the actual work of art: "Les peintres dessinent d'après un modèle intérieur auquel ils plient les formes du modèle extérieur" ("Du Beau," p. 140). This inner model results from sensations and memories of exterior reality transfigured by the artist's intuition of spiritual beauty. The artist is not an inventor of forms, since they all exist in nature; he remakes them into an ideal image. For Gautier, as it did for Hugo, the myth of Prometheus becomes once again an exemplary version of the creative process; the great artists, he claims: "Au lieu de donner une forme à l'idéal, ils donnent un idéal à la forme; ce n'est plus l'âme qui prend un corps, c'est le corps qui prend une âme: ce dernier procédé paraît même le plus simple. Le Titan qui souffrit sur la croix du Caucase les douleurs du Calvaire, quand il eût modelé sa statue d'argile, ravit la flamme du ciel, et appliqua une torche au flanc muet du fantôme pétri par ses mains" ("Du Beau," p. 155). Proceeding from the material to the spiritual, from exterior reality to the inner vision of the ideal, the beauty of the model comes not alone from the world of things nor from the artist's imaginative world, but from a transformation of the real through the inner vision of the ideal: "les manifestations du beau caché doivent se soumettre à la règle des formes sensibles: seulement que l'artiste, à travers les peintures de la vie ou du monde matériel poursuive son rêve idéal, pense au ciel en peignant la terre, et à Dieu en peignant l'homme; sans quoi ses ouvrages, quelque curieuse qu'en soit l'exécution, n'auront pas ce caractère général, éternel, immuable, qui donne la consécration aux chefs-d'oeuvre: il leur manquera la vie" ("Du Beau," p. 161).

Prometheus is not treated as the Hugoesque figure of revolt and suffering for humanity's progress but as a molder of ideal forms. He resembles more closely Diderot's great actress la Clairon, who carries within her a "grand fantôme" or inner model of the character she will recreate, a model similarly composed of observation of real people and imaginative idealization that produces a universal type.

It could be claimed that the major shift in neoclassical aesthetics in the eighteenth century is signaled by Diderot's notion of the inner model of the artist. He prepares for romanticism by insisting that art is neither a mimetic imitation of exterior reality nor a slavish copy of inherited forms (neither realism nor classicism), but that the artist is truly a creator who gives form to his own inner model through the materials of his medium. Gautier and Baudelaire, we should add, essentially adopt the same theory. In his effort to defend, once again, art for art's sake, Gautier claims: "tous sujets sont indifférents et ne valent que par l'idéal, le sentiment et le style que chaque artiste y apporte" ("Du Beau," p. 150). What counts is the expression of a certain ideality produced by the individual genius of each artist.

His final justification of the value of art brings us back again to Hugo and the romantic idea of the artist as a privileged interpreter of the divine. The intuition he carries within him is the special faculty that enables him to glimpse a higher truth; the final product of his imagination and craft contains a revelation of spiritual reality, which gives the work of art its superiority as a cultural product and its only moral value: the great artists have: "fait concevoir l'idéal à des gens qui d'eux-mêmes ne l'auraient jamais soupçonné et introduit cet élément divin dans des esprits jusque-là matériels" ("Du Beau," p. 153).

When the satire of *Les Jeunes-France* is considered in the light of "Du Beau dans l'art" it is clear that Gautier was mocking the would-be artists who imitated the outward trappings and exaggerated signs of romantic art. Subjects for parody are those who are unaware that the true source of creativity is a kind of sixth sense, the special intuition of ideal beauty that makes the artist capable of creating "le sublime modèle qu'il porte au-dedans de lui-même" ("Du Beau," p. 134).

In his introduction to a recent edition of *Les Jeunes-France*,[3] Jasinski explains the history of these satirical pieces and offers an interpretation of Gautier's intention; each one deals in a curiously ambivalent manner and in a bittersweet tone with a different aberration resulting from the young generation's fascination with romantic attitudes toward life and art. Ambiguous, as we shall see, because the bourgeois alternative to romantic excess is even more unacceptable to the narrator of these tales. Regretful, because although these "romans goguenards" are rich with Rabelaisian humor and grotesque situations, their narrator's irony seems often to be against his grain.

For our purposes, only the preface and those stories dealing specifically with creative activity and artist figures will be analyzed. "Onuphrius," "Daniel Jovard," and "Celle-ci ou celle-là" are all representations of the creative process in action. The first is one of his best in the genre of "Contes fantastiques," and the latter two stories are surprisingly "modernist" in technique and tone.

With the preface to *Les Jeunes-France* alone the modern reader enters a world curiously attuned to our sensibilities. An example of the metaliterature found throughout Gautier's works, this text is self-reflective and has as frame of reference the context of literary prefaces so important in the French tradition, especially since the notorious *Préface de Cromwell* (1827).

A preface that is a meditation on the esthetic value of prefaces is presented by an author who claims to be a nonauthor. Ironic and familiar in tone, he addresses the reader directly, questioning the need for long prefaces, preparing him for the demystification of romantic themes he will find in the stories, and mocking the idea of a romantic author itself! The "je" of the preface at first describes himself as cynical and without illusions, above all bourgeois and antiartistic in temperament; he does not have a rich and original personality; he hates nature and never travels. He claims to love only cats and writes poetry simply to relieve the immense boredom of his empty bourgeois existence (almost a caricature of the Baudelairean stance twenty years in advance). Art is defined as nothing more than a "jonglerie pure" (*Jeunes-France*, p. 3), although he admits his esteem for the acrobats.

The ironic portrait of the bored author of an unnecessary preface offers, of course, an amusing contrast to the contemporary image of the romantic artist—passionate, fiercely individualistic, and in revolt against his society. The portrait is doubly satirical, however, since the author claims that his life was completely changed when his young romantic friends succeeded in transforming him into a dandy—Jeune-France—replete with the famous "gilet rouge" (red vest) and other requisite outward signs of the artist's life.

The preface is thus a clever satire of contemporary attitudes toward art that corresponds exactly to Gautier's theories; the author of the preface has no inner life from which to produce an oeuvre, he has only the excessive and empty outward signs currently conveying an artist's image. The confessional tone of the preface would suggest that the author is also mocking himself; a contemporary reader would have immediately recognized the allusion to the red vest and the vogue for long polemical prefaces. The irony is even more subtle, since the preface actually parodies the precise situations and structures of many of the stories that it introduces. The "je" of the preface, who has nothing to write about, discovers through the mediation of a friend, already initiated into the arcane world of romantic literature, how to become a romantic writer. This is the fictional framework for the plots of both "Daniel Jovard" and "Celle-ci ou celle-là," in which the mediation of others and especially other texts stands between the aspiring romantic and the world. Desire is mediated through the other (love and the creative impulse are modeled on the concepts of initiates), and literature becomes the unique frame of reference for all experience and all writing. The preface is consequently an ironic parody of romantic prefaces in which the author refuses to take seriously his position as a presenter of texts. Contrary to the famous model of the *Préface de Cromwell,* which introduced a philosophy of history as well as a new aesthetic and completely overshadowed the play, the stories that follow parody romantic texts and satirize conventions, values, and styles characteristic of the new romantic literature.

Daniel Jovard is an ironic and humorous spin-off from the preface, in which Gautier presents a dull bourgeois young man who learns "la gaie science du romantisme" (*Jeunes-France,* p. 104) through the intermediary of Ferdinand, a young imitator of Victor Hugo. Ferdinand serves as a model, teaching him how to become a writer by changing costume, name, and the size of his forehead, and especially through the acquisition of a new vocabulary. Daniel learns the formulas for different styles such as the "intime," "artistique," "dantesque," "fatal" (*Jeunes-France,* p. 103), a new language or set of signs that in current Parisian society signify a romantic artist like Hugo:

> Il lui apprit à avoir un air moyen-âge, il lui enseigna les moyens de se donner de la tournure et du caractère, il lui révéla le sens intime de l'argot en usage cette semaine-là; il lui dit ce que c'était que ficelle, chic, galbe, art, artiste et artistique; il lui apprit ce que voulait dire cartonné, égayé, damné; il lui ouvrit un vaste répertoire de formules admiratives et réprobatives, phosphorescent, transcendental, pyramidal, stupidifiant, foudroyant, annihilant, et mille autres qu'il serait fastidieux de rapporter ici. (*Jeunes-France,* pp. 101–2)

The text becomes a parodic satire[4] in which the false artist without originality or inner life becomes the dandy, making literature "à recettes" by imitating a human model, himself a falsified version of the true artist, Victor Hugo. The whole centrifugal process of exteriorization and trivialization—which Gautier terms "l'Hugolâtrie"—is directly opposed to the movement toward the self-center and potential source of creativity of the serious artist.

The product of this unfortunate imitation of cultural signs and literary texts is the proliferation of romantic clichés as well as artificiality and exaggeration in the dress and attitudes of the artist. In fact the most original aspect of this satire of the young romantic à la Hernani is use of language. If irony results from the conflict of two incompatible discourses, then the reader of "Daniel Jovard" is faced with the conflict of at least four sets of discourses—the classical language of the outmoded theater being mocked by the Jeunes-France, the excesses of romantic phraseology and vocabulary, the linguistic platitudes of the bourgeois (represented by Daniel's parents), and finally, the cynical, "realistic" speech of the narrator, who addresses himself directly to the reader and distances himself from the other language spaces. The epigraph of the story, a parody of classical verse followed by a romantic parody of the same themes suggests the juggling of tones and discourses that is to follow. In the last analysis, Gautier is satirizing the empty rhetoric of romantic language divorced from any real experience of human emotion as well as bourgeois conformity and classical pomposity. Before his "conversion" Daniel writes in colorless classical style of his desire to be inspired by the "muse":

> Je veux boire à longs traits les eaux de l'Hippocrène,
> Et couché sur leurs bords au pied des myrtes verts,
> Occuper les échos à redire mes vers.
> (*Jeunes-France*, p. 90)

After conversion, Daniel represents his desire to destroy the muse in violent, romantic imagery:

> Par l'enfer! je me sens un immense désir
> De broyer sous mes dents sa chair, et de saisir

Avec quelque lambeau de sa peau bleue et verte
Son coeur demi pourri dans sa poitrine ouverte.
(*Jeunes-France*, p. 90)

The destruction of the muse, announced in this epigraph, is precisely
the effect Gautier's satire predicts if poorly imitated literary models continue to intervene between the artist's expression and his
experience.

"Celle-ci ou celle-là," somewhat marred by redundancy and excessive length, is nevertheless the most complex of the fictions in *Les
Jeunes-France*. It contains a metaliterary function that defines its structure, as the narrator himself declares in the final paragraphs. Once
again the story of a young artist (already converted to romanticism)
and his wise companion, Albert (apparently a spokesman for the author), its content is explained as an allegory of the situation of literature in 1833. In an ironic tone the narrator indicates that the young
protagonist, Rodolphe, whose goal is to transform reality into a romantic drama, represents the soul in youth "plein de vagues désirs"
(*Jeunes-France*, p. 192); Madame de M., the cold and rich bourgeoise
he seduces, is classical poetry, whereas Mariette the servant girl, with
whom Rodolphe finally settles down, is true poetry—natural, human, and intimate. Madame de M.'s husband, the liberal and stupid
bourgeois who quotes Racine but refuses to be jealous of his wife's
infidelity, is contrasted with Albert, who stands for reason—a friend
of true poetry.

This simplistic schema is offered by the narrator to interpret the
story as a corrective to romantic excess and a suggestion that intim-
ism in poetry—the style of the *Vie, poésies et pensées de Joseph Delorme*
(1829) by Sainte-Beuve, or the *Feuilles d'automne* (1831) by Hugo—is
currently the appropriate development for romantic literature. Albert and Rodolphe are compared to Don Juan offering his hand to
Childe Harold: a union of two poets, the first understanding reality
and appreciating the sensuous beauty of the world, the second endowed with a rich and mysterious inner life. Together they might
produce the necessary equilibrium for a new kind of literary creation,
a poetry fully attuned to both the beauty of natural objects and the
intuition of spiritual reality within the artist's nature.

The text is indeed another presentation of Gautier's own aesthetic
and a parody of this very aesthetic. "Du Beau dans l'art" tells us that

true art transforms real forms into an approximation of ideal beauty according to an inner model or personal vision; Rodolphe, however, learns the absolute impossibility of transforming bourgeois reality into romantic beauty. His vision of the ideal is simply borrowed from texts and contexts foreign to his own world, and never corresponds to a personal or original intuition of truth.

This parody of Gautier's own aesthetic is a true parody this time, since there is a specific text incorporated into "Celle-ci ou celle-là." Rodolphe is searching for inspiration, the raw materials of an artistic creation; from the point of view of the protagonist, this story is that of his own creative process. He sets out to force reality to resemble the very successful romantic drama *Antony* by Alexandre Dumas. He quite lucidly exposes his plan: to discover an unusually passionate woman, and then drive her husband into a jealous rage in order to provoke intense dramatic conflicts that will be the source of subjects for poetic elegies and perhaps another "drame romantique." The scenario he adopts is quite close to the actual plot of *Antony,* which has a contemporary, Parisian setting and a similar cast of actors.

The irony, of course, results from the contrast between his expectations, based on the passionate emotions experienced by the characters of *Antony,* and the total deception offered by his reality. Rodolphe's creative activity is based on a false premise, and in this sense is a negative parody of Gautier's aesthetic; instead of developing his own instinct for beauty, he ignores the richness of the humble lives and objects around him and seeks to impose a romantic model on a bourgeois reality that stubbornly resists all such efforts at idealization. His error is double, since he both denies the world surrounding him and refuses to define his own intuitive and imaginative world, his longing for love and beauty. The reader cannot refrain from the thought that characters like the future Madame Bovary could have profited enormously from this book! Had they read of Rodolphe's failure to transform bourgeois reality into art according to a romantic model, instead of reading the sentimental "lamentateurs de l'école de Lamartine" (*Jeunes-France,* p. 131) (as Gautier himself calls them) they might have renounced romantic illusions.

For Rodolphe makes the mistake that Emma later repeats: that of seeking romantic passion in the banality of bourgeois life. Since his vision comes from texts and is always mediated (perhaps inevitably) by the desire of the other and does not develop from his own inner life, he is never able to compose the "interior model" for the new work. Every attempt to give bourgeois reality an ideal form fails comically and miserably.

One could study in detail the parallels between Rodolphe's project (the "parodiant" or text that parodies) and the plot of *Antony* (the "parodié" or text parodied); the parody was certainly an obvious one to any contemporary reader, due to the enormous popularity of Dumas's play in 1831. Two examples of the relationship between the two texts will suffice: Rodolphe's attempt to seduce the willing Madame de M. and his futile efforts to render her husband jealous. Rodolphe had decided he needed to experience the true passion of an artist in Byron's image in order to sharpen his sensibilities. The beautiful, sensuous woman must be Spanish or Italian and provide a source for the experience of violent emotions. Madame de M., whom he meets at the opera, was born at Chateau-Thierry in France and accepts his advances readily without the haughty disdain he had expected. In fact, she loves him in spite of his "donquichotisme de passion" (*Jeunes-France*, p. 143). The title, twice interpreted in the story, refers again to Rodolphe's error. The ideal romantic woman cannot exist in reality, and the cold, classical beauty he discovers is a total disappointment. Only imperfect representations of the ideal are to be found disseminated in the real women of the world, "celle-ci" or "celle-là" captures certain aspects of this dream upon which the artist can then build his model.

The plot of *Antony* hinges on the theme of jealousy and the ensuing conflict between Antony's mad love for Adèle and her sentiment of horror concerning her marriage to the old colonel (a situation quite similar to that of Hernani and Doña Sol, to which Gautier also alludes). The main actions in Rodolphe's scenario consist in futile efforts to make the husband jealous. An anonymous letter denouncing Rodolphe and the husband's unexpected arrival in the midst of the facile seduction scene provoke neither the expected duel nor a cathartic intensification of emotions. The famous fifth act or violent conclusion anticipated by Rodolphe is replaced by a banal discussion about literature! Instead of exhibiting jealousy like Othello (another favorite of the Jeunes-France), the husband remains imperturbable, reasonable, profoundly bourgeois; indeed he: "n'avait guère le physique d'un mari comme il faut dans les drames" (*Jeunes-France*, p. 117).

This section of the text is presented as a dialogue with many authorial intrusions, emphasizing the undramatic quality of the supposed drama. At this point the dialogue also reveals the other subtexts or discourses whose conflict causes irony and humor. The husband, still enamored of the classics, first quotes from Racine, recalling the resemblance between the situation of Theseus and Hippolytus and their own; Rodolphe replies with a quotation from *Hernani* concerning the old man who loves Doña Sol; the husband, unwittingly accurate, adds a reference to a contemporary bourgeois novel entitled *Le Cocu* (*The Cuckold*) of Paul de Kock! Once again three discourses are present: the classical and the romantic are obviously too noble (*Phèdre*) or too exotic (*Hernani*) for the reality at hand; the bourgeois in its banality appears much more appropriate.

The narrator's discourse and role here are much more complex than those found in "Daniel Jovard." He addresses the reader directly throughout the text and reveals that he too had wanted to write a romantic story; like his hero, who is thus an author in the second degree, he had wanted to fashion contemporary reality into an ideal romantic image. "Celle-ci ou celle-là" is therefore also the record of his own creative process, the story of his efforts to fashion ideal forms of beauty and love. Similar to his protagonist, "il croyait que les situations énergiques allaient abonder sous sa plume" (*Jeunes-France*, p. 160).

After presenting the scene with the complacent husband the narrator in "celle-ci ou celle-là" excuses himself to the reader for the banality of such events and the language used. He admits the impossibility of transforming the platitudes of quotidian, bourgeois life into romantic art; he claims to be a realist who cannot lie by falsifying the facts through fictional exaggeration or romantic idealization. His protagonist, however, has not yet renounced his efforts; he tells himself: "tu n'avais qu'à vouloir pour faire de l'antonysme première qualité" (*Jeunes-France*, p. 160).

Thus the narrator-writer distances himself for the most part from the protagonist-writer, with whom, however, he occasionally identifies. Early in the story he establishes an antiromantic stance and enunciates a "realist" discourse; he claims to be basically cynical,

Rabelaisian, and in love with his own healthy servant girl, Mariette. The possession of a woman is always preferable, he claims, to a tirade on the union of souls. In short, his antiromantic discourse, equally opposed to the pettiness of bourgeois society, is the real point of reference with which the classical, romantic, and bourgeois languages come into comic and ironical juxtaposition.

At the conclusion of the story he discusses his narrative and creative problem with the reader, again humorously anticipating that of Flaubert and *Madame Bovary*. He realizes that to write a story centered on a banal situation unfortunately requires banality in tone and style; the situation at hand has no conventional romantic elements: setting suns, haunted castles, and descriptions of moonlit forests have no place in the story of a Parisian seduction. He lists the clichés of romantic fiction, its images and themes that by 1833 have become empty formulas. They are no longer viable, he declares, and concludes that contemporary bourgeois reality cannot support the falsification of romantic idealization.

Protagonist and narrator are both disappointed when faced with their failure to produce romantic literature—it has become, regrettably unwritable:

> Considérez, lecteurs et lectrices, que je n'ai pas, comme les autres auteurs mes confrères, la ressource des clairs de lune et des couchers de soleil, pas la plus petite description de château, de forêt ou de ruines. Je n'emploie pas de fantômes, encore moins de brigands; j'ai laissé chez le costumier les pantalons mipartis, et les surcots armoriés; ni bataille, ni incendie, ni rapt, ni viol. Les femmes de mon livre ne se font pas plus violer que le vôtre ou celle de votre voisin, ni meurtre, ni pendaison, ni écartellement, pas un pauvre petit cadavre pour égayer la narration et étouper les endroits vides. (*Jeunes-France*, p. 174)

In a sense Gautier is writing self-parody as well; his narrator, who comments often on the resistance of the matter or subject he has chosen, compares Rodolphe's uninteresting love affair in a dull Parisian drawing room to the exotic *Contes d'Espagne* with their scintillating "couleur locale." Gautier also reminds the reader of Albertus, the tormented and passionate medieval hero of his poem *Albertus ou l'âme et le péché* (Albertus has metamorphosed into the reasonable Albert in "*Celle-ci ou celle-là*").

Self-conscious about his text, Gautier's narrator often interrupts the flow of narration to comment disappointedly on the action and the lack of progress of his characters. In a like manner Rodolphe judges his own seduction scene to be mediocre; it belongs in a vaudeville rather than in the famous fifth act.

Rodolphe nevertheless retains his ambition to rise to the "sommités les plus inaccessibles de la passion délirante" (*Jeunes-France*, p. 148). Even in the conclusion, when he abandons his romantic project and finally becomes aware of the beauty of his immediate surroundings—including the attractions of the wholesome servant girl, Mariette—he persists, incorrigible, in his artistic desire to idealize reality and to imitate literary models: together they will relive the pastoral love of Daphnis and Chloé. Curiously enough, the classical discourse reappears; even as Rodolphe rediscovers reality, he attempts to adapt it to an ideal version of humble love. It is his alter ego, Albert, who at last offers the lesson of the text. True poetry is personal and intimate; the poet's immediate milieu is therefore the microcosm of which his soul is the center. Albert concludes that to explore this soul and this environment is the real source of creativity—travel to exotic lands is not necessary, for his own rooms contain his dreams and visions.

In spite of the far-reaching satire of romantic excesses, the advocacy of an intimist poetry in 1833 manifests once again Gautier's adherence to a Hugoesque model. His story even suggests a humanitarian and social preoccupation that is found in *Les Feuilles d'automne* but will be later rejected by Gautier. The criticism of bourgeois banality and stupidity is accompanied with the suggestion that the artist should concern himself with the plight of the poor; Mariette is not only a source of natural beauty and humble poetry, but a rather eloquent reminder of the unjust treatment the new bourgeois monarchy continues to accord its working classes. Seen in the context of the evolution of romantic social and political philosophy, "Celle-ci ou celle-là" reflects the growing disillusionment with the new regime, and signals a serious rupture between the artist and the bourgeois public. Rodolphe rejects the bourgeois "players" of his drama and turns to what Sartre terms the virtual audience, the lower classes. Mariette, with her unaffected beauty and simple generosity, becomes the possible source of artistic emotion.

"Onuphrius ou les vexations fantastiques d'un admirateur d'Hoffman" originally appeared in 1832 in *La France littéraire;* it was considerably reworked for publication in *Les Jeunes-France* a year later. Generally serious in tone and incorporating elements of E. T. A. Hoffman's style and thematics, it is a "conte fantastique," as well as a parody and presents a view of the artist's experience quite opposed to that found in "Celle-ci ou celle-là." The protagonist is a painter, a Jeune-France given to romantic excess, and a poet whose vivid imagination has fallen prey to his reading of fantastic literature. He has been transformed by romantic books into a visionary: "Il se faisait, au milieu du monde réel bourdonnant autour de lui, un monde d'extase et de vision où il était donné à bien peu d'entrer. Du détail le plus commun et le plus positif, par l'habitude qu'il avait de chercher le côté surnaturel, il savait faire jaillir quelque chose de fantastique et d'inattendu."[5] He has indeed lost control of his rich imagination, and his attraction to fantasy leaves him at the edge of madness. The narrator himself interprets its destructive influence: "Il eût été capable sans cette tendance funeste, d'être le plus grand des poètes" (*ON,* p. 61).

Onuphrius has lost himself on the path of the supernatural and its "profondeurs nébuleuses" (*ON,* p. 61) uncovered by his poetic faculties. This fragmented personality suggests Balzac's Louis Lambert as the narrator describes his childlike appearance, his love for a mother figure, Jacinta, and his obsession with the world of metaphysics. His vision of himself as a double in the form of Satan torments him to the point of paralysis. Living in a state of fear, frustration, and impotence, he is finally incapable of distinguishing between his anxiety-causing dreams and exterior reality. Literally persecuted by his visions, nature and inanimate objects are metamorphosed into hostile forces, "chaque lanterne était un oeil sanglant qui l'espionnait" (*ON,* p. 59).

The imagination overstimulated by macabre and fantastic texts leads to self-destruction instead of creativity, as it transforms nature into a monstrous enemy of the artist. The particular exploration of the poetic, irrational faculties of the artist's inner world recorded in this story is clearly a negative version of the discovery and intuition of beauty to be described later in "Du Beau dans l'art." The necessary equilibrium for creative work between the imaginative self and the self capable of assessing reasonably the value of forms and objects outside the mind is destroyed by the "first poet," or irrational persona. Here, this persona is symbolized by an incarnation of the devil, who dominates the life of Onuphrius and literally prevents any synthesis of form and idea capable of producing a work of art. Onuphrius's satanic vision distorts real objects into nightmare images rather than endowing them with an ideal form: "Tant les yeux de son âme et de son corps avaient la faculté de déranger les lignes les plus droites et de rendre compliquées les choses les plus simples, à peu près comme les miroirs courbes ou à facettes qui trahissent les objets qui leur sont présentés, et les font paraître grotesques ou terribles. (*ON*, p. 31).

Unlike Rodolphe—who made no effort to explore the inner resources of intuition, imagination, and reverie, where, according to Gautier, the primary impetus for creativity exists—Onuphrius is totally immersed in this irrational world, living in a perpetual hallucination. Like Rodolphe, however, he is also the victim of literary models and texts and cannot seek his motivation in exterior reality, which he gradually loses the power to observe objectively.

One could, of course, interpret his madness as a result of drug abuse or other artificial stimulants and view the satanic elements of the text as metaphor. Indeed, biographical critics have found in this story an autoportrait; the dream that plunges him into a state of perpetual hallucination is a recurring, obsessional motif in Gautier's works—the hero is buried alive, and his spirit witnesses his betrayal by friends and his lover. The adventures of Onuphrius also recall the excesses of Petrus Borel, Nerval, and other members of the Petit Cénacle that Gautier frequented. Their desperate desire to revolt against bourgeois life through the experience of the extreme limits of human sensibility (drug-induced hallucination, cruelty, crime, and exaggerated linguistic innovation) has been aptly characterized as the "courant frénétique" of French romanticism.

A visionary gone mad, the pathetic fallacy of Hugo's nature alive with signs of spiritual order, is now turned into a hellish prison, as the poet personifies the world around him:

les arbres de la route avaient l'air de grands spectres tendant les bras; de temps en temps un feu follet traversait le chemin, le vent ricanait dans les branches d'une façon singulière. (*ON*, p. 38)

Les clochers s'inclinaient sur le chemin creux pour le regarder passer, ils le montraient au doigt, lui faisaient la nique et lui tendaient par dérision leurs cadrans dont les aiguilles étaient perpendiculaires. Les cloches lui tiraient la langue et lui faisaient la grimace, sonnant toujours les six coups maudits. (*ON,* p. 37)

The language of correspondences, metaphors, and symbols used to give form to his vision translates only the disorder of a paranoid, profoundly troubled mind. Church bells do not evoke a superior level of experience as they might in a poem of Hugo, but are a projection of the artist's isolated and damned inner life. Poetic language does not have the power to reveal spiritual order, as the romantic conception prescribes, it only confirms the disorder experienced by the artist within himself. Parts of this text readily suggest the "Spleen" sequence in Baudelaire's *Les Fleurs du mal;* "La Cloche fêlée," for example, expresses the same opposition between the poet's desire to "sing" a spiritual song and the metaphoric transpositions of his own states of anguish he succeeds in producing:

> Moi, mon âme est fêlée, et lorsqu'en ses ennuis
> Elle veut de ses chants peupler l'air froid des nuits,
> Il arrive souvent que sa voix affaiblie
> Semble le râle épais d'un blessé qu'on oublie
> Au bord d'un lac de sang, sous un grand tas de morts,
> Et qui meurt, sans bouger, dans d'immenses efforts.[6]

The romantic model for the creative process is thus negatively parodied as the imagination becomes the source of folly rather than of a new creation: "Sorti de l'arche du réel, il s'était lancé dans les profondeurs nébuleuses de la fantaisie et de la métaphysique; mais il n'avait pu revenir avec le rameau d'olive; il n'avait pas su retrouver le chemin par où il était venu; il ne put, quand le vertige le prit d'être si haut et si loin, redescendre comme il l'aurait souhaité, et renouer avec le monde positif." (*ON,* p. 61) A modern Noah incapable of refinding solid ground, Onuphrius's poetic faculty is compared to an extinguished lamp: "La lumière s'était éteinte dans la lampe; cette belle imagination, surexcitée par des moyens factices, s'était usée en de vaines ébauches; à force d'être spectateur de son existence Onuphrius avait oublié celle des autres, et les liens qui le rattachaient au monde s'étaient brisés un à un." (*ON,* p. 61) Excessive exercise of the imagination's capacity to transform reality, now turned in upon itself, has become self-destructive: "Pour avoir trop regardé sa vie à la loupe, car son fantastique, il le prenait presque toujours dans les événements ordinaires, il lui arriva ce qui arrive à ces gens qui aperçoivent, à l'aide du microscope, des vers dans les aliments les plus sains, des serpents dans les liqueurs les plus limpides. Ils n'osent plus manger; la chose la plus naturelle grossie par son imagination lui paraissait monstrueuse" (*ON,* p. 61).

An exaggerated dependence on texts that are themselves a distortion of reality, a denial of reason and lucid observation of concrete forms, or an equally unfruitful refusal to investigate the inner world of intuition and imagination—these are the artistic abuses that the satirical pieces of *Les Jeunes-France* and some of the fantastic tales propose to criticize and perhaps to correct. In the final analysis, Daniel Jovard, Rodolphe, and Onuphrius all fall victim to current forms of romantic literature that ruin their creative enterprise.

VIII

Alfred de Musset: Split Personalities and the Romantic Abuse of Adjectives—*Le Fils du Titien* and the *Lettres de Dupuis et Cotonet*

> Un seul homme a bien peu de
> force quand tout un siècle
> lutte contre lui.
>
> (*Le Fils du Titien*)

Alfred de Musset presents creative persons in many of his works, often directly, as in the play *Andréa del Sarto,* the novella *Le Fils du Titien,* and the poems of *Les Nuits,* in which the persona of the poet dialogues with his muse. Many of the other works also deal with important aspects of the creative process or study characters who attempt to transform life through art. Fantasio (*Fantasio,* 1834), for example, uses his remarkable imaginative faculty to solve the amorous problems of the beautiful fairy-tale princess. This relatively simple Shakespearean fantasy nevertheless contains the major theme that dominates all of Musset's work—the apparent dichotomy between the worlds of art and experience. Musset's creative persons almost always discover that they must choose between the exigencies of an artist's commitment and the desire to lead a life of sensual and sentimental fulfillment. Devotion to art or devotion to love, both considered to be superior goals, seem mutually exclusive.

It is true that the comic figure Fantasio succeeds in using his creative faculty to produce a successful love situation for the unhappy princess, but only in the neglected *Le Fils du Titien* does the artist hero himself actually succeed in both art and love. This story, to be analyzed in detail, offers Musset's own ideal model of the creative process in which the artist's personality is fully integrated: the son of Titian articulates a coherent concept of creativity, actually paints a masterpiece, and also succeeds in love and "life."

Many of Musset's other works offer variations of this paradigm, "deconstructions" of the model that present the artistic personality in disarray or fragments and the hero as a "raté." The problem of the double in Musset, the splitting of his characters often noted and studied since Otto Rank's[1] work in 1914, can be seen as peculiarly the result of the artistic personality's anxiety. There is of course an obvious or manifest use of the double in *Les Nuits,*[2] which assumes the form of a dialogue between the two selves of the poet. The poet's personality is divided into the creative muse, or anima, and the self who desires only to experience the pleasures of love. In the "Nuit de Décembre" an actual double appears, a mirrorlike projection of the poet's solitude, or a personification of the "mal du siècle" that isolates and paralyzes him in his work. Few critics have analyzed in detail, however, the less obvious use of doubles throughout Musset's oeuvre. This could easily furnish the topic for another essay, and therefore my discussion will be limited to examples of doubling specifically related to the creative process.

In *La Confession d'un enfant du siècle* (1836) Musset's protagonist-narrator offers the famous explanation for his failure to love and to succeed in art that underlies all of the works dealing with artists; a society that had lost its spiritual values, failed in all its efforts to transform itself (revolution, empire, restoration), and now accepted the materialistic conclusions of the reigning bourgeoisie could offer only the meaningless and uncomprehending present to the young generation: "Il leur restait donc le présent, l'esprit du siècle, ange du crépuscule qui n'est ni la nuit ni le jour; ils le trouvèrent assis sur un sac de chaux plein d'ossements, serré dans le manteau des égoïstes, et grelottant d'un froid terrible. L'angoisse de la mort leur entra dans l'âme à la vue de ce spectre, moitié momie et moitié foetus."[3] The spirit of the century, a specter who is a double of the lost generation, is death itself projecting the poet's disillusionment and despair. This is the "secret sharer" that Musset himself seemed to have carried with him throughout his own life, taking the form of anguishing experiences of autoscopy and a disenchanting sentiment of the death in all life, the meaninglessness of existence when defined in its tragic limits, and the never-ending destruction by time. A secret sharer who is also a welcome guest, the death instinct figures powerfully in the many manifestations of personality splitting in Musset's works. Victim of his "century," physically weak and mentally anguished, the ego-subject finds through his double, who represents a complacent acceptance of corruption and the corrosion of life, an offer of the consolation of nothingness.

The fragmentation of the personality caused by the pressure and stress of a society in decadence, according to Musset, takes the form of negative and destructive doubling (the opposing self in Roger's terminology), and also can be found in projections of positive and desirable traits and drives. The muse, or animalike spiritual guide, in *Les Nuits* encourages the poet to write and represents the possibility of renewal and rebirth through a deeper comprehension of nature's processes. Tebaldeo, the young artist in *Lorenzaccio,* is an idealistic version of Lorenzo himself, believing in the religious function of art and the sanctity of the mother-city, Florence. He appears as a projection of the best instincts of the youthful Lorenzo before he had adopted a mask of corruption, doubling and thus condemning himself to a tragic end.

Andréa del Sarto (1833) presents a "second generation" artist, a disciple of Raphael, whose overwhelming passion for his wife Lucrèce has consumed his energy and talent and led him to waste the money François I had offered him in commission. He represents the first stages in the degeneration of Renaissance art since the time of the great masters, and Florence in decadence can be seen, as it is in *Lorenzaccio,* as an analogue of contemporary Paris after the collapse of the empire. His love has made him weak, dishonest, and finally guilty of murder when he kills Cordiani, his wife's lover. Cordiani is actually a latent double of Andréa, since he is also a painter, but above all he is characterized as a great lover; he succeeds with Lucrèce where Andréa fails. The artistic personality is thus irreconcilably split into opposing components; the talented self, Andréa, and the alter ego capable of inspiring love, personified in Cordiani (he knows no spiritual life other than that of love for women), destroy each other. There is no integration of the need to experience human love and the desire to create in one personality; the tragic conflict of the drama is constructed on the warring fragments within Andréa del Sarto.

Two plays that do not deal specifically with artists, *Les Caprices de Marianne* (1833) and *On ne badine pas avec l'amour* (1834), should also be included as revelations of the multiple personality. In *Les Caprices* the good and evil instincts are clearly split between Octave and Celio, doubles who are responsible for each other's ruin through an unfortunate reversal of identity in a game of love. Camille and Perdican, the hapless protagonists of *On ne badine pas,* both have doubles in the caricatural forms of the priggish Dame Pluche and the loutish Maître Blazius, figures who have deformed their original, authentic selves and serve to warn the young couple of the inevitable distortions of time. More significantly, there is also a curious doubling within Perdican that resembles that of Lorenzaccio; his authentic self ("le moi-centre" in Starobinski's terms[4]), the simple child of nature, capable of communicating openly and transparently with others, has been obfuscated by the mask of society's artificiality. The "moi" of the present, transformed by society's falsity, is unable to express itself without the frivolous game playing that results in the tragedy of Rosette's death and the consequent failure of love between Perdican and Camille.

Finally in *Les Lettres de Dupuis et Cotonet* (1836–37), a satirical study of romantic conventions and modes, the authorial "nous" suggests a harmonious integration of two aspects of the creative personality—the writer and the critic. Musset is able at last to take distance from both art and love in the form of criticism that itself constitutes another "dédoublement." As we shall see, the composite narrator, Musset's surrogate, examines the literature of romanticism, very similar to that which Musset himself had written, from a detached and decidedly ironic perspective. The voice or self of Musset's own early romanticism is juxtaposed with the mature stance of the disillusioned couple. Their voice doubles in parody that of the youthful artist.

In *Le Fils du Titien* (1838) we discover the only representation of creativity in Musset's entire canon where the artist's personality is made whole; the tragic fragmentations found in the other variations of the artist figure are overcome in this fiction, which can serve as Musset's model.

The conception of the artist expressed in *Le Fils du Titien* is considerably less heroic than that of the Hugo version. The great artist is not a visionary or prophet; indeed, the best art results from hard work, from long apprenticeship with the forms of the past, and above all from the unique inner world of the artist's imagination and the richness of his personal life. Titian and Raphael are the admired models, not Da Vinci or Michelangelo; the superb craftsman is clearly preferred to the visionary genius. Titian's son inherits his vision of art from the past, just as Lorenzo admired the rebellious courage of his ancestors. Here, as is frequently the case in Musset's oeuvre, the artist-protagonist is a second-generation figure who admires his father but despairs of equalling him; indeed, this ambivalent attitude toward the father is perhaps the real source of anxiety and personality splitting in *Le Fils du Titien* and the other works considered. In *La Confession* the same complex of admiration, inferiority, and distress is expressed by the narrator, who feels that the life of his generation has been determined and undermined by the examples of greatness and failure inherited from the fathers of the empire and the grandfathers of the revolution.

Although narrated in the third person, the story is often focalized in the perspective of Titian's son, who presents a theory of artistic creation close to Musset's own conception. "Raphaël a eu tort de devenir amoureux étant peintre";[5] a projected portrait of Raphael dying, seen with his mistress, becomes an icon of Tizianello's philosophy. He explains that a portrait of the anguished and aged painter clinging to his young mistress would symbolize the suffering of the creative person and the realization that love is finally superior to "la gloire" of being an artist. This icon projects the major ideas of Musset's aesthetic philosophy into a condensed visual form: the poetics of suffering found throughout his works, and the final choice of life and love over art. Personal suffering as necessary to the enrichment of artistic sensitivity is indeed the central theme of *Les Nuits;* Tebaldeo also proclaims that the growth of the artist results from the suffering of his people. Of course the simplification of this notion has become an unfortunate romantic cliché often attributed to supposedly self-pitying artists like Musset.

The problem is more complex than has generally been acknowledged, however, since Musset's protagonist is quite conscious of the tragic loss of creative energy due to "suffering" in love, and advocates the choice of sublimation (without using that precise term) or, as alternative, a healthy renunciation of art. Like Balzac, he understands that thought consumes the thinker, and that energy devoted to sentimental and sensual love quite literally uses up the mysterious inner sources of creative vitality. The great Raphael, according to Tizianello, had attempted to create and to continue his amorous exploits even as an old man; his excessive consumption of energy finally exhausted and killed him. The true artist must therefore make the choice to sacrifice sensual experience and channel his given quota of energy into art; his own father, Titian, becomes the ideal model, he who "s'occupa constamment de son art" (*Fils du Titien*, p. 184) for ninety-nine years!

Three qualities are considered essential to the elaboration of a masterwork: patience, the creative role of time, and what Musset calls "recueillement," or a special concentration of energy transformed (sublimated) into creative goals and hard work.

The problem of the conciliation of the needs of art and those of life central to Musset is thus resolved in this fiction alone. Tizianello and the narrator criticize the deplorable facility of current Venetian painting, "premier signe de la décadence des arts" (*Fils du Titien*, p. 184). Titian's son refuses to profit from this easy imitation of past models to achieve success. He declares that were he to devote himself to painting, it would require twenty years of study and a total concentration of energy on art, in order to oppose this decadent trend.

He concludes that this effort would represent too great a sacrifice of his vitality—in effect, the acceptance of a life of suffering to communicate with an uncomprehending public uninterested in his authenticity: "Un seul homme a bien peu de force, quand tout un siècle lutte contre lui" (*Fils du Titien*, p. 185). The break between public and artist seems already irrevocable, and like Musset in the *Confession,* he believes himself to be the victim of a materialistic society that has lost its values.

Although both art and love cannot, therefore, be served and realized by the artist without a destructive consumption of energy (the case of Raphael) or the tragic fragmentation of the artistic personality (as Andréa del Sarto is profoundly torn between painting and love for his wife), the son of Titian rather remarkably achieves a sense of wholeness and realizes his true artistic potential, at least for a brief moment.

The story fairly demands a Jungian interpretation, for its structure provides one of the most illuminating literary examples to be found of Jung's theory of individuation.[6] The process through which a person integrates into his conscious self the voices of his unconscious, and consequently is able to tap the source of his deepest psychic energy, is followed precisely by Titian's son in his quest for self-fulfillment.

According to Jung, whose depth psychology with its spiritualist implications has a particular affinity with romantic literature,[7] the figures of the shadow, the anima, and the "great man" represent elements of the unconscious portion of the psyche in every man's effort to achieve a whole and integrated personality. The shadow (or double) personifies in dreams and other signs from the unconscious the negative aspects of the subject's being; the anima, or feminine principle of the male psyche, becomes a spiritual and moral guide. Finally the "great man" figures the essential spiritual self or cosmic spirit that the subject or ego must discover within himself and that he shares with all other men. For Jung, imaginative literature, religion, and myth offer many examples of the objectification of these archetypes: Dante's Beatrice, and we would add Nerval's Aurélia for the anima; spiritual leaders like Christ and Buddha; and "great men" like Ghandi embody the difficult reconciliation of opposing spiritual forces into a meaningful whole necessary to complete psychic development.

Titian's son is first introduced as an undisciplined but talented adolescent dissipating his energy and his father's fortune (the sign of his power and fame) in gambling and through the familiar pastime of Musset's heroes, "la débauche." The same atmosphere of moral decadence and corruption found in *Lorenzaccio* and *La Confession* is established with the first description of ruins in the Venice of 1580, "un spectacle de destruction": "Des poutres, des pierres, d'énormes blocs de marbre, mille débris encombraient le canal des Prisons. Un incendie récent venait de détruire, au milieu des eaux, la demeure d'un patricien. Des gerbes d'étincelles s'élevaient par instants, et à cette clarté sinistre on apercevait un soldat sous les armes veillant au milieu des ruines" (*Fils du Titien*, p. 131).

Gambling symbolizes the personal and social degradation of Tizianello's generation and is constantly placed in opposition to art: "le jeu résume presque toutes les émotions" (*Fils du Titien*, p. 177). The narrator analyzes in detail its special attraction; for the gambler it offers an extraordinary exaltation of the mind through an intense concentration of desire that renders all other sensations insipid. This exaltation is abstract and fleeting, however, as opposed to that of art, in which it finds a concrete, permanent form, and is thus a waste of creative energy, a characteristic form of a society in decline.

Although he is devoting his energy to society's distractions, Titian's son had already proved his merit as a painter by producing one masterpiece, unfortunately destroyed by fire. In a state of reverie he imagines the portrait of his future lover, Béatrice Loredano Donato, thus revealing a profound desire to realize his artistic potential and at the same time giving visual form to his own anima, in Jungian terms. He dreams her before she appears at dawn, the noble, perfect beauty, an ideal redemptive figure who intends to save him from the disorder of his life. Attracted by the religious mystery of art that she senses in him, she comes to offer the gift (the name Donato means to give) of her love in order to make of him a truly great painter: "elle espérait que l'amour ranimerait la divine étincelle" (*Fils du Titien*, p. 162).

She contributes her love as a treaty in exchange for his work in art, and he begins to paint his final and unique masterpiece—her portrait. What she offers, in a Jungian perspective, is the opportunity to release his spiritual gift, buried still in the recesses of his unconscious. The personification of his anima, she alone can provide him with a means of access to the spiritual source of creativity deep within his psyche, through the liberating experience of generosity in love.

In concrete terms, the effectiveness of the anima's guidance is proved by Tizianello's ability to rediscover his childlike sense of beauty and wonder: "Les choses qui nous ont été jadis familières nous le redeviennent aisément" (*Fils du Titien*, p. 174). Working in his studio, he recovers his authentic "moi-centre." A kind of miraculous return to his childhood apprenticeship with his loving father is effected, which becomes an experience of wholeness and leads him to a superior level of creative work. Unlike Perdican in *On ne badine pas avec l'amour,* who is unable to rid himself of the mask of society's deformity and thus to recapture his childhood sentiment for Camille, Tizianello is given the extraordinary chance to begin anew, reborn through the love of his Béatrice.

He continues to gamble his time and energy, however, and before completing the portrait, he must kill the dragon of his double. Not only is he presented as a dual personality, the frivolous gambler and the true artist capable of a "vivacité extraordinaire" (*Fils du Titien,* p. 176), he actually encounters his shadow figure in the person of an impostor, the false Tizianello. This phony son of Titian is successful through his facile imitations of the masters, his trickery, and his complacency with the immorality of Venetian society. He profits shamelessly from the reputation of his assumed father.

The false Tizianello, shadow, or opposing self is certainly a projection in the text of the true son's bad instincts; his alter ego represents a fear and a danger, for the laziness, vice, and superficiality that characterize him are a source of anxiety in the true son as well.

Now strengthened by his love for Béatrice, the "moi profond," or authentic Tizianello, is prepared to rid himself of the "moi superficiel," the facile and corrupted alter ego. He achieves this through a struggle reminiscent of Jacob's battle with the angel: he attacks him, literally knocking him off the painter's scaffold, which easily symbolizes the false masculine power he had usurped from the father, the real Titian. The fight with his double takes place in church in front of the paintings dedicated to religious values; he is, of course, struggling to preserve the integrity of his own spiritual nature—that is, his creative power as a painter—and to make whole his divided personality. Like the false Tizianello, he had wasted his talent, dispersed his energies, and thereby betrayed his father.

The third and final step in the Jungian scheme enacted in *Le Fils du Titien* is quickly sketched. Titian himself is the complete artistic personality, the "great man" whose exemplary life and art gave expression to the extraordinary complexity of his time. It united, through the rich sensuality of painterly forms and the spiritual insight of his themes, the diverse strains of pagan or mythological, religious, and historical realities that defined the Renaissance sensibility. His son finishes the portrait, which is deemed a masterwork. Thus he incorporates into his conscious life the profound creative impulse or essence imprinted in his unconscious through the father, achieving the wholeness of his personality in the Jungian view by bringing together the social ego and the inner self.

True to his philosophy, however, the son of Titian renounces art; after having achieved the Jungian synthesis of the voices of his unconscious and proved himself deserving of his father's name, he: "resta jusqu'à sa mort fidèle à sa paresse" (*Le Fils du Titien,* p. 189).

Contrary to Louis Lambert, he consciously chooses life over art and devotes all of his energy to the beloved anima figure, Béatrice. He recognizes the necessity for the sublimation of sensual love in order to produce a body of works, but concludes that the sacrifice is too great. In the last analysis, he does not have enough energy to sustain the delicate equilibrium that had rendered him capable of giving a permanent artistic form to his sentiment for Béatrice. He had, in effect, reconciled briefly the needs of art and life, indeed nourishing his painting with his love for her. Blame again falls on society, as it does in the other works dealing with artist figures in Musset. Society is considered incapable of appreciating the kind of art he would hope to produce, and has already disillusioned him with its spiritual bankruptcy and dissipated his strength through its corruption.

> Nous récapitulons maintenant et concluons: c'est faute de connaître l'esprit de notre temps, qu'une foule de talents distingués tombent continuellement dans l'exagération la plus burlesque; c'est faute de se rendre compte à soi-même de ce qu'on vaut, de ce qu'on veut, et de ce qu'on peut, qu'on croit tout pouvoir, qu'on veut plus qu'on ne peut, et que finalement on ne vaut rien. Toute imitation du passé n'est que parodie et niaiserie; on a pu autre fois faire de belles choses sans simplicité; aujourd'hui ce n'est plus possible.[8]

The novella *Le Fils du Titien* contains Musset's most mature statement about the nature of creativity. Its criticism of artificiality and facile imitation and its emphasis on the artist's need to recognize his own limits are forms of demystification or demythification of the romantic, heroic model. *Les Lettres de Dupuis et Cotonet,* written in 1836–37, immediately preceding his series of "nouvelles," forms an amazing document—auto-criticism, satire of romantic conventions and modes, and an almost modernist, pre-Flaubertian treatise on the inadequacy of language. The *Lettres* actually constitute an attempt at a rudimentary type of sociological criticism as well, in which Musset examines the correlation, or more precisely the lack of correspondence, between the operative cultural codes and the mental structures[9] of his group of contemporaries living during the monarchy of Louis-Philippe.

Writers and artists in general, he claims, have not understood the true spirit of the period and have exaggerated and deformed its expression through artificial languages. The cultural codes, which his protagonists examine satirically, are therefore a distortion of reality that ruins the talent of those who work within them and who are in turn determined by them. He discovers the dominant mental structure of his generation to be defined by a new "simplicity" in thought and expression, a refusal of the ideologies of the past (Titian's son will arrive at the same conclusion). A new spirit of emptiness and despair results from disillusionment with society's present forms and its failures of the previous forty years. Materialistic, atheistic, resolutely modern, the new society projects its loss of values and profound disenchantment even in the simple black costume of its young men, an accurate cultural sign.

This ironic text was prepared while Musset was in correspondence with Stendhal, who apparently suggested the typical bourgeois names Dupuis and Cotonet. Critics have often remarked on the resemblance between the tone of Musset's iconoclasm and eighteenth-century Voltairean irony. It is true that many of Musset's techniques—emphasis on incompatibility and inconsistency in situation and language, reductio ad absurdum of complicated arguments (such as those found in Hugo's famous *Préface de Cromwell*), the juxtaposition of contrasting and contradictory voices (exaggerated romantic and flat provincial naiveté)—are those of eighteenth-century satire and parody. A modern reader is perhaps more impressed with the anticipatory aspects of the text. In its form and approach to language it immediately suggests Flaubert's *Bouvard et Pécuchet*. Consisting of four letters written to the editor of *La Revue des deux mondes,* the text presents two provincial gentlemen (even the rhythm of their names resembles that of Flaubert's characters) who are indistinguishable as personalities, since they speak in one voice. Instead of studying the encyclopedia, they attempt to comprehend the current cultural phenomenon—Romanticism. The provincial naiveté of their tone contrasts

ironically and comically with the rather vast knowledge they have accumulated, all to no avail. Letter one concludes with the famous definition of romanticism as an abuse of adjectives, which results from
the protagonists' detailed examination of recent literary history. It
also provides a satire of the romantic school of writers, and a close
reading of examples of romantic style: "Las d'examiner et de peser,
trouvant toujours des phrases vides et des professions de foi in-
compréhensibles, nous en vînmes à croire que ce mot de *romantisme*
n'était qu'un mot, nous le trouvions beau, et il nous semblait que
c'était dommage qu'il ne voulût rien dire" (*Lettres*, p. 875).

Letter two foreshadows *Bouvard et Pécuchet* even more precisely as
Musset's duo examine a series of words in contemporary usage; like
Flaubert's protagonists and their systematic study of the encyclopedia, Dupuis et Cotonet make great efforts to determine the meaning
and possible applicability to their society of the terms *Humanitaire*
and *Perfectibilité,* central concepts of the new philosophico-reformist
schools of St. Simon and Fourier.

The first word is found to be a useless neologism, since the term
philanthropist exists with a precise signification. The second word is,
according to Dupuis and Cotonet, a typical example of the false and
meaningless language of the romantic humanitarian or progressivist
thinkers. In effect, they claim (without using our contemporary terminology) that it is a signifier whose pretended signifieds are contradictory—is it man or things that are capable of being perfected? Perfecting carts and plows is an ancient concept; perfecting man is a
mockery, since men are and always will be "singes plus la parole dont
ils abusent" (*Lettres,* p. 826).

Romantic language is thus characterized by the figure of hyperbole,
neologism, and "mots futiles" (*Lettres*, p. 885); the signs or signifiers
of romantic writing clearly do not correspond to any meaningful signifieds or correct apprehension of "reality" in society's current frame
of reference. Musset severely reduces the philosophies of his contemporaries to the absurd. He displays a conservative political stance
through the use of sharp Voltairean irony and emphasizes in a modern way the arbitrary quality of the exaggerated system of signs that
represents the "new" thought. He insists, through his spokesmen,
that the reformist philosophies currently in fashion are not new at
all; their ideas are quite contradictory and lacking in originality,

since the Greeks had already tried out most of them. In a mocking description of the inconsistencies in the reformers' thought, he announces Flaubert's "club de l'intelligence" in the *Education sentimentale,* where a profusion of contradictory, confusing, and incomprehensible phrases cancel each other out: "qu'ils ne revêtent pas de mots futiles le squelette des temps passés" (*Lettres,* p. 885). Not only are the reformist ideas inconsistent and empty, but they have already been proved useless through the negative experience of ancient societies like Lacedemonia!

In letter three the protagonists attack contemporary journalists who take advantage of this inflated language to produce a discourse capable of dangerous consequences. Irresponsibly, they provoke political discord and confusion in order to create a power structure for themselves based on the use of inflammatory catchwords designed to disguise their duplicity.

Letter four is the most important for my purposes, since Musset now deals directly with creative persons and the process by which the current situation of language transforms them into false artists and "ratés." They are quite literally the victims of romantic discourse, cultural codes composed of false signs that correspond to no recognizable referent or truth about life itself. In a series of satirical and parodic portraits, he singles out a novelist, painter, singer, and woman in love who imitate models lacking in substance and simplicity with disastrous results.

It is in this final letter, the logical outcome of the progression established, that the sociological interpretation of the current situation of language is developed in detail. According to Musset's pair of writers, a historical time when men live without illusions, whether political or metaphysical, cannot foster belief in anything, not even discourse itself. They offer the example of an eloquent speech given by an ancient Greek to convert a sinner; moral discourse happily succeeded in transforming reality. Today, they affirm, no one would believe or be moved by language used in a similar way: "en France, avec nos moeurs et nos idées, après ce que nous avons fait et détruit, avec notre horrible habit noir, il n'y a plus de possible que le simple, réduit à sa dernière expression" (*Lettres,* p. 892).

Actions as well as language are determined by environment, and although truth never changes according to Musset, its form varies:

"or je dis qu'aujourd'hui sa forme doit être simple, et que tout ce qui s'en écarte n'a pas le sens commun" (*Lettres*, p. 892). Contemporary discourse, literature, and language itself, however, fail to represent the truth of an epoch without illusion: "tâchons de parler simplement à propos de simplicité: il n'y a plus, en France de préjugés" (*Lettres*, p. 892).

His examples of contemporary discourse that are empty of substance include the political, the religious, the literary, and the philosophical (humanitarian). The parodic portraits destined to illustrate his theory are brief and masterly in the choice of precise, telling detail and introduce a group of Parisian romantics who are victims of the exaggerated models they seek to imitate. All of these romantic models, which mediate between the world and the character who would experience reality, are faulty in identical ways; they distort the signs of their discourse, thus creating a rupture between cultural codes and their referents, between signifiers and signifieds. When Musset mocks the romantic models of the artist in the name of a desired simplicity, he is invoking the possibility of a direct and nonmediated expression of feeling and ideas. This is a fundamental and characteristic form of nostalgia for an ideal past, before the fall of man and the corruption of his language (the failure of ideologies and systems) that can be found throughout his work. Perdican, for example, yearns for the natural expression of his lost childhood love; Lorenzaccio, for the ability to act without the paralysis his adult knowledge of men has brought; and Titian's son dreams of the harmony and wholeness he experienced as a child learning the language of painting in his father's studio.

Letter four offers the reader a series of humorous sketches of eccentric young romantics. We meet the student Garnier, who behaves like Casanova, only to incur enormous debts. Narcisse, who is "malade d'exagération au troisième degré" (*Lettres*, p. 293), imitates the tormented dandy Byron one day and the more galant Crébillon fils another. He is afflicted with a double personality, comically changing his costume like a madman.

The novelist Evariste and the painter Vincent, who might very well be parodic portraits of Balzac and Delacroix respectively, offer the problem of the artist who deforms his work through an excessive search for ultimate meaning. They both fail to realize that the languages of fiction and painting have their own internal laws and structures; they plan to use them only to discover through them a source of philosophical and metaphysical insight. Constituting a critique of the visionary pretention or ambition of the romantics with which I began this study, these portraits present artists who distort their sign systems and thereby falsify the medium in which they work: "au lieu de se contenter de peindre ce qu'il voit et de constater les nuances, Evariste veut saisir un fil qui puisse tout réunir et tout concentrer; son ambition est d'être le *criterium*, le *nec plus ultra* de l'époque, et d'en posséder seul une clef unique" (*Lettres*, p. 894). Much like Balzac in his search for the essential unifying law behind all social phenomena, Evariste, "qui fait des romans presque lisibles" (*Lettres*, p. 894), learned in 1825 that a genius must be the expression of his century. Following this inflated model: "il n'a repos ni trève qu'il ne découvre l'esprit de son siècle, afin d'en être l'expression; il cherche les moeurs du temps pour les peindre, et ne peut réussir à les trouver" (*Lettres*, p. 894). According to Musset the complexity and variety of these "moeurs" systematically refuse to reveal a philosophical essence.

Vincent, the misunderstood painter, commits the same error: he neglects the beauty of painterly forms and colors in favor of a "pensée profonde" (*Lettres*, p. 894). What is important for him, unfortunately, is not beauty or the painting itself, "ce n'est pas le tableau, c'est ce que le peintre pensait en le faisant, c'est l'idée philosophique qui l'a guidé, c'est l'incalculable suite de méditations *théosophistiques* qui l'ont amené, décidé et contraint à faire un nez retroussé plutôt qu'un nez aquilin" (*Lettres*, p. 894).

The current model of the romantic artist as seer or prophet, Musset concludes, can only lead to a destructive misunderstanding. The languages of the arts are distorted, since signs are made to convey meanings that they cannot possibly formulate, and the value of artistic language as a play of beautiful forms and surfaces is ignored in the search for impossible essences.

Musset is certainly aware of a painful separation between romantic words and the things they are supposed to represent; he has lost all confidence in the hyperbolic language of his time to convey the simple truths about reality as he perceived it. In at least one instance he uses the very terms a modernist might choose to convey this dichotomy: "Voilà de beaux codes d'amour, qu'une pluie de romans où on ne voit que des amoureux phtisiques et des héroïnes échevelées" (*Lettres,* p. 895). Julie, sick with passion, has transformed a healthy sentiment into an unnatural frenzy under the influence of novels that distort the language of love: "Croyez-vous donc qu'il peignent rien d'humain, ces livres absurdes dont on nous inonde, et qui, je le sais, irritent vos nerfs malades? Les romanciers du jour vous répètent que les vraies passions sont en guerre avec la société, et que, sans cesse faussées et contrariées, elles ne mènent qu'au désespoir. Voilà le thème qu'on brode sur tous les tons" (*Lettres,* p. 895). Lelio the singer, whose song is false because his language deforms human emotions, and Julie, who seems to announce Emma Bovary, are deceived by cultural codes consisting of false signs, exaggerated and empty phrases.

Gautier's *Les Jeunes-France* and Musset's *Lettres de Dupuis et Cotonet* represent reasonable and salutary critiques of romantic models of creativity. Although Musset makes no direct reference to his own works, as Gautier does in obvious examples of self-parody, the simplification of style and the relative realism in subject matter found in the later *Nouvelles* would suggest that the writing of the *Lettres* had a therapeutic effect. The tone and florid style of much of his early poetry, and certainly the frenzied excesses of love in *La Confession,* belong to the same cultural codes Dupuis and Cotonet deplore. In any case, the son of Titian will adopt a rational approach to art and to his own limitations. His rejection of the visionary model seems to symbolize an awareness in Musset of a danger inherent in the current practice of romantic art: the tendency of the artist to relinquish control over his medium and thus prevent the development of his own individual potential. By transforming his language into a tool for metaphysical speculation instead of aesthetic beauty, or by adopting cultural codes that ignore the realities of his social context, he deforms the truths of human nature and misrepresents the real needs of the group for which he is a spokesman.

The satires of Gautier and Musset considered alone almost constitute a critique of the metaphysics of "presence" in the sense Derrida attaches to it. The writers featured in *Les Jeunes-France* have no rich, essential being behind the empty facades of their models they imitate. The languages of the romantic cultural codes singled out in Musset's *Lettres* cannot carry the authority to reveal transcendental truth (as could be the case in the poetic language of Victor Hugo's visionary artist), for they are arbitrary, empty of significance, and purely self-referential.

Conclusion

In the last thirty years literary criticism has witnessed the demise of the author as an original presence and the gradual shift in interest from the narrator's point of view to the role of reader response in the interpretation of fiction. The notion of the "text" as an open field of "signifiers" has replaced the concept of a unified work whose "signifieds" can be readily understood thematically. The concept of representation itself has been questioned as the poststructuralists, following Barthes and Derrida, place in doubt the rigid categorization of Saussurean linguistics, thus attempting to "decenter the sign."[1] Contemporary critics (such as those who practice "deconstruction") reintroduce the role of referentiality in texts by emphasizing, not the author, but the influence of ideology, philosophy, and other thought systems on the structure of the signs of art, and the perception of "things" in the real world to which they may sometimes refer.

In spite of their abiding interest in the individual personality of the creative artist, the fallacy of autonomous originality as it might now be termed, the writers of the romantic period in France (from Rousseau's *Rêveries* to the Nervalian world of dream and myth) were also particularly preoccupied with the complex problems of artistic production. They were, as my study has demonstrated, profoundly troubled by the equivocal role of the artist in the new bourgeois society and seriously questioned the function of his work.

My analysis of the romantic representation of creativity included only the male model or version. It was indeed the dominant one in the patriarchal, bourgeois society that issued from the upheavals of 1789 and 1830. There was a perceived need in the new society to fortify the family structure against the development of a free exercise of individual rights, seemingly authorized by successive revolutions and even fostered by many romantic thinkers. Balzac's utopian novel *Le Médecin de campagne* (1833), for example, offers an ideal rural society presided over by a benign and omnipresent father figure. *La Recherche de l'absolu* (1834), on the other hand, presented the dangerous consequences for the family and the social group when the father loses himself in the excesses of creative enterprise. It was incumbent upon Marguerite, the daughter, to assume the male role in order to maintain and support family unity and community values.

The woman as artist is usually represented by the male romantic group as an anomalous figure, androgynous at best, monstrous when she seems to threaten male prerogatives by abandoning her traditional role in marriage. Félicité des Touches, Balzac's fictionalized version of George Sand and a recurring character in the *Comédie humaine*[2] is treated as a superior woman intellectually. Her ideas about the creative process, however, are never developed, although she is a successful artist. Eventually she renounces writing, not for love, but for the convent. Her great intellect and novelistic talent are primarily revealed through her ability to manipulate people (Calyste and Béatrix in the novel *Béatrix*), much as Balzac himself plots the lives of his fictional characters. Ultimately she is presented as an outsider, being an unmarried female writer in the male-dominated world of Parisian letters. Dinah de la Baudraye, the "muse du département,"[3] in spite of her intellectual superiority and, like Mlle des Touches, a capacity for magnanimity, is ridiculed by society and the narrator for her literary pretensions.

George Sand herself, although befriended by Balzac and later treated with respectful admiration by Flaubert, is vilified by Vigny in the *Journal d'un poète* and mocked by Baudelaire.

Another book obviously needs to be written from the perspective of current feminist and sociological criticism to analyze the particular characteristics of the romantic woman's experience of the creative process. Marceline Desbordes Valmore, Delphine Gay, Daniel Stern,

George Sand, and, of course, Mme de Staël would form an important group for consideration.[4]

Balzac's term *muse* is, I am afraid, generally characteristic of the male romantic writer's conception of the role of woman in creativity. As we have seen, the figure of the mysterious Eva rescues Vigny's poet from the impotence of spiritual isolation. Musset's poetic persona enters into dialogue with the inspirational, or "feminine" (sensitive, intuitive), side of his creative personality in the famous series of *Les Nuits*.

André Breton presents the function of Nadja in much the same way, almost one hundred years later. The fragile heroine will represent the head and heart (imagination, compassion), while the poet's strong creative hand structures the materials of art in the famous "autobiographical" fiction *Nadja* (1928). The "feminine" and "masculine" qualities of the mind are both deemed necessary to produce art. But for the romantic poets as for Breton, these qualities are still defined in the stereotypes—feminine sensitivity, intuition, and irrationality vs. masculine rationality, intelligence, and creative force.

French romantic writing about artists and the creative process thus exhibits the self-conscious and self-reflective quality we have come to associate with contemporary approaches to art, found already in the early novel of the first modernist. In *Novembre* (1842), Flaubert presents a typically romantic love story in the first part, which is substantially undermined by the ironic reflections of his narrator in part 2. It is, of course, Flaubert who will maintain and project this double approach to the romantic worldview—admiration for the beauty of its myths, dreams, and illusions and parody of its excesses and its linguistic and literary conventions and clichés.

The German romantics were not alone in correcting the high seriousness and mystical aspirations of their writing with the subversive discourse of "romantic irony" and satire. Of the authors studied here, only Vigny seems to have lacked a comic vein. All of them, however, are deeply moved by the aspirations and great potential of the creative personality. In an age of enormous social upheaval (industrial revolution and the new dominance of the bourgeoisie) and the loss of traditional values amid political instability, the artist did assume heroic proportions even in the real world: witness Lamartine's role as provisional president of the Second Republic, and the importance of Hugo's voice politically and socially even during his exile. At the same time, however, these writers are anguished by the restrictions imposed on the artist in his social milieu (Stello) and the limitations of his personal quota of creative energy (Lambert, Claës). They are disturbed as well by the inadequacies of artistic media to represent their perceptions of reality (*Les Jeunes-France*) and even the arbitrariness of language itself (*Lettres de Dupuis et Cotonet*).

This double postulation of French romanticism we have identified indeed persists until our time. The romantic myth of the artist as seer will be continued through the belief in the power of poetry of Rimbaud's "voyance" and the surrealists' search for a richer and more meaningful reality through art. Even the existential commitment of the prose writer to the specific needs of a chosen audience—Sartre's early view of *engagement* in *Qu'est-ce que la littérature?*—seems to concretize the more abstract and idealistic romantic concept of the artist's function as spiritual guide.

On the other hand, the romantic disenchantment with contemporary forms of experience, cultural codes, and uses of language will find its exponent in Flaubert and twentieth-century thinkers and writers. For the modernists it is imperative to understand first how literature and art function as self-regulating systems before analyzing the relationships among texts, possible referents, and audience. The "nouveaux romanciers" and structuralist theoreticians, for example, tended to view literary forms and language itself as arbitrary tools or sources of invention that are essentially self-referential in nature.

The author as unique originator of his text may indeed be dead, as contemporary critics have pronounced. Consequently, the romantics' preoccupation with artistic personality and vision might seem limited to an outdated form. The myths they engendered, however, about the artist's possibilities and the questions they raised concerning his limitations and those of his media and function in society have dominated our thinking about creativity since the beginning of the nineteenth century. They now form an essential part of the historical development of literature as a cultural institution, which my study has been an attempt to investigate.

Notes

Introduction

1. Henri Evans, *Louis Lambert et la philosophie de Balzac* (Paris: Corti, 1951), p. 247.

2. Albert Béguin, *L'Ame romantique et le rêve* (Paris: Corti, 1939).

3. Many poems of Lamartine, especially the unfinished *Les Visions* and the *Harmonies poétiques et religieuses* (1830), treat poetry as a privileged interpretation of nature. His role as president was an actualization of the romantic myth—a poet in political power. George Sand deals with art and artists, particularly poets and singers—who are protagonists in several works. Music is the form that, for her, becomes a metaphor for art in general: *Les Sept cordes de la lyre.* See Thérèse Marix-Spire, *Les Romantiques et la musique: Le cas de George Sand* (Paris: Nouvelles Editions Latines, 1954).

4. The classic study of English romantic theory is Meyer H. Abrams, *The Mirror and the Lamp: Romantic Theory and the Critical Tradition* (Oxford: Oxford University Press, 1953).

5. Maurice Schroder, *Icarus: The Image of the Artist in French Romanticism* (Cambridge: Harvard University Press, 1961); Gwendolyn Bays, *The Orphic Vision: Seer Poets from Novalis to Rimbaud* (Lincoln: University of Nebraska Press, 1964); Raymond Trousson, *Le Thème de Prométhée dans la littérature européenne,* 2 vols. (Geneva: Droz, 1964); and Bettina Knapp, *The Prometheus Syndrome* (Troy, N.Y.: Whitson Publishing Co., 1979).

6. In the chapters entitled "The Concept of Romanticism in Literary History," and "Romanticism Re-examined," René Wellek, in his *Concepts of Criticism* (New Haven: Yale University Press, 1963), furnishes a critical commentary on the major theoretical studies of romanticism until 1961.

7. Morse Peckham is the major proponent of the concept of romanticism as a new mode of thought based on a dynamic and organic view of man and nature, supplanting the static, mechanistic worldview of the eighteenth century. See his articles

"Towards a Theory of Romanticism," *PMLA* 66 (March 1951): 5–23, and "Towards a Theory of Romanticism: II. Reconsiderations," *Studies in Romanticism* 1 (Autumn 1961): 1–8.

8. François Germain, *L'Imagination d'Alfred de Vigny* (Paris: Corti, 1961).

9. Baudelaire, in a celebrated essay in *L'Art romantique*, declared: "J'ai maintes fois été étonné que la grande gloire de Balzac fût de passer pour un observateur; il m'avait toujours semblé que son principal mérite était d'être visionnaire, et vision-naire passionné. Tous ses personnages sont doués de l'ardeur vitale dont il était animé lui-même. Toutes ses fictions sont aussi profondément colorées que les rêves" (Charles Baudelaire, "Théophile Gautier" in *Curiosités esthétiques* and *L'Art roman-tique* [Paris: Garnier, 1962], pp. 678–79).

Albert Béguin studied the theme of the visionary in Balzac's novels and its rela-tionship to traditional mythical figures such as Satan and Faust in *Balzac visionnaire* (Geneva: Skira, 1947).

10. Balzac, *Louis Lambert*, in *Oeuvres complètes*, 28 vols. (Paris: Guy le Prat, 1901), 20:601.

Chapter I

1. François Germain, *L'Imagination d'Alfred de Vigny* (Paris: Corti, 1961).

2. Alfred de Vigny, *Le Journal d'un poète*, in *Oeuvres complètes*, 2 vols. (Paris: Pléiade, 1948), 2:1218. All future references to the *Journal* are to pages in volume 2 of this edition.

3. A résumé of Vigny's political and social thought in 1829 contains this theme of combat: "Tout le travail de l'humanité qui fermente est le combat de l'ordre contre la liberté. Elle marche vers leur accord. Le désir de l'être isolé est la liberté, le désir de l'être social est l'ordre par besoin de protection. L'empire toujours croissant de l'in-telligence amènera la société à ce point que nul désir de liberté ne soit gêné et que l'ordre l'assure invariablement" (*Journal*, p. 888).

4. George Poulet develops this concept in his article "Timelessness and Roman-ticism," *Journal of the History of Ideas* 15 (1954): 3–22, and in *Les Métamorphoses du cercle* (Paris: Plon, 1961).

5. Vigny compares the movement of the mind, or *esprit*, in the work of creation to an Icarian flight; his language recalls the religious connotation of Baudelaire's "Elévation" in this entry of 1853:

> De l'Esprit. — La marche de l'Esprit n'est pas directe. Si son vol était en droite ligne sans détours, il se perdrait dans l'Infini, au delà de l'atmosphère, où la fa-tigue le ferait tomber épuisé et sans haleine.
>
> Dès le réveil, chaque jour, l'esprit de l'homme est errant et glisse comme l'hirondelle, en tournant, montant, descendant, s'abattant, pointant tout à coup au plus haut du ciel.
>
> L'âme armée du gouvernail de la volonté retient à la poupe et surveille ce vol égaré sans cesse, mais ce n'est que dans les têtes fortes que ce gouverneur est de-bout, en ferme commandant.
>
> Dans les autres têtes, le moment l'emporte sur le travail intérieur et l'étouffe à jamais, ou le rend vulgaire, ainsi qu'il est dans presque tous les hommes. (*Journal*, p. 1305)

"L'Esprit pur" and "La Maison du berger" of *Les Destinées* both present spiritualist affirmation through the theme of the creative mind as a divine force:

Mais notre esprit rapide en mouvements abonde:
Ouvrons tout l'arsenal de ses puissants ressorts.
L'Invisible est réel. Les âmes ont leur monde
Où sont accumulés d'impalpables trésors.
Le Seigneur contient tout dans ses deux bras immenses,
Son Verbe est le séjour de nos intelligences,
Comme ici-bas l'espace est celui de nos corps.
(Vigny, "La Maison du berger," in *Oeuvres*, 1 : 179)

6. Biographical critics have, for example, often insisted on the influence of Marie Dorval in Vigny's creation of female figures, and attribute the apparent contradiction between woman as angelic Kitty Bell and treacherous Delila to his unfortunate affair with the actress.

7. The central section of "La Maison du berger," for example, develops the role of the poet's imagination. Germain has studied in depth the various meanings of imagination for the writers of the first half of the nineteenth century as an introduction to his *L'Imagination d'Alfred de Vigny*.

8. Vigny, "La Beauté idéale," *Oeuvres*, 1 : 235.

Vigny's poem "Le Déluge" (composed in 1823) is an interesting, if largely unsuccessful, attempt at a "transposition d'art" before similar efforts by Gautier. Inspired by Girodet's painting of the Deluge (as well as Poussin's), he attempts to transpose into words the pictorial effects and emotions evoked by the painting. He realizes, however, the almost insurmountable difficulty of the task in view of the complexity and grandeur of the subject, particularly when he considers the need to suggest the sounds and movement of this cosmic drama. It is at this point that he dreams of a more complete art form in which music, poetry, and painting would function together, complementing and interpenetrating each other to produce a more evocative, expressive, complete art. The Pléiade edition of Vigny's poetry omits an important section of "La Beauté idéale," where he explains the need for such forms. These verses immediately precede the lines I have quoted in my text beginning "Descends donc, triple lyre . . ."

Mais quels vastes concerts, quels mots, quelles couleurs
D'un monde châtié traceront les douleurs
Et graveront pour nous sur le flot du déluge
La grandeur du coupable et celle de son juge?
A ce dessin sublime et sur un mont jeté
Manquent le mouvement, les bruits, l'immensité;
Le concert où serait cette scène tracée
Regretterait encor la forme et la pensée,
Et si la poésie essayait ces tableaux
Pour suivre le ravage et la marche des eaux,
Seule et sans les couleurs, les voix mélodieuses,
Elle demanderait ses soeurs harmonieuses.
(*Poésies complètes* [Paris: Garnier, 1962], p. 236)

The mention of music is particularly pertinent when we consider that Vigny admired Berlioz; in fact, he wrote to the Count d'Orsay that he dreamed of Poussin's painting of the Deluge while listening to the dramatic music of Berlioz. Berlioz, of course, attempted to evolve artistic forms that extended the boundaries of pure music. He was inspired by poetry and drama, as his *Mémoires* attest, in an attempt to suggest color and emotion through musical timbre and phrasing.

9. Vigny contrasts the work of the historian with that of the historical novelist through an analogy based on painting: "L'historien doit se placer pour considérer le passé comme le peintre d'un Panorama sur la plus haute élévation de la terre; le romancier doit descendre dans la vallée comme le peintre de genre, s'asseoir dans les chaumières et sous les buissons. Le premier dominera le vieux siècle qu'il veut peindre, de toute la hauteur du sien; le second se transportera au coeur de ce siècle même et l'habitera" (*Journal,* p. 886). In the last stanzas of "La Maison du berger," the poet, regenerated through his love for Eva and his new confidence in his own creative power, prepares to "see" again the richness of the world:

> Viens du paisible seuil de la maison roulante
> Voir ceux qui sont passés et ceux qui passeront.
> Tous les tableaux humains qu'un Esprit pur m'apporte
> S'animeront pour toi, quand devant notre porte
> Les grands pays muets longuement s'étendront.
> (*Oeuvres,* 1:181–82)

10. Charles Baudelaire, "Le Peintre de la vie moderne," in *Curiosités esthétiques* (Paris: Garnier, 1962).

11. The great actor, according to Diderot, is not the one who relives his own emotions on the stage but the one who painstakingly creates each role. The formation of a role, just like that of a poem or painting, involves primarily the creation of a model, or "grand fantôme," by the imagination that is different from nature and from the artist's own personality. Describing the great talent of the actress Clairon, Diderot writes: "sans doute elle s'est fait un modèle auquel elle a d'abord cherché à se conformer; sans doute elle a conçu ce modèle le plus haut, le plus grand, le plus parfait qu'il lui a été possible; mais ce modèle qu'elle a emprunté de l'histoire, ou que son imagination a créé comme un grand fantôme, ce n'est pas elle; si ce modèle n'était que de sa hauteur, que son action serait faible et petite!" (Denis Diderot, *Paradoxe sur le comédien* [Paris: Garnier-Flammarion, 1967], p. 129).

Chapter II

1. Maud Bodkin in *Archetypal Patterns in Poetry* (Oxford: Oxford University Press, 1934) explains the special power of the rebirth archetype: "we may say that all poetry, laying hold of the individual through the sensuous resources of language, communicates in some measure the experience of an emotional but supra-personal life; and that poetry in which we re-live, as such a supra-personal experience though in terms of our own emotional resources, the tidal ebb toward death followed by life renewal, affords us a means of increased awareness, and of fuller expression and control, of our own lives in their secret and momentous obedience to universal rhythms" (p. 89).

2. In major statements about romantic theory, Lovejoy, Peckham, and Wellek have essentially accepted this concept. See Arthur O. Lovejoy, "Romanticism and Plenitude," in *The Great Chain of Being* (New York: Harper and Brothers, 1963), pp. 288–314; Morse Peckham, "Towards a Theory of Romanticism," *PMLA* 66 (1951):5–23; and René Wellek, *Concepts of Criticism* (New Haven: Yale University Press, 1955).

In a recent article entitled "The Rise of Modern Science and the Genesis of Romanticism" (*PMLA* 97 [1982]:8–25), Hans Eichner places in a contemporary perspective the romantic emphasis on a world in a state of "becoming"; in a rather revisionist mode he argues that eighteenth-century science with its comprehension of the mechanistic and determinist laws of nature was closer to the truth and much more productive scientifically than the organicist view of the nineteenth century.

3. Frank P. Bowman, "The Poetic Practices of Vigny's Poèmes philosophiques," *Modern Language Review* 60 (1964):359–68; Maurice Schroder, *Icarus: The Image of the Artist in French Romanticism* (Cambridge: Harvard University Press, 1961); George Bonnefoy, *La Pensée religieuse et morale d'Alfred de Vigny* (Paris: Hachette, 1944). A brief but impressive article on Vigny from a phenomenological perspective is Jean-Pierre Richard's in his *Etudes sur le romantisme* (Paris: Seuil, 1970).

4. Vigny himself, in an entry in the *Journal* of 1836, pointed out the role of irony in his largely misunderstood "Consultation": "Ce qui me surprendrait le plus, si quelque négligence des critiques pouvait surprendre, ce serait de voir que pas un d'eux ne s'est aperçu que l'originalité de *Stello* tient au mélange d'ironie et de sensibilité du Docteur Noir dans ses récits" (*Journal*, pp. 1046–47). In other references to *Stello* he notes the originality of its composition when compared to the taste for symmetrical patterns of unimaginative critics: "Je l'ai dit et pensé souvent, *Stello* a donné le vertige à la critique. — Personne n'a laissé voir qu'il eût senti ni le fond ni la forme même. Comment n'ont-ils pas vu qu'un livre de désespoir devait être désespéré dans sa forme même et dégoûté même de la symétrie des compositions ordinaires, qu'il devait laisser tomber ses récits et ses réflexions feuille à feuille comme un arbre qui se dépouille?" (*Journal*, p. 965). He also analyzes with remarkable precision the element of unresolved tension that constitutes the real originality of *Stello*—the opposition between sacred fount (Docteur Noir) and ivory tower (Stello), life and poetry—which defines the structural as well as the thematic levels of the work. "Le Docteur Noir, c'est la vie. Ce que la vie a de réel, de triste, de désespérant, doit être représenté par lui et par ses paroles, et toujours le malade doit être supérieur à la triste raison de tout ce qu'a la poésie de supérieur à la réalité douloureuse qui nous enserre; mais cette raison selon la vie doit toujours réduire le sentiment au silence et ce silence sera la meilleure critique de la vie" (*Journal*, p. 969). Subsequent references to the works of Vigny are to volumes 1 or 2 of the Pléiade edition.

5. See his defense of the historical novel, "Réflexions sur la vérité dans l'art" (*Oeuvres complètes*, 1:19–25) and his essay on *Chatterton*, "Dernière nuit de travail" (*Oeuvres complètes*, 2:811–21).

6. François Germain, "Les Idées du Docteur Noir," part 6 of *L'Imagination d'Alfred de Vigny* (Paris: Corti, 1961), pp. 443–526.

7. Carl J. Jung, "On the Relation of Analytical Psychology to Poetry" (pp. 65–83) and "Psychology and Literature" (pp. 84–105), in *The Spirit in Man, Art, and Literature* (Princeton, N.J.: Princeton University Press, 1966).

8. Pierre G. Castex, *Vigny, l'homme et l'oeuvre* (Paris: Boivin, 1952).

9. The idea of sacrifice is at the core of Vigny's concept of morality; he never ceased to admire the Christian concept of sacrifice, and the stoical renunciation of personal desires is a recurrent theme in the last pages of his *Journal*. In 1863 he writes of his devotion to his wife: "Jamais mon esprit de sacrifice n'a trouvé de sentiment de reconnaissance proportionné, excepté dans la tendresse de Lydia pour moi" (*Journal*, p. 1381).

In one of the final entries he concludes that his life and work have been devoted to the celebration of the tragic sacrifice in modern society of the noble, the poet, and the soldier. He reiterates the three great themes of his fiction and poetry, and provides a résumé of his understanding of the meaning of his life:

> Etant poète, j'ai montré l'ombrage qu'a du poète tout plaideur d'affaires publiques et le vulgaire des salons et du peuple.
> Officier, j'ai peint ce que j'ai vu: le gladiateur sacrifié aux fantaisies politiques du peuple ou du souverain.
> J'ai dit ce que je sais et ce que j'ai souffert.
> (*Journal*, pp. 1390–91)

10. Vigny, "Les Destinées," in *Poèmes philosophiques*, 1:172.

11. René Wellek, "The Concept of Romanticism in Literary History" (pp. 128–98), in *Concepts of Criticism* (New Haven: Yale University Press, 1963), pp. 188–89.

12. "La Flûte," 1:202.

13. "L'Esprit pur," 1:222.

14. "La Bouteille à la mer," 1:210.

15. All references to "La Maison du berger" are to Volume 1 of the Pléiade edition of Vigny's works and will be designated hereafter in the text as MB.

16. This concept of the human spirit as a dynamic, divine force is found delineated in the *Journal* as early as 1829: "Soumettre le monde à la domination sans borne des esprits supérieurs en qui réside la plus grande partie de l'intelligence divine doit être mon but — et celui de tous les hommes forts du temps" (*Journal*, p. 897).

17. Eva is both goddess and child:

> Viens donc! le ciel pour moi n'est plus qu'une auréole
> Qui t'entoure d'azur, t'éclaire et te défend;
> La montagne est ton temple et le bois sa coupole.
> La terre est le tapis de tes beaux pieds d'enfant.
> (MB, p. 180)

18. The recurrent myth of Prometheus in romantic writing has been studied by Raymond Trousson in *Le Thème de Prométhée dans la littérature européenne*, 2 vols. (Geneva: Droz, 1964) and by Bettina Knapp in *The Prometheus Syndrome* (Troy, N.Y.: Whitson Publishing Co., 1979). Associated with Napoleon and with other figures of rebellion, the image of Prometheus is not considered too heroic to be applied to one's private experience, as Vigny does occasionally in his *Journal*. In this entry he compares his stoic sense of duty and the sacrifice of himself during his army career to the suffering of Prometheus: " — Je marchai une fois d'Amiens à Paris par la pluie avec mon Bataillon, crachant le sang sur toute la route et demandant du lait à toutes les chaumières, mais ne disant rien de ce que je souffrais. Je me laissais dévorer par le vautour intérieur" (*Journal*, p. 960).

19. This letter is found in a collection entitled *Lettres à des poètes*, in *Oeuvres complètes*, 1:996.

Chapter III

1. "Le cristal neuf orné de symboles nouveaux et préservateurs." Alfred de Vigny, *Daphné*, in *Oeuvres complètes*, 2 vols. (Paris: Pléiade, 1948), 2:843. Subsequent references to *Daphné* (D) are to pages in volume 2 of this edition and will be cited in the text.

2. Some biographers insist that Vigny never did renounce his ambition to play an active role in the political life of France; he has even been accused of working for the secret police during the Second Empire.

3. George Bonnefoy, *La Pensée religieuse et morale d'Alfred de Vigny* (Paris: Hachette, 1944), p. 209.

4. Trivulce, a resident of the *pays latin* had been endowed with an appropriate name, since *vulsus* can mean to have an unusual softness of the soul.

5. Bonnefoy, *La Pensée religieuse*, p. 247.

Chapter IV

1. Victor Hugo, *William Shakespeare* (Paris: Hetzel, 1864), p. 35. All subsequent references are to this edition and will be cited as *W.S.* in the text.

2. Morse Peckham, "Towards a Theory of Romanticism," *PMLA* 66 (March 1951): 5–23. This is the first in an important series of articles and books by Peckham that present romanticism in its cultural context. He defines it as a far-ranging new mode of thought based on a "dynamic" and "organic" concept of nature.

3. Paul Bénichou, *Le Sacre de l'écrivain, 1760–1830* (Paris: Corti, 1973).

4. Victor Brombert analyzed the function of the image and theme of the prison in romantic literature in *La Prison romantique* (Paris: Corti, 1975). See particularly the chapter on Hugo: "Victor Hugo: Prison de la pensée, prison de l'espace," pp. 93–125.

5. Susanne Nash, *"Les Contemplations" of Victor Hugo: An Allegory of the Creative Process* (Princeton, N.J.: Princeton University Press, 1977).

6. Ernst Kris and Otto Kurz, *Legend, Myth, and Magic in the Image of the Artist* (New Haven: Yale University Press, 1979). This work first appeared in 1934.

7. Victor Hugo, "Pasteurs et troupeaux," in *Les Contemplations* (1856) (Paris: Garnier, 1962), p. 229.

8. Silvano Arieti, *Creativity, the Magic Synthesis* (New York: Harper, Colophon Books, 1976), p. 12.

9. Ibid., p. 186.

10. Jean-Bertrand Barrère comments on Hugo's *Post-scriptum de ma vie* in his *Hugo: L'homme et l'oeuvre* (Paris: Boivin, 1952), pp. 245–46.

11. Carl Jung distinguishes between two modes of creative activity, the "personalistic" and the "visionary," in his essay "Psychology and Literature" in *The Spirit of Man, Art, and Literature* (Princeton, N.J.: Princeton University Press, 1971), pp. 84–105. Hugo as a visionary artist has been studied by Gwendolyn Bays in *The Orphic Vision: Seer Poets from Novalis to Rimbaud* (Lincoln: University of Nebraska Press, 1964). Hermine Riffaterre, in *L'Orphisme dans la poésie romantique, thèmes et style surnaturalistes* (Paris: Nizet, 1970), includes an extensive bibliography of the subject, but no detailed discussion of Victor Hugo.

12. See chapter 3, "Pour qui écrit-on?" in Jean-Paul Sartre's *Qu'est-ce que la littérature* (1948) for a discussion of the writer's complex relationship with his public (Paris: Gallimard, Collection Idées, 1978).

13. The Marxist critic Lucien Goldmann made a similar assertion; great art, including the realist novel, is by definition "critique" and "oppositionnel." It constitutes a form of resistance to reification in the dominant social ideology, in the name of authentic, transindividual values. (*Pour une sociologie du roman* [Paris: Gallimard, Collection Idées, 1964], p. 52.)

Chapter V

1. The writer who is the head of the Cénacle and even offers a theory of fiction in *Les Illusions perdues*. Artist figures play a central role in the following major works of Balzac: *Béatrix, La Muse du département, Illusions perdues, Pierre Grassou, La Cousine Bette, Massimila Doni, Le Chef-d'oeuvre inconnu, Louis Lambert, Gambara, Les Proscrits, Sarrasine.*

2. See Charles Affron, *Patterns of Failure in the "Comédie humaine"* (New Haven: Yale University Press, 1966). Pierre Laubriet, in his very detailed, scholarly study of the concepts of artistic creation in Balzac, *L'Intelligence de l'art chez Balzac* (Paris: Didier, 1958), devotes a chapter to "Les Types d'artiste: 1. les ratés."

3. One of the most important visionary figures in Balzac's fiction, Frenhofer, is presented in *Le Chef-d'oeuvre inconnu* (1831).

4. *Gambara* (1837) is another of the *Etudes philosophiques* that develops in detail the tragic results for the creative person, in this case a composer, of an obsession with theorizing.

5. ". . . pour Balzac, l'expérience religieuse et l'expérience esthétique sont une seule et même chose. Il croit à la significance métaphysique de l'art, à la transfiguration magique de la matière par l'art. . . . Même il n'est pas loin de penser que l'art est la véritable religion du monde moderne, et que le voyant futur c'est l'artiste. Ceci est chez lui une idée vécue, une intuition née de sa propre expérience d'artiste créateur. Cette certitude est d'ailleurs universelle chez les romantiques, elle est le fond même du romantisme." (Henri Evans, *"Louis Lambert" et la philosophie de Balzac* [Paris: Corti, 1957], p. 247.)

6. Balzac, *La Peau de chagrin* (Paris: Garnier, 1955), pp. 309, 310.

7. Ibid., pp. 310–11.

8. Ibid., p. 310.

9. Henri Evans's *"Louis Lambert" et la philosophie de Balzac* is a detailed study of the genesis of the novel as well as the philosophical thought it contains.

10. Balzac, *Louis Lambert,* in *Oeuvres complètes,*28 vols. (Paris: Guy le Prat, 1961), 20:558. All subsequent references are to this edition and will be cited in the text as *LL*.

11. He is the protagonist of a short story entitled "Jean-François les bas-bleus" and first published in 1832 by Charles Nodier in a collection of "contes et nouvelles."

12. The prototype of these letters from Paris is probably Saint-Preux's letter to Julie in *La Nouvelle Héloïse,* or Rousseau's own impressions of Parisian life found in the *Confessions.*

13. See Arthur O. Lovejoy, *The Great Chain of Being* (Cambridge: Harvard University Press, 1936; especially chapter 10, "Romanticism and the Principle of Plenitude."

14.

L'idée première de la Comédie humaine fut d'abord chez moi comme un rêve, comme un de ces projets impossibles que l'on caresse et qu'on laisse s'envoler; une chimère qui sourit, qui montre son visage de femme et qui déploie aussitôt ses ailes en remontant dans un ciel fantastique. Mais la chimère, comme beaucoup de chimères, se change en réalité, elle a ses commandements et sa tyrannie auxquels il faut céder.

Cette idée vint d'une comparaison entre l'Humanité et l'Animalité.

"Avant-propos à *La Comédie humaine,*" in *Anthologie des préfaces de romans français du XIXᵉ siècle,* ed. Herbert S. Geishman and Kernan B. Whitworth, Jr. [Paris: Juilliard, 1964], p. 190. Balzac's "Avant-Propos" was first published in 1842.)

15. Rousseau in the "Troisième promenade" of the *Rêveries* describes the spiritual crisis he experienced as a result of his contemporaries' philosophical thoughts:

Souvent des arguments nouveaux que j'entendais faire me revenaient dans l'esprit à l'appui de ceux qui m'avaient déjà tourmenté. Ah! me disais-je alors dans des serrements de coeur prêts à m'étouffer, qui me garantira du désespoir si dans l'horreur de mon sort je ne vois plus que des chimères dans les consolations que me fournissait ma raison? Si, détruisant ainsi son propre ouvrage, elle renverse tout l'appui d'espérance et de confiance qu'elle m'avait ménagé dans l'adversité? Quel appui que les illusions qui ne bercent que moi seul au monde?

Combien de fois dans ces moments de doute et d'incertitude je fus prêt à m'abandonner au désespoir.

(J. J. Rousseau, *Les Rêveries du promeneur solitaire* (Paris: Garnier, 1960), pp. 36–37). Nerval's narrator in *Aurélia*, attempting to reconstruct an acceptable version of Christian belief, presents his anguished situation in these terms: "Mes premières années ont été trop imprégnées des idées issues de la Révolution, mon éducation a été trop libre, ma vie trop errante, pour que j'accepte facilement un joug qui, sur bien des points, offenserait encore ma raison. Je frémis en songeant quel chrétien je ferais si certains principes empruntés au libre examen des deux derniers siècles, si l'étude encore des diverses religions ne m'arrêtaient sur cette pente" (Gérard de Nerval, *Aurélia*, in *Oeuvres complètes,* 2 vols. [Paris: Garnier, 1958], 1:797–98.)

16. The narrator records Lambert's early meditations on language and its origins, in which he emphasizes the mysterious unity of words, ideas, and things; or as we would now say, the strong links between signifiers and their signifieds and referents: "La plupart des mots ne sont-ils pas teints de l'idée qu'ils représentent extérieurement?" (*LL*, p. 507). "Tous sont empreints d'un vivant pouvoir qu'ils tiennent de l'âme, et qu'ils y restituent par les mystères d'une action et d'une réaction merveilleuse entre la parole et la pensée. . . . Par leur seule physionomie, les mots raniment dans notre cerveau les créatures auxquelles ils servent de vêtement." (*LL*, p. 508).

17. See Jean Starobinski's illuminating study *Jean-Jacques Rousseau, La Transparence et l'obstacle* (Paris: Gallimard, 1970).

18. Jean Mourot in his *Chateaubriand: Le génie d'un style, rythme, et sonorité dans les "Mémoires d'outre-tombe"* (Paris: Armand Colin, 1960) claims that 2,700 sentences out of 3,300 in the *Mémoires d'outre-tombe* repeat the same "existential" pattern, translating in their rhythm the essence of Chateaubriand's melancholy, his eloquent obsession with the death of all things already informing every vital movement. Examples of this "respiration éloquente de la mort," according to Mourot, are "Vieux chêne / le temps a fauché sur ta racine jeune fille et jeune fleur." "Dans les bruyères armoricaines, / elle n'était qu'une solitaire avantagée de beauté, de génie et de malheur."

19. Without using the term *sublimation* specifically, Balzac frequently deals with that phenomenon. *Le Curé de Tours,* for example, offers the clear case of a priest (l'Abbé Birotteau) who has transformed his sexual desires into an inordinate passion for furniture—"la convoitise mobilière." The opening pages of the novel present a classic example of Balzac's anticipation of Freud's concept.

Chapter VI

1. Quoted from Balzac's *Une Fille d'Eve,* by Albert Béguin in *Balzac lu et relu* (Paris: Seuil, 1965), p. 94.

2. Andre Dabezies, in his comprehensive survey *Le Mythe de Faust* (Paris: Colin, 1972), identifies three distinct variants, which he examines historically, psychologically, and, finally, in a symbolic context. The Renaissance sorcerer-magician figure becomes the disenchanted searcher for the infinite in the nineteenth century, to be followed in the twentieth by the superman or conqueror (p. 65). Charles Dédéyan studied the presence of Faustian figures and themes in specific works in his four-volume *Le Thème de Faust dans la littérature européenne* (Paris: Minard, 1954).

3. The actual source of the etymology of the name Claës is "Nicolaus," of which it is a shortened version: Albert Carnoy, *Origines des noms de famille en Belgique* (Louvain: Louvain Publications Universitaires, 1953). Balzac frequently chose the names of his characters for their symbolic connotations.

4. Madeleine Fargeaud, *Balzac et "La Recherche de l'absolu"* (Paris: Hachette, 1968).

5. Balzac, *La Recherche de l'absolu* (Paris: Albin Michel, 1951), p. 149. All subsequent references are to this edition and will be cited in the text as *RA*.

6. Emmanuel is compared to Christ, and it is, of course, he, through marriage with Marguerite, who redeems the Claës family. The possibility of this rebirth is foreseen at the moment of Josephine's death; Emmanuel will "save" Marguerite from her father. Their alliance signals the beginning of a new family unit under the sign of Christ and through a humble or Christian acceptance of nature. Emmanuel is a son but also Solis—"soleil"—sun, offering Christian light to the Claës family. This image is contrasted by the narrator with the pagan images of Promethean fire and solar energy associated with Balthazar.

7. On Balthazar's side, in addition to the devilish stranger who inaugurates his search for the absolute, there is also the figure of his trusted servant, Lemulquinier, who recalls the companion Wagner in Goethe's *Faust*. Lemulquinier's name, according to our narrator, means merchant of flaxen thread, and he symbolizes "l'histoire de la Flandre, de son fil et de son commerce" (*RA*, p. 79). In his unshakable devotion to his master throughout the quest, he seems to represent the simple faith of the common people in the future benefits to be accrued from the work of genius.

8. Lucien Goldmann, in his *Pour une sociologie du roman* (Paris: Gallimard, 1964).

9. Tzvetan Todorov studies the narrative function of the enigma or secret in the chapters on Henry James in his *Poétique de la prose* (Paris: Seuil, 1971). See also Roland Barthes's analysis of the code of the enigma in his *S/Z* (Paris: Seuil, 1970).

10. In particular *La Peau de chagrin* (1831) dramatizes Balzac's theory of human energy consumed by thought and contains yet another example of the Faustian pact.

11. *Les Martyrs ignorés,* in vol. 27, *Oeuvres complètes,* 28 vols. (Paris: Guy le Prat, 1961), p. 473.

12. André Allemand studies Balzac's many strategies to unify his fictional world in *Unité et structure de l'univers balzacien* (Paris: Plon, 1965).

13. Sociological explanations for the changing meanings of the pattern that defines this quest for values would be the subject of another study. George Lukács, Pierre Barbéris, and other Marxist critics have already studied Balzac's work in view of his portrait of the new capitalist economy, particularly the phenomenon of reification and the rise and fall of the liberal bourgeoisie.

Balzac's own pessimism about the effects of exaggerated materialism and individualism, which he, however, views as direct results of the French Revolution and the degeneration of the traditional social structure, is clearly manifest in his final novels dealing with Parisian society: *Les Parents pauvres* comprising *La Cousine Bette* (1846) and *Le Cousin Pons* (1847).

Chapter VII

1. Théophile Gautier, "Du Beau dans l'art," in *L'Art moderne* (Paris: Michel Levy, 1856). All subsequent references are to this edition and will be cited in the text.
2. Meyer Howard Abrams, *The Mirror and the Lamp: Romantic Theory and the Critical Tradition* (Oxford: Oxford University Press, 1953).
3. Théophile Gautier, *Les Jeunes-France, romans goguenards* (1833), ed. René Jasinski (Paris: Nouvelle Bibliothèque romantique, Flammarion, 1974). Subsequent references are to this edition and will be cited in the text.
4. Linda Hutcheon has neatly clarified the distinctions and interrelationships between irony, parody, and satire in her article "Ironie, satire, parodie: Une approche pragmatique de l'ironie," *Poétique* 36 (1978):467–77.
5. Théophile Gautier, "Onuphrius," in *Contes fantastiques* (Paris: Corti, 1969), p. 31. Subsequent references are to this edition and will be cited in the text as (*ON*).
6. Charles Baudelaire, "La Cloche fêlée," in *Les Fleurs du mal* (Paris: Garnier, 1961), p. 78.

Chapter VIII

1. Otto Rank, *The Double: A Psychoanalytic Study,* trans. and ed. Harry Tucker, Jr. (Chapel Hill: University of North Carolina Press, 1971).
2. *Les Nuits* is discussed by Rank and is also analyzed briefly by Robert Rogers in *A Psychoanalytic Study of the Double in Literature* (Detroit: Wayne State Press, 1970), pp. 23–24. He uses the term *decomposition* to characterize the splitting off of personality and distinguishes between latent and manifest examples of multiple personality traits in his examination of many literary characters.
3. Alfred de Musset, *La Confession d'un enfant du siècle* (Paris: Classiques Garnier, 1956), pp. 7–8.
4. Jean Starobinski distinguishes between the authentic soul-center (or "moi-centre") and the self at the circumference of life, or the social self. Using this terminology, he analyzes J.-J. Rousseau's troubled efforts to move from the transparent solitude of his "moi-centre" to communication with others in the outer circle of social experience, where he encounters insuperable obstacles. See his *J.-J. Rousseau: La Transparence et l'obstacle* (Paris: Gallimard, 1971).
5. Alfred de Museet, *Le Fils du Titien,* in *Nouvelles* (Paris: Classiques Garnier, 1948), p. 182. All subsequent references are to this edition and will be cited in the text. This "nouvelle" was first published in May 1838 in *La Revue des deux mondes.*
6. Carl Jung, "Contributions to the Symbolism of the Self," part 1 in *Psyche and Symbol* (New York: Doubleday Anchor Books, 1958).
7. See Ross Woodman, "Shaman, Poet, and Failed Initiate: Reflections on Romanticism and Jungian Psychology," *Studies in Romanticism* 19, no. 1 (1980):51–82.
8. Alfred de Musset, *Lettres de Dupuis et Cotonet* in *Oeuvres complètes* (Paris: Seuil, 1963), p. 895. All subsequent references are to this edition and will be cited in the text.
9. Musset is examining these cultural codes in a manner that suggests Lucien Goldmann's definition of the relationship between fictional works and society: "Le grand écrivain est précisément l'individu exceptionnel qui réussit à créer dans un cer-

tain domaine, celui de l'oeuvre littéraire (ou picturale, conceptuelle, musicale, etc.), un univers imaginaire, cohérent ou presque rigoureusement cohérent, dont la structure correspond à celle vers laquelle tend l'ensemble du groupe" (*Pour Une Sociologie du roman* [Paris: Gallimard, Collection Idées, 1964], p. 347).

Conclusion

1. See the anthology of essays including poststructuralist and deconstructionist criticism entitled *Textual Strategies,* edited by Josué Harari (Baltimore: Johns Hopkins University Press, 1980), especially Roland Barthes, "From Work to Text," and Michel Foucault, "What Is an Author?"

2. Félicité des Touches, or Camille Maupin, her pseudonym, is a protagonist in *Béatrix* (1839). She also appears in *Illusions perdues* (1835–43) and *Splendeurs et misères des courtisanes* (1837–43) as well as in *Honorine* (1843). Always presented as a magnanimous spirit and a beautiful woman, she aids Lucien de Rubempré financially and renounces the poet Calyste to the desirable Béatrix.

3. Balzac's other major female literary figure, Dinah de la Baudraye, protagonist of *La Muse du département* (1843), also appears in *Un Prince de la bohème* (1840). Her attempts at independence and literary creativity alternate with a return to her aristocratic and mediocre husband. Although viewed as spiritually and morally superior to the mediocrities in her milieu, her artistic efforts are treated with irony and scorn.

Unfortunately, "La Femme auteur" is only a fragment of a work begun in Russia in 1847. Mme Hannequin, the author in question, is compared to Camille Maupin, but the text does not deal with the problem of creativity in any detail.

4. Interesting examples of work already done on the subject of the female writer and creativity include the following studies, which deal in part with romantic women in England and France:

Bellet, Roger, ed. *La Femme au dix-neuvième siècle: Littérature et idéologie* (Lyon: Presses Universitaires de Lyon, 1979).

Brée, Germaine. *Women Writers in France: Variations on a Theme* (New Brunswick, N.J.: Rutgers University Press, 1973).

Gilbert, Sandra M., and Susan Gubar. *The Madwoman in the Attic: The Woman Writer and the Nineteenth-Century Literary Imagination* (New Haven: Yale University Press, 1979).

Gutwirth, Madelyn. *Madame de Staël, Novelist: The Emergence of the Artist as Woman* (Urbana: University of Illinois Press, 1978).

Moers, Ellen. *Literary Women: The Great Writers* (Garden City, N.Y.: Doubleday, 1976).

Spacks, Patricia Meyer. *The Female Imagination* (New York: Knopf, 1975).

Selected Bibliography

Abrams, Meyer Howard. *The Mirror and the Lamp: Romantic Theory and the Critical Tradition.* Oxford: Oxford University Press, 1953.
———. *Natural Supernaturalism, Tradition, and Revolution in Romantic Literature.* New York: W. W. Norton, 1971.
Abt, Lawrence E., and Rosner, Stanley, eds. *The Creative Experience.* New York: Dell, 1970.
Affron, Charles. *Patterns of Failure in the "Comédie humaine."* New Haven: Yale University Press, 1966.
Albouy, Pierre. *La Création mythologique chez Victor Hugo.* Paris: Corti, 1963.
Allemand, André. *Unité et structure de l'univers balzacien.* Paris: Plon, 1965.
Allen, James Smith. *Popular French Romanticism: Authors, Readers, and Books in the Nineteenth Century.* Syracuse: Syracuse University Press, 1981.
Arieti, Silvano. *Creativity, the Magic Synthesis.* New York: Harper, Colophon Books, 1976.
Balzac, Honoré de. *La Recherche de l'absolu.* Paris: Albin Michel, 1951.
———. *Le Curé de Tours,* in vol. 6, *Oeuvres complètes,* 28 vols. Paris: Guy le Prat, 1961.
———. *Illusions perdues,* in vol. 12, *Oeuvres complètes,* 28 vols. Paris: Guy le Prat, 1961.
———. *Louis Lambert,* in vol. 20, *Oeuvres complètes,* 28 vols. Paris: Guy le Prat, 1961.
———. *Les Martyrs ignorés,* in vol. 27, *Oeuvres complètes,* 28 vols. Paris: Guy le Prat, 1961.
———. "Avant-propos à *La Comédie humaine,*" in *Anthologie des préfaces de romans français du XIXᵉ siècle.* Edited by Herbert S. Geishman and Kernan B. Whitworth, Jr. Paris: Julliard, 1964.

Barbéris, Pierre. *Balzac et le mal du siècle: Contribution à une physiologie du monde moderne.* Tome 1: *1799–1829, Aliénations et prises de conscience.* Tome 2: *1830–1833, Une expérience de l'absurde: De la prise de conscience à l'expression.* Paris: Gallimard, 1970.

———. *Balzac: Une mythologie réaliste.* Paris: Larousse, 1971.

———. *Mythes balzaciens.* Paris: Colin, 1972.

Barrère, Jean-Bertrand. *Hugo: L'Homme et l'oeuvre.* Paris: Boivin, 1952.

Barricelli, Jean-Pierre, and Gibaldi, Joseph. *Interrelations of Literature.* New York: Modern Language Association of America, 1982.

Barthes, Roland. *S/Z.* Paris: Seuil, 1970.

Bays, Gwendolyn. *The Orphic Vision: Seer Poets from Novalis to Rimbaud.* Lincoln: University of Nebraska Press, 1964.

Baudelaire, Charles. *Curiosités esthétiques* and *l'Art romantique.* Paris: Garnier, 1962.

Béguin, Albert. *L'Ame romantique et le rêve.* Paris: Corti, 1939.

———. *Balzac visionnaire.* Geneva: Skira, 1946.

———. *Balzac lu et relu.* Paris: Seuil, 1965.

Bellemin-Noël, Jean. *Psychanalyse et littérature.* Paris: Presses Universitaires de France, 1978.

Bellet, Roger, ed. *La Femme au dix-neuvième siècle: Littérature et idéologie.* Lyon: Presses Universitaires de Lyon, 1979.

Bénichou, Paul. *Le Sacre de l'écrivain, 1760–1830.* Paris: Corti, 1973.

———. *Le Temps des prophètes: Doctrines de l'âge romantique.* Paris: Gallimard, 1977.

Berger, John. *Art and Revolution.* London: Weidenfeld and Nicolson, 1969.

Besser, Gretchen, R. *Balzac's Concept of Genius: The Theme of Superiority in the "Comédie humaine."* Geneva: Droz, 1969.

Bodkin, Maud. *Archetypal Patterns in Poetry.* Oxford: Oxford University Press, 1934.

Bolster, Richard. *Stendhal, Balzac, et le féminisme romantique.* Paris: Lettres Modernes, 1970.

Bonaparte, Marie. *Edgar Poe.* Paris: Denoël et Steele, 1935.

Bonnefoy, George. *La Pensée religieuse et morale d'Alfred de Vigny.* Paris: Hachette, 1944.

Bourgeois, René. *L'Ironie romantique: Spectacle et jeu de Mme de Staël à Gérard de Nerval.* Grenoble: Presses Universitaires de Grenoble, 1974.

Bousquet, Jacques. *Les Themès du rêve dans la littérature romantique.* Paris: Didier, 1964.

Bowman, Frank P. "The Poetic Practices of Vigny's *Poèmes philosophiques.*" *Modern Language Review* 60 (1964): 359–68.

———. *Le Christ romantique.* Geneva: Droz, 1974.

Brée, Germaine. *Women Writers in France: Variations on a Theme.* New Brunswick, N.J.: Rutgers University Press, 1973.

Brombert, Victor. "The Artist as Hero." *The Hero in Literature.* Greenwich, Conn.: Fawcett Publications, 1968.

————. *La Prison romantique*. Paris: Corti, 1975.

————. *Victor Hugo and the Visionary Novel*. Cambridge: Harvard University Press, 1984.

Brooks, Peter. *The Melodramatic Imagination, Balzac, Henry James, Melodrama, and the Mode of Excess*. New Haven: Yale University Press, 1976.

Carnoy, Albert. *Origines des noms de famille en Belgique*. Louvain: Louvain Publications Universitaires, 1953.

Charleston, D. G., ed. *The French Romantics*. Cambridge: Cambridge University Press, 1984.

Chasseguet-Smirgel, Jeanne. *La Psychanalyse de l'art et de la créativité*. Paris: Payot, 1971.

Culler, Jonathan. *Structuralist Poetics*. Ithaca, N.Y.: Cornell University Press, 1975.

Dabezies, André. *Le Mythe de Faust*. Paris: Colin, 1972.

Dédéyan, Charles. *Le Thème de Faust dans la littérature européenne*. 4 vols. Paris: Minard, 1954.

Donoghue, Denis. *The Sovereign Ghost: Studies in Imagination*. Berkeley and Los Angeles: University of California Press, 1976.

Duchet, Claude, and Neefs, Jacques, eds. *Balzac: L'Invention du roman*. Paris: Belfond, 1982.

————. "Ecrivains et artistes en 1830." *Romantisme* 12 (1983): 151–59.

Eichner, Hans. "The Rise of Modern Science and the Genesis of Romanticism." *PMLA* 97 (1982): 8–25.

Engell, James. *The Creative Imagination: Enlightenment to Romanticism*. Cambridge: Harvard University Press, 1981.

Evans, Henri. *"Louis Lambert" et la philosophie de Balzac*. Paris: Corti, 1951.

Fargeaud, Madeleine. *Balzac et "La Recherche de l'absolu."* Paris: Hachette, 1968.

Fehrman, Carl. *Poetic Creation: Inspiration or Craft*. St. Paul: University of Minnesota Press, 1980.

Felman, Shoshana. *La Folie et la chose littéraire*. Paris: Seuil, 1978.

Fischer, Ernest. *The Necessity of Art*. Baltimore: Penguin Books, 1963.

Fizaine, Jean-Claude. "Génie et Folie dans *Louis Lambert, Gambara*, et *Massimila Doni*." *Revue des sciences humaines* 175 (1979): 61–75.

Foucault, Michel. *L'Ordre du discours*. Paris: Gallimard, 1971.

Frappier-Mazur, Lucienne. *L'Expression métaphorique dans la "Comédie humaine": Domaine social et physiologique*. Paris: Klincksiek, 1976.

Freud, Sigmund. *On Creativity and the Unconscious*, including "The Relation of the Poet to Day-Dreaming," "The Occurrence in Dreams of Material from Fairy Tales," and "The 'Uncanny.'" New York: Harper and Row, 1958.

————. *The Interpretation of Dreams*. New York: Basic Books, 1960.

Furst, Lilian R. *The Contours of European Romanticism*. Lincoln: University of Nebraska Press, 1979.

Gans, Eric. *Musset et le drame tragique*. Paris: Corti, 1974.

Garvin, Harry. *The Arts and Their Interpretation.* Lewisburg, Pa.: Bucknell University Press, 1979.

Gastinel, Pierre. *Le Romantisme d'Alfred de Musset.* Paris: Hachette, 1933.

Gautier, Théophile. *Les Jeunes-France, romans goguenards.* Edited by René Jasinski. 1833; reprint, Paris: Nouvelle Bibliothèque Romantique, Flammarion, 1974.

―――. *Contes fantastiques* (1857). Paris: Corti, 1969.

―――. "Du Beau dans l'art" in *L'Art moderne.* Paris: Michel Levy, 1856.

Germain, François. *L'Imagination d'Alfred de Vigny.* Paris: Corti, 1961.

Ghiselin, Brewster. *The Creative Process: A Symposium.* Los Angeles: University of California Press, 1954.

Gilbert, Sandra M., and Susan Gubar. *The Madwoman in the Attic: The Woman Writer and the Nineteenth-Century Literary Imagination.* New Haven: Yale University Press, 1979.

Goldmann, Lucien. *Pour une sociologie du roman.* Paris: Gallimard, Collection Idées, 1964.

Gombrich, Ernst Hans. *Art and Illusion.* Princeton, N.J.: Princeton University Press, 1960.

Grant, Richard B. *The Perilous Quest: Image, Myth, and Prophecy in the Narratives of Victor Hugo.* Durham, N.C.: Duke University Press, 1968.

Gutwirth, Madelyn. *Madame de Staël, Novelist: The Emergence of the Artist as Woman.* Urbana: University of Illinois Press, 1978.

Haig, Stirling. "From Cathedral to Book, from Stone to Press: Hugo's Portrait of the Artist in *Notre-Dame de Paris.*" *Stanford French Review* 3 (Winter 1979): 343–50.

Harari, Josué, ed. *Textual Strategies.* Baltimore: Johns Hopkins University Press, 1980. See especially Roland Barthes, "From Work to Text," and Michael Foucault, "What Is an Author?"

Hauser, Arnold. *The Social History of Art.* 4 vols. New York: Vintage Books, 1958–60.

Houston, John Porter. *The Demonic Imagination: Style and Theme in French Romantic Poetry.* Baton Rouge: Louisiana State University Press, 1969.

Hugo, Victor. *Les Contemplations* (1856). Paris: Garnier, 1962.

―――. *William Shakespeare.* Paris: Hertzel, 1864.

Hutcheon, Linda. "Ironie, satire, parodie: Une approche pragmatique de l'ironie." *Poétique* 36 (1978): 467–477.

Juden, Brian. *Traditions orphiques et tendances mystiques dans le Romantisme français.* Paris: Klincksiek, 1971.

Jung, Carl J. *The Spirit in Man, Art, and Literature.* Princeton, N.J.: Princeton University Press, 1966.

―――. "Contributions to the Symbolism of the Self." Part I in *Psyche and Symbol.* New York: Doubleday Anchor Books, 1958.

Kanes, Martin. *Balzac's Comedy of Words.* Princeton, N.J.: Princeton University Press, 1975.

Knapp, Bettina. "Louis Lambert: The Legend of the Thinking Man." *Nineteenth Century French Studies* 6 (1977–78): 21–35.

———. *The Prometheus Syndrome.* Troy, N.Y.: Whitson Publishing Co., 1979.

Kofman, Sarah. *L'Enfance de l'art (une interprétation de l'esthétique freudienne).* Paris: Petite Bibliothèque Payot, 1970.

Kris, Ernst, and Kurz, Otto. *Legend, Myth, and Magic in the Image of the Artist.* New Haven: Yale University Press, 1979.

Langer, Suzanne. *Feeling and Form: A Theory of Art.* New York: Scribners, 1953.

Laubriet, Pierre. *L'Intelligence de l'art chez Balzac.* Paris: Didier, 1958.

Lock, Peter W. "Origins, Desire, and Writing: Balzac's *Louis Lambert.*" *Stanford French Review* 1 (1977): 289–311.

Lovejoy, Arthur O. *The Great Chain of Being* (1936). New York: Harper and Brothers, 1963.

Majewski, Henry F. "Alfred de Vigny and the Poetic Experience: From Alienation to Renascence." *Romanic Review* 67 (November 1976): 268–89.

———. "Alfred de Vigny and the Creative Experience: *Le Journal d'un poète.*" *Hebrew University Studies in Literature* 7 (Summer 1979): 94–112.

———. "The Function of the Mythic Patterns in Balzac's *La Recherche de l'absolu.*" *Nineteenth Century French Studies* 9 (1980–81): 10–27.

———. "Alfred de Vigny's *Daphné* and the Power of Symbols: The Second Consultation of the Docteur Noir. *Studies in Romanticism* 20 (Winter 1981): 461–74.

Marceau, Félicien. *Balzac et son monde.* Paris: Gallimard, 1970.

Marcuse, Herbert. "The Aesthetic Dimension," in *Eros and Civilization.* New York: Vintage Books, 1955.

Mauron, Charles. *Des métaphores obsédantes au mythe personnel.* Paris: Corti, 1963.

Mehlman, Jeffrey. *Revolution and Repetition: Marx, Hugo, Balzac.* Berkeley: University of California Press, 1977.

Michel, Arlette. "Le Statut du romancier chez Balzac: Intercession et destruction." Pp. 257–71 in Marc Fumaroli, ed., *Le Statut de la littérature: Mélanges offerts à Paul Bénichou.* Geneva: Droz, 1982.

Moers, Ellen. *Literary Women: The Great Writers.* Garden City, N.Y.: Doubleday, 1976.

Moreau, Pierre. *Ames et thèmes romantiques.* Paris: Corti, 1965.

Mourot, Jean. *Chateaubriand: le génie d'un style, rythme, et sonorités dans les "Mémoires d'outre-tombe."* Paris: Armand Colin, 1960.

Musset, Alfred de. *Andréa del Sarto* (1833) in *Oeuvres complètes,* 1 vol. Paris: Seuil, 1963.

———. *La Confession d'un enfant du siècle* (1836). Paris: Classiques Garnier, 1956.

———. *Lettres de Dupuis et Cotonet* (1836–37) in *Oeuvres complètes,* 1 vol. Paris: Seuil, 1963.

———. *Le Fils du Titien* (1838) in *Nouvelles.* Paris: Classiques Garnier, 1948.

Nash, Suzanne. *Les Contemplations of Victor Hugo: An Allegory of the Creative Process.* Princeton, N.J.: Princeton University Press, 1977.

Neumann, Erich. *Art and the Creative Unconscious.* Princeton, N.J.: Princeton University Press, 1960.

Peckham, Morse. "Towards a Theory of Romanticism." *PMLA* 66 (March 1951): 5–23.

———. "Towards a Theory of Romanticism: II. Reconsiderations." *Studies in Romanticism* 1 (Autumn 1961): 1–8.

———. *The Triumph of Romanticism: Collected Essays.* Columbia: University of South Carolina, 1971.

———. *Romanticism and Behavior.* Columbia: University of South Carolina Press, 1976.

Pelles, Geraldine. *Art, Artists, and Society: Origins of a Modern Dilemma.* Englewood Cliffs, N.J.: Prentice-Hall, 1963.

Porter, Laurence M. "The Present Directions of French Romantic Studies, 1960–75." *Nineteenth-Century French Studies* 6 (1977–78): 1–20.

———. *The Renaissance of the Lyric in French Romanticism: Elegy, "Poème," and Ode.* Lexington, Ky.: French Forum, 1978.

———. *The Literary Dream in French Romanticism: A Psychoanalytic Interpretation.* Detroit: Wayne State University Press, 1979.

Poulet, George. "Timelessness and Romanticism." *Journal of the History of Ideas* 15 (1954): 3–22.

———. *Les Métamorphoses du cercle.* Paris: Plon, 1961.

———. *Etudes sur le temps humain.* 3 vols. Paris: Plon, vol. I, 1950; vol. 2, 1952; vol. 3, 1968.

Pugh, Anthony R. *Balzac's Recurring Characters.* Toronto: University of Toronto Press, 1974.

Rank, Otto. *The Double: A Psychoanalytic Study.* Translated and edited by Harry Tucker, Jr. Chapel Hill: University of North Carolina Press, 1971.

Read, Herbert. *Icon and Idea: The Function of Art in the Development of Human Consciousness.* Cambridge: Harvard University Press, 1955.

Richard, Jean-Pierre. *Etudes sur le romantisme.* Paris: Seuil, 1970.

Riffaterre, Hermine. *L'Orphisme dans la poésie romantique: thèmes et styles surnaturalistes.* Paris: Nizet, 1970.

Riffaterre, Michael. *Text Production.* New York: Columbia University Press, 1983. (See "The Poem as Representation: A Reading of Hugo," chap. 11, pp. 181–201.)

Robert, Marthe. *Roman des origines et origines du roman.* Paris: Grasset, 1972.

Rogers, Robert. *A Psychoanalytic Study of the Double in Literature.* Detroit: Wayne State University Press, 1970.

Roland, Alan, ed. *Psychoanalysis, Creativity, and Literature: A French-American Inquiry.* New York: Columbia University Press, 1978.

Ruitenbeek, Hendrick, ed. *The Literary Imagination: Psychoanalysis and the Genius of the Writer.* Chicago: Quadrangle Books, 1965.

Sartre, Jean-Paul. *Qu'est-ce que la littérature?* (1948). Paris: Gallimard, Collection Idées, 1978.

Schor, Naomi. *Breaking the Chain: Women, Theory, and French Realist Fiction.* New York: Columbia University Press, 1985.

Schroder, Maurice. *Icarus: The Image of the Artist in French Romanticism.* Cambridge: Harvard University Press, 1961.

Showalter, Elaine, ed. *Essays on Women, Literature, and Theory: The New Feminist Criticism.* New York: Pantheon, 1985.

Skura, Meredith. *The Literary Use of the Psychoanalytic Process.* New Haven: Yale University Press, 1981.

Snell, Robert. *Théophile Gautier: A Romantic Critic of the Visual Arts.* Oxford: Clarendon, 1982.

Spacks, Patricia Mayer. *The Female Imagination.* New York: Knopf, 1975.

Spector, Jack. *The Aesthetics of Freud: A Study in Psychoanalysis and Art.* New York: Praeger, 1972.

Starobinski, Jean. *Jean-Jacques Rousseau: La transparence et l'obstacle.* Paris: Gallimard, 1970.

Stein, Jack Madison. *Richard Wagner and the Synthesis of the Arts.* Detroit: Wayne State University Press, 1960.

Sypher, Wylie. *Loss of Self in Modern Literature and Art.* New York: Random House, 1962.

Todorov, Tzvetan. *Introduction à la littérature fantastique.* Paris: Seuil, 1970.

———. *Poétique de la prose.* Paris: Seuil, 1971.

———. *Théories du Symbole.* Paris, Seuil, 1977.

Trousson, Raymond. *Le Thème de Prométhée dans la littérature européenne.* 2 vols. Geneva: Droz, 1964.

Vigny, Alfred de. *Stello* (1832). In vol. 1, *Oeuvres complètes,* 2 vols. Paris: Pléiade, 1948.

———. *Daphné* (1837). In vol. 2, *Oeuvres complètes,* 2 vols. Paris: Pléiade, 1948.

———. *Le Journal d'un poète* (1864). In vol. 2, *Oeuvres complètes,* 2 vols. Paris: Pléiade, 1948.

———. *Poésies complètes.* Paris: Garnier, 1962.

Weber, Jean-Paul. *Genèse de l'oeuvre poétique.* Paris: Gallimard, 1960.

Wellek, René. "The Concept of Romanticism in Literary History" and "Romanticism Re-examined." Pp. 128–98, 199–221. In *Concepts of Criticism.* New Haven: Yale University Press, 1963.

Winner, Ellen. *Invented Worlds: The Psychology of the Arts.* Cambridge: Harvard University Press, 1982.

Wiskel, Thomas. *The Romantic Sublime: Studies in the Structure and Psychology of Transcendence*. Baltimore: Johns Hopkins University Press, 1976.

Woodman, Ross. "Shaman, Poet, and Failed Initiate: Reflections on Romanticism and Jungian Psychology." *Studies in Romanticism* 19, no. 1 (1980): 51–82.

Index